THE
PSYCHOLOGY
of the
FRUIT OF THE SPIRIT

The Biblical Portrayal
of the Christlike Character
and Its Development

Zoltán Dörnyei

ZONDERVAN
ACADEMIC

ZONDERVAN ACADEMIC

The Psychology of the Fruit of the Spirit
Copyright © 2022 by Zoltán Dörnyei

Requests for information should be addressed to:
Zondervan, *3900 Sparks Dr. SE, Grand Rapids, Michigan 49546*

Zondervan titles may be purchased in bulk for educational, business, fundraising, or sales promotional use. For information, please email SpecialMarkets@Zondervan.com.

ISBN 978-0-310-12847-2 (audio)

Library of Congress Cataloging-in-Publication Data

Names: Dörnyei, Zoltán, author.
Title: The psychology of the Fruit of the Spirit : the biblical portrayal of the Christlike character and its development / Zoltán Dörnyei.
Description: Grand Rapids : Zondervan, 2022. | Includes bibliographical references and index.
Identifiers: LCCN 2022021298 | ISBN 9780310128458 (paperback) | ISBN 9780310128465 (ebook)
Subjects: LCSH: Bible. Galatians, V, 22-23—Criticism, interpretation, etc. | Fruit of the Spirit—Biblical teaching. | Christian life—Biblical teaching.
Classification: LCC BS2685.6.C48 D67 2022 | DDC 227/.406—dc23/eng/20220705
LC record available at https://lccn.loc.gov/2022021298

Cover design: Brian Bobel
Cover art: Leos Moskos / Public Domain; Pannawish Jarusilawong / Getty Images
Interior design: Sara Colley

Printed in the United States of America

22 23 24 25 26 27 28 29 30 31 32 /TRM/ 12 11 10 9 8 7 6 5 4 3 2 1

Contents

FOREWORD

Daniel J. Treier

The present book offers new insight into the fruit of the Spirit by integrating the theological interpretation of Scripture with modern psychology. "Integration of faith and learning" has become an axiom in many Christian institutions of higher education, especially in the United States. Although it can easily degenerate into a tired cliché, here a worked example fulfills this noble aspiration thanks to a Hungarian psycholinguist who taught in the United Kingdom and who obtained a second doctoral degree in theology.

The challenges of doing "integration" are sizable. On one hand, integration is not mere assimilation of a subordinate perspective into a dominant framework. Both the authoritative sources for Christian faith and the disciplines of modern learning must be engaged with intellectual integrity. On the other hand, Christian faith claims final epistemic authority (e.g., 1 Cor 1:18–2:16; 3:11). When identifying the locus of "faith," some approaches prioritize biblical or doctrinal content whereas others prioritize the experience or practice of piety. Even so, Christian scholars across that spectrum acknowledge the ultimate authority of the special divine revelation in the Scriptures. Yet identifying the loci of "learning" comprises another challenge: The possibilities for integration are manifold, not monolithic, when it comes to the various disciplines' cultural impact, personal formation, conceptual frameworks, or even specific details.

Psychology poses such challenges in distinctive ways. Its object of study, the human person, has natural, social, and theological dimensions. All of the major academic "cultures" joust in this arena. Some Biblicist Christians have virtually rejected psychology out of hand, fearing a Trojan horse that would smuggle secularism into the city of God. Others have quickly surrendered to the triumph of the therapeutic. Thus, Christian psychologists have generated their own discourse about the prospects and pitfalls of integration.

The present book does not labor in those methodological weeds. Instead, it gets busy harvesting the material fruit of integrative engagement. It carefully addresses a neglected biblical motif, while avoiding naïve equivalences between biblical concepts and English-language terms. It creatively appropriates psychological concepts to cultivate theological understanding, while avoiding the eisegetical overlay of external frameworks onto Scripture. Professor Dörnyei has engaged the existing biblical scholarship on the fruit motif while explaining its relative neglect: theologians have struggled to find an overarching vision of the forest rather than focusing on the tree bark, or they have simply fit the fruit into another framework like classic virtue theory. Hence, integration with psychology catalyzes fresh pursuit of a unifying perspective with which to harvest biblical teaching on human transformation.

As for *what this biblical motif means*, Professor Dörnyei's account finds the fruit of the Spirit to be "the ideal outcome of a divinely orchestrated transformation process to produce a Christlike character in the believer." This character sketch fleshes out the meaning of love, the apex of such spiritual transformation. Despite having affinities with virtue theory, this account notices the biblical contrast with straightforward eudaimonism: by grace Christians find ultimate joy in God rather than directly seeking their own happiness, however ethically they might do so. Without generically reducing the fruit to love, Dörnyei's account articulates an ordered unity rather than simply leaving us with nine discrete elements from Gal 5:22–23. The categories of (1) loving compassion, (2) spiritual contentment, and (3) steadfast perseverance mediate broad yet concrete understanding of human transformation. This ordered unity is rooted in two supporting soils: detailed biblical study establishes the comprehensive, interrelated character of the Pauline list, while psychological resonances enable the distinct categories to unfold. The resulting model has the added virtue of relating personal formation to communal life.

Professor Dörnyei's account also illuminates *how the Spirit's fruit grows*. While reflecting the unity of the virtues, this biblical motif avoids virtue's paradox regarding how new dispositions could arise without accompanying habits. Here the mysterious intersection of divine and human agency both contributes explanatory power and is further clarified with reference to self-control. Although the terminology for that fruit is relatively infrequent in the New Testament, the concept is vitally important. Divine sovereignty and human responsibility are manifest in its psychological complexity—as both a "trait" that distinctively characterizes and benefits some persons and a "skill" that can be learned and enhanced. Relatedly, hope is one of three theological virtues in 1 Corinthians 13 yet is absent from the list of fruit in Galatians 5, which are more directly manifest. Nevertheless, hope is a nourishing root of the self-control that is ingredient within Christlike love. Again, psychology plays a supporting role at this point—corroborating that personality traits can be changed, skills can be acquired through stages of intentional action, and beliefs about the possibility of change influence actual change. Thus Dörnyei has identified three broad motivational strategies with which the New Testament fosters hopeful self-control: (1) linking virtue to divine rewards, (2) contrasting moral darkness and light, and (3) amplifying the attractiveness of role models. Consistent with the theological mysteries involved, a "fine line" ensues between unbiblical legalism and necessary perseverance in self-regulating practices.

This book's disciplinary integration both plants the seed of a worked example and harvests psychological insight to enrich theological understanding. Used carefully and corrigibly, psychology supplies lenses for seeing more that is present in the Scriptures, conceptual links for synthesizing the revelation encountered there, and language for sharing this teaching clearly and creatively. With deeper understanding of the Spirit's fruit, we may hope for ourselves and others to grow in loving compassion, spiritual contentment, and steadfast perseverance.

The goal of this foreword has been to whet readers' appetites for the ensuing intellectual feast. But I conclude with a note of gratitude for the "second career" of Zoltán Dörnyei as a Christian theologian. In God's providence, project-related email became the occasion for us to "meet" and to find mutual encouragement in Christ. Such literary fellowship has not only enriched me with this book but also testifies to the Holy Spirit's fruitful ministry of divine love. I am sad that Zoltán lost his battle with cancer before the printed version of this book could reach his hands, but I am pleased that he saw a draft of this foreword as faithfully articulating his aims.

1

INTRODUCTION AND RATIONALE

The "fruit of the Spirit" is a well-known concept in Christian circles, with the phrase originally coined by the apostle Paul in his epistle to the Galatians, where he states, "The fruit of the Spirit is love, joy, peace, forbearance [patience[1]], kindness, goodness, faithfulness, gentleness and self-control" (5:22–23). This list of nine human "virtues"—as they are frequently referred to—is contrasted in the letter with a preceding list of fifteen human "vices" (vv. 19–21) in order to illustrate the difference between the "acts of the flesh" (v. 19) and being "led by the Spirit" (v. 18). The fruit of the Spirit is undoubtedly a popular notion, as evidenced by the existence of numerous books published on the subject,[2] including dedicated collections of sermons.[3] As Scot McKnight summarises, a common feature

---

1. The NIVUK translates the Greek word *makrothymia* as "forbearance" rather than "patience"; the exact meaning of the term will be discussed in chapter 3, but in general references to the nine facets of the fruit of the Spirit in this book, the more familiar "patience" will be used.

2. E.g., Don M. Aycock, *Living by the Fruit of the Spirit*, expanded ed, (Grand Rapids: Kregel, 2016); Philip D. Kenneson, *Life on the Vine: Cultivating the Fruit of the Spirit in Christian Community* (Downers Grove, IL: InterVarsity, 1999); Thomas E. Trask and Wayde I. Goodall, *The Fruit of the Spirit: Becoming the Person God Wants You to Be* (Nashville: Emanate, 2000); Stephen F. Winward, *Fruit of the Spirit* (Leicester: Inter-Varsity, 1981); Christopher J. H. Wright, *Cultivating the Fruit of the Spirit: Growing in Christlikeness* (Downers Grove, IL: IVP Books, 2017).

3. E.g., C. Thomas Hilton, *Ripe Life: Sermons on the Fruit of the Spirit*, Protestant Pulpit Exchange (Nashville: Abingdon, 1993); Warren W. Wiersbe, ed., *Classic Sermons on the Fruit of the Spirit* (Grand Rapids: Kregel, 2002).

of these works has been that they "focus on the individual dimensions of the fruit of the Spirit and . . . seek to make this list a character-building piece of instruction."[4] In other words, these books typically present a largely practical and ethically-oriented message to facilitate Christian character building by offering separate accounts of the nine Christian virtues listed in Gal 5:22–23. They usually foreground the nine virtues' normative nature, illustrate their significance with biblical references and real-life examples, and suggest concrete methods for cultivating them.

Given the richness of the available publications, what justifies writing another book on the fruit of the Spirit? Rather than replicating existing work, the current volume intends to add two novel aspects to the discussion:

- First, it will be argued that the theological significance of the fruit is not limited solely to forming the biblical foundation of ethical recommendations. Instead, it will be shown (in chapter 4) that Paul's list of virtues in Gal 5 outlines a *composite character* that can be seen as a representation of an ideal, Christlike personality for believers to aspire to and to approximate as much as possible. Moreover, once we consider the nine attributes collectively as a unified theological concept, this positions the fruit of the Spirit at the intersection of several important theoretical themes related to spiritual growth and human transformation (e.g., creation in the likeness of God; justification and sanctification; being conformed to the divine image; new creation and the advancement of the kingdom of God), thereby promising novel insights.
- Second, in order to uncover the full meaning of the fruit and its facets, the current work adopts an *interdisciplinary approach*, whereby theological reflections are complemented with findings from the field of *psychology*.

The rest of this introduction looks at these two points more closely, before addressing a final question: If the fruit of the Spirit does indeed

---

4. Scot McKnight, *Galatians*, The NIV Application Commentary (Grand Rapids: Zondervan, 1995), 277.

have theoretical significance, has this been duly reflected in theology? It will be argued that despite its popularity in Christian circles, the notion of the fruit of the Spirit has remained somewhat peripheral in the theological mainstream, and several reasons will be provided to explain this imbalance.

Why Is the Composite Fruit Important?

The nine human attributes included in Gal 5:22–23—love, joy, peace, patience, kindness, goodness, faithfulness, gentleness, and self-control— unquestionably involve essential Christian values and virtues, and therefore the list has often been used both in preaching and writing as a vehicle for discussing ethical aspects of the believer's conduct. While this practice has been understandable and has formed the basis of helpful pastoral teaching, one may wonder whether the fruit of the Spirit is solely about the nine individual characteristics it subsumes. An important indication that this may not be the case is offered by the very fact that the phrase has become a well-known part of the Christian vocabulary over the past two millennia, which suggests that many people have used it to refer to something more general than the nine individual facets—that is, to a whole that is larger than the sum of its parts. In other words, the mere fact that the "fruit of the Spirit" has become a frequently used phrase evidences people's belief that it expresses some important aggregate meaning related to a Christlike character in general. In further support of this observation, chapter 4 will show first that the description of the Christian character outlined in Gal 5 is not *ad hoc* but comprehensive (not in the sense that the list is exhaustive of every possible virtue that one could exhibit in life, but in the sense that all the other virtues mentioned elsewhere in the Scriptures are covered by it one way or another); and second that the nine facets of the fruit of the Spirit form a coherent whole by being interrelated in multiple ways. It will also be argued that the function of the nine attributes within the specific context of Gal 5 is not so much to present a list of virtues for Christians to emulate as to *paint a larger picture* in order to illustrate the Spirit-led alternative to gratifying the flesh. We should note, however, that these arguments do not reduce the significance of the nine individual virtues—after all, those include core Christian concepts such as love, peace, and self-control—and therefore a balanced account of the fruit of the Spirit also requires an exegesis of the nine terms listed in Gal 5:22–23, a task that will be carried out in chapter 3.

In order to illustrate the potential theological significance of the composite fruit, let us consider one aspect as a preliminary example. We shall see in the next chapter in detail that all the nine virtues listed in Gal 5:22–23 are mentioned elsewhere in the Scriptures in relation to either God the Father or the Son (or both), and therefore most commentators would agree with Philip Kenneson's summary that the fruit of the Spirit reflects divine attributes: "The fruit that the Spirit desires to produce in our corporate and individual lives therefore, is not merely a hodgepodge of admirable character traits or virtues that are universally admirable or commendable. Rather, God desires to produce this fruit through the Spirit—and the community of Jesus Christ desires to have this fruit produced in its life—because these dispositions reflect *the very character of God*."[5]

This understanding underlies James Dunn's comparison of the fruit of the Spirit to "a kind of 'character-sketch' of Christ"[6] that develops in Christian believers through the direct intervention of the Holy Spirit, and Christopher Wright further reminds us that earlier in Galatians Paul already alluded to this view when he said, "My dear children, for whom I am again in the pains of childbirth until *Christ is formed in you*" (Gal 4:19; emphasis added).[7] Accordingly, Craig Keener concludes that "the fruit of the Spirit is the character of the Spirit of God's Son living in us, God's image in his children."[8]

This perspective offers an important link between the fruit of the Spirit and the creation of humans *in the divine image/likeness* (Gen 1:26),

---

5. Kenneson, *Life on the Vine*, 32; emphasis added.

6. James D. G. Dunn, *The Epistle to the Galatians*, BNTC (Peabody, MA: Hendrickson, 1993), 310.

7. C. Wright, *Cultivating the Fruit of the Spirit*, 14.

8. Craig S. Keener, *Galatians: A Commentary* (Grand Rapids: Baker Academic, 2019), 516.

and while it is not implied here that the fruit represents this likeness in full, its development in believers can be seen as part of the process of being "conformed to the image of his Son" (Rom 8:29; see also 2 Cor 3:18). This process is paraphrased in Col 3:10 as "the new self . . . being renewed in knowledge in the image of its Creator," and N. T. Wright underlines this process of renewal as a central thrust of the Scriptures: "The whole New Testament insists that the point of Christian living is the remaking of humans in God's image."[9] Consequently, the notion of a communion with divine likeness is not alien to Christian theology, as witnessed by the existence of a range of relevant theological terms concerning some form of "sanctification," "deification," or "union with God," and chapter 6 will offer an overview of the biblical portrayal of such spiritual growth, describing how the fruit of the Spirit fits into it as its aspired-to outcome.

How Can Psychology Complement Theology in Exploring the Fruit of the Spirit?

In order to uncover the full meaning and significance of the fruit of the Spirit, the current book has adopted an interdisciplinary approach, whereby theological reflections are complemented with findings from the field of *psychology*. Taking an interdisciplinary approach when exploring the fruit of the Spirit has been a frequently employed practice in past scholarship, but the theological understanding has usually been augmented by philosophical rather than psychological insights, most notably concerning virtue ethics. In reflecting on the benefits of drawing on philosophy in this area, Keener offers the following explanation:

> Examining Paul's usage elsewhere offers the surest clue for determining how Paul understands the terms on his list. Nevertheless, some of Paul's examples of the fruit of the Spirit in his virtue list in Gal 5 are

---

9. N. T. Wright, *After You Believe: Why Christian Character Matters* (New York: HarperOne, 2010), 251.

harder to define in Pauline terms than others. Because philosophers were often meticulous about defining their ethical language, we may compare and contrast some of Paul's ethical language here with that of other intellectuals, especially often with that of the dominant philosophic school of his era, namely the Stoics.[10]

That is, complementing biblical exegesis with insights from philosophy concerning human virtues offers a profitable avenue to uncover the full content of the ninefold fruit. A similar argument can also be made about turning to *psychology* for further clarification: human attributes such as the ones subsumed by the fruit of the Spirit have been subject to substantial research in personality psychology (see EXCURSUS 1) and therefore psychological insights can contribute meaningfully to specifying the various concepts in question. In order to illustrate the potential benefits of such an integrated approach, let us briefly look at three concrete areas where psychological findings may be helpful in illuminating theological understanding:

(1) Clarifying individual virtues. The nine attributes listed in Gal 5:22–23 vary in how frequently they are mentioned in the Scriptures and how thoroughly they are expounded by the biblical authors. For example, the term "self-control" (*enkrateia*) and its cognates occur only in five other verses in the whole of the New Testament,[11] and the word does not appear in the canonical books of the Greek translation of the Hebrew Bible, the Septuagint, at all. This has led several commentators to conclude that the term is rare in the Scriptures,[12] which is at odds with its prominent position in concluding the list of the facets of the fruit of the Spirit (since the final position in a Greek structure is a

---

10. Craig S. Keener, "A Comparison of the Fruit of the Spirit in Galatians 5:22–23 with Ancient Thought on Ethics and Emotion," in *The Language and Literature of the New Testament: Essays in Honor of Stanley E. Porter's 60th Birthday*, ed. Lois Fuller Dow, Craig A. Evans, and Andrew W. Pitts (Leiden: Brill, 2017), 574.

11. As a noun: Acts 24:25; 2 Pet 1:6 (2x); as an adjective (i.e., self-controlled): Titus 1:8; as a verb (i.e., to exercise self-control): 1 Cor 7:9; 9:25.

12. E.g., Hans Dieter Betz, *Galatians: A Commentary on Paul's Letter to the Churches in Galatia* (Philadelphia: Fortress, 1979), 288; Thomas R. Schreiner, *Galatians*, Zondervan Exegetical Commentary on the New Testament (Grand Rapids: Zondervan Academic, 2010), 350.

place for emphasis[13]). Psychology can help to clarify this curious incongruity: as we shall see in chapter 3, the broad psychological domain of self-control/persistence subsumes a large variety of closely interrelated concepts in personality psychology, from "grit" and "resilience" to "perseverance" and "self-regulation," with the different but considerably overlapping labels signifying only relatively subtle dissimilarities.[14] If we approach the Scriptures with such an awareness, we will find that the notion of "self-control" also appears in the New Testament in several different forms related to the broader semantic domain of self-discipline/mastery, and pooling these occurrences—as is typically done in psychology—will result in a much larger corpus of biblical examples. Thus, integrating psychological knowledge with the available biblical records can offer a systematic way of widening one's investigative lens and can thus effectively fill any possible gaps in our understanding of the fruit's facets.

(2) Defining broader psychological dimensions. There have been several attempts in the past to divide the nine facets of the fruit of the Spirit into fewer clusters, usually into three triplets: love–joy–peace, patience–kindness–goodness, and faithfulness–gentleness–self-control. As we shall see in chapter 5, these classifications raise certain issues: First, it is not entirely straightforward how the attributes in each group are related to each other, and when scholars attempted to identify a unifying theme for each cluster,[15] some of the attributes did not readily fit into these groupings. Second, the meaning of the individual attributes is often complex and overlapping, which makes it difficult to group them neatly under a single rubric. A potentially more productive classification may be achieved not by dividing the attributes into distinct clusters but by establishing broad *dimensions* underlying them. The advantage of this approach is that it

---

13. Richard N. Longenecker, *Galatians*, WBC 41 (Dallas: Word, 1990), 260; see also Betz, *Galatians*, 288; Richard B. Hays, "The Letter to the Galatians," in *New Interpreter's Bible*, ed. L. E. Keck (Nashville: Abingdon, 2000), 328.

14. The differences largely concern how broadly the particular constructs are defined, what timescale they occupy, what kind of adversity they are concerned with, and how they navigate the difficulty in question.

15. E.g., (1) habits/dispositions of the mind; (2) qualities affecting human relations; and (3) principles that guide human conduct. For a discussion, see chapter 5.

does not exclude the possibility of an attribute relating to more than one dimension. This procedure has been the standard methodology in personality psychology in the twentieth century to identify the main components of human personality, and the approach has also been successfully applied in the positive psychological movement over the past decade to establishing dimensions underlying human virtues in general. Chapter 5 will review the most important previously proposed virtue models and will then present a threefold division of the composite fruit into three underlying dimensions: *loving compassion*, *spiritual contentment*, and *steadfast perseverance*.

(3) Offering lessons for cultivating the fruit of the Spirit. Stanley Hauerwas submitted some forty years ago that "philosophers and theologians have for too long left the analysis of moral development to educators and psychologists."[16] While there have been some advances in this respect over the past decades,[17] it is still the case that (educational) psychology has a lot of accumulated knowledge in the area of moral education that might be relevant to the cultivation of Christian virtues: as will be shown in chapter 7, methods for modifying personality traits and forming various habits have been the subject of a great deal of recent research in the social sciences. In Gal 6:8–9, Paul exhorts Christian believers to "sow to the Spirit" in order to "reap at harvest time" (NRSVA), and an integrated theological-psychological discussion can provide valuable lessons concerning what the process of "sowing" may specifically involve.

Psychological insights might also be useful in addressing a long-standing dilemma in biblical studies regarding the fact that the nine virtues of the fruit of the Spirit are described both as endowments/gifts received from the sovereign Holy Spirit and as attributes that need to be consciously cultivated by humans.[18] For example, the introduction of a recent

---

16. Stanley Hauerwas, *A Community of Character: Toward a Constructive Christian Social Ethic* (Notre Dame, IN: University of Notre Dame Press, 1981), 129.

17. See e.g., Catharine Darnell et al., "Phronesis and the Knowledge–Action Gap in Moral Psychology and Moral Education: A New Synthesis?," *Human Development* 62, no. 3 (2019): 101–29; Gopal Sreenivasan, "Character Education and the Rearguard of Situationism," in *Virtue and Character*, ed. Walter Sinnott-Armstrong and Christian B. Miller, vol. 5 of *Moral Psychology* (Cambridge, MA: MIT Press, 2017); Graham Tomlin, *Spiritual Fitness: Christian Character in a Consumer Society* (London: Continuum, 2006).

18. E.g., while Fung rightly points out that "the phrase directly ascribes the power of fructification not to the believer himself but to the Spirit," we shall see in chapter 7 that elsewhere in the

edited volume on *Character: New Directions from Philosophy, Psychology, and Theology* concludes about virtues that "it is not clear how to understand the contribution that both human beings and God are supposed to make in fostering them."[19] This dilemma can be related to an established contrast in personality psychology, the difference between *trait* and *state* characteristics. "Traits" (e.g., intelligence) are relatively enduring dispositions and are thought to be inherited to a large extent (hence a divinely endowed virtue could be seen to fall under this rubric), whereas "state characteristics" (e.g., motivation) are more situation-specific, transitory, and temporary, and are to some extent under the person's conscious control. As we shall see in the next chapter, research has shown that the two aspects are not mutually exclusive, as most personality features involve both a more established dimension of general propensity (i.e., trait-like) and a more contextualised layer of individuality that can be brought under human control (i.e., state-like). Lessons emerging from this duality can usefully inform the understanding of the twofold nature of the fruit of the Spirit.

Excursus 1: Psychological Research on Virtues

In a recent book on theological psychology, Matthew LaPine rightly points out that "it is easy to miss the fact that categories of virtue ethics like 'virtue' or 'vice' are psychological categories, having to do with the habits of the soul's powers."[20] Indeed, the moral aspects of personal characteristics (including vices and virtues) have been featured topics not only in theological and philosophical discourse but also in psychological research, and there is even a subfield in the social sciences, "moral psychology," which specifically focuses on questions related to moral development and identity. The main

---

Bible all the facets of the fruit of the Spirit are commanded of the believer. Ronald Y. K. Fung, *The Epistle to the Galatians*, NICNT (Grand Rapids: Eerdmans, 1988), 262.

19. Christian B. Miller et al., "Introduction," in *Character: New Directions from Philosophy, Psychology, and Theology*, ed. Christian B. Miller et al. (New York: Oxford University Press, 2015), 5.

20. Matthew A. LaPine, *The Logic of the Body: Retrieving Theological Psychology* (Bellingham, WA: Lexham, 2020), 5.

difference between theology and modern psychology primarily concerns the method of inquiry and the type of evidence that is accepted as valid. Modern academic psychology is based on *empirical research*—that is, the collection and analysis of quantitative or qualitative *data*—but this does not mean that it is incompatible with theology; as LaPine succinctly puts it, while the latter attends to reality "by way of the book of Scripture" and the former by "the book of nature," both sources of revelation are divinely given.[21]

Research on character, virtues, and morality flourished during the first decades of modern scientific psychology at the beginning of the twentieth century,[22] and in fact, as renowned psychologist Gordon Allport explains, the field of personality psychology was specifically initiated to explore human "character," defined as "the personality evaluated according to prevailing standards of conduct."[23] It was only because of the moral dimension attached to the term "character" that its study gradually fell out of favour and was replaced by the 1930s with the more neutral "personality."[24] Until relatively recently, academic psychologists have largely avoided the study of moral virtues; as Dan McAdams explains, the topic seemed "too philosophical, even theological, for their intellectual tastes, and many may have worried that venturing into the virtue domain might compromise their scientific objectivity."[25] The tide turned around the turn of the new millennium, and in a review paper published by the prestigious *Annual Review of Psychology*, Emmons and Paloutzian highlighted in 2003 that "the study of

---

21. LaPine, 5.

22. Wiebke Bleidorn, "Moving Character Beyond the Person-Situation Debate," in *Character: New Directions from Philosophy, Psychology, and Theology*, ed. Christian B. Miller et al. (New York: Oxford University Press, 2015), 131.

23. Gordon W. Allport, "Personality and Character," *Psychological Bulletin* 18, no. 9 (1921): 443.

24. See e.g., Nicole B. Barenbaum and David G. Winter, "History of Modern Personality Theory and Research," in *Handbook of Personality: Theory and Research*, ed. O. P. John, R. W. Robins, and L. A. Pervin (New York: Guilford, 2008), 5.

25. Dan P. McAdams, "Psychological Science and the Nicomachean Ethics" in *Cultivating Virtue: Perspectives from Philosophy, Theology, and Psychology*, ed. Nancy E. Snow (New York: Oxford University Press, 2014), 307.

virtue is making a comeback in psychology and is at the nexus of the psychology of religion, personality psychology, moral philosophy, and the psychology of emotion."[26] A clear manifestation of the changing perception was the fact that the American Psychological Association (APA) launched the journal *Psychology of Religion and Spirituality* in 2009 as the official publication of its Division 36, the "Society for the Psychology of Religion and Spirituality."

The growing interest among psychologists in matters of spirituality was accompanied by a complementary trend, the emergence of "positive psychology" as a prominent strand within psychological science. It was formally inaugurated by Martin Seligman's presidential address to the 1998 APA convention, and was more widely launched by a subsequent special issue of the journal *American Psychologist* in 2000. A central research focus of the new movement included the exploration of human virtues and character strengths, and the existing knowledge in this area was summarised in a landmark volume by Peterson and Seligman in 2004, published by the APA, on *Character Strengths and Virtues: A Handbook and Classification.*[27] Thus, positive psychology and the psychology of religion share an interest in virtues,[28] and this interest has been further advanced over the past decade through substantial funding by the Templeton Foundation for interdisciplinary research on the subject, resulting in a number of edited volumes integrating relevant scholarship from psychology, philosophy, and theology.[29]

---

26. Robert A. Emmons and Raymond F. Paloutzian, "The Psychology of Religion," *Annual Review of Psychology* 54 (2003): 386.

27. Christopher Peterson and Martin E. P. Seligman, *Character Strengths and Virtues: A Handbook and Classification* (Washington, DC: American Psychological Association, 2004).

28. For recent overviews, see Lindsey M. Root Luna, Daryl R. Van Tongeren, and Charlotte vanOyen Witvliet, "Virtue, Positive Psychology, and Religion: Consideration of an Overarching Virtue and an Underpinning Mechanism," *Psychology of Religion and Spirituality* 9, no. 3 (2017): 299–302; Sarah A. Schnitker and Robert A. Emmons, "The Psychology of Virtue: Integrating Positive Psychology and the Psychology of Religion," *Psychology of Religion and Spirituality* 9, no. 3 (2017): 239–41.

29. E.g., Christian B. Miller, *Moral Character: An Empirical Theory* (Oxford: Oxford University Press, 2013); Christian B. Miller et al., eds., *Character: New Directions from Philosophy, Psychology, and Theology* (New York: Oxford University Press, 2015); Christian B. Miller and Walter

Why Is the Fruit of the Spirit Relatively Peripheral to Theological Reflection?

Even a brief review of the literature on the fruit of the Spirit reveals a curious phenomenon regarding the perception of the subject in contemporary Christian circles: while there are literally dozens of books on the topic geared at non-specialist Christian readers, academic theology has been less forthcoming about the fruit's significance, with most theological discussions of the fruit being relatively short and confined largely to commentaries on the relevant passage in Paul's epistle to the Galatians.[30] Thus, one may not be altogether wrong in getting the impression that there are two strikingly different assessments of the notion: on the one hand, from a practical perspective, the fruit of the Spirit has been widely seen as an important concept that represents a set of essential Christian values whose exposition and cultivation are beneficial for the church; on the other hand, academic theology has attached only limited unique theoretical meaning to the notion of the fruit of the Spirit.[31] A good illustration of the prevailing practice-oriented preference is Christopher Wright's recent book on *Cultivating the Fruit of the Spirit*: while the author has an impressive academic record and this excellent book has a solid foundation in theology and scriptural citations, the text has been consciously framed as nonacademic discourse, aimed primarily at "preachers" and "general Christian readers."[32] This practice reflects a common pattern, with no academic monographs dedicated to the subject to date.

What explains this asymmetry? Why has the theological significance of the fruit not been sufficiently acknowledged in mainstream theology? There are at least four main reasons for this: (1) the seemingly open-ended nature of the list in Gal 5:22–23, (2) the existence of the classical

---

Sinnott-Armstrong, eds., *Virtue and Character*, vol. 5 of *Mortal Psychology* (Cambridge, MA: MIT Press, 2017); Jennifer Cole Wright, Michael T. Warren, and Nancy E. Snow, *Understanding Virtue: Theory and Measurement* (New York: Oxford University Press, 2021).

30. For a valuable recent exception, see Keener, "Fruit of the Spirit."

31. E.g., McGrath's classic *Christian Theology* does not list the fruit of the Spirit in its detailed Index. Alister E. McGrath, *Christian Theology: An Introduction*, 6th ed. (Oxford: Wiley-Blackwell, 2017).

32. C. Wright, *Cultivating the Fruit of the Spirit*, 10.

Greek genre of virtue lists that has often hijacked the discussion, (3) the danger of not being able to see the forest (i.e., the composite fruit) for the trees (i.e., the nine facets), and (4) the absence of an overarching theological theory of human transformation to accommodate the notion of the fruit of the Spirit. Each of these points will be addressed in the following chapters in more detail, but a brief summary might be useful here to set the scene:

(1) Open-ended nature of the list. One reason why scholars have not attached more theological significance to the fruit of the Spirit is that they have not seen it as a self-contained whole: Virtually all commentators consider the nine facets to constitute a somewhat *ad hoc* and incomplete collection of attributes on the basis of a short phrase—"such things"—that Paul includes in a comment after the list: "Against *such things* there is no law" (v. 23; emphasis added).[33] That is, the nine virtues are not considered by scholars to represent an all-inclusive, self-contained theological notion, and this perception of randomness is further strengthened when the Galatians list is compared with catalogues of virtues in other NT books that offer somewhat different itemisation (e.g., Col 3:12–13; 2 Pet 1:5–7). This is a valid concern, because if we regard the Gal 5:22–23 passage merely as a list of commendable human qualities—and not even a comprehensive one at that—it is understandable that the list does not feature highly in theological reflection. To address this concern, chapter 4 offers a comprehensive survey of all the virtues mentioned in the New Testament to demonstrate that the broader Christian persona outlined in Gal 5 is sufficiently comprehensive to accommodate or represent all the outstanding virtues. Moreover, if we view the list of attributes in Gal 5:22–23 as a character sketch of the Christian ideal, the issue of open-endedness largely disappears: when we describe someone's personality, we can do it using any number of adjectives and it will still be the same person—sometimes we offer some shorthand of his/her character, at other times we produce a

---

33. Keener's ("Fruit of the Spirit," 576) conclusion in typical: "The phrase 'such things' in 5:21 (τα τοιαῦτα) and 23 (τῶν τοιούτων) makes explicit that Paul offers only samples here." See also Wesley L. Gerig, "Fruit of the Spirit," in *Evangelical Dictionary of Biblical Theology*, ed. Walter A. Elwell (Grand Rapids: Baker, 1996), 274–275; J. Louis Martyn, *Galatians: A New Translation with Introduction and Commentary*, AB 33a (New Haven, CT: Yale University Press, 1997), 498.

more detailed portrayal or, alternatively, focus only on a specific personality aspect, but the length of the description does not change the overall nature of the referent as we are still talking about the same person.

(2) Hijacked by the popular classical genre of virtue lists. Chapter 2 will explain that virtue lists used for character building constituted a common genre in antiquity and that such lists were highly popular in Greek ethical and philosophical writings (with the most famous of these being the "catalogue of cardinal virtues" attributed to Plato[34]). The relevance of these lists to the current discussion is that we find marked similarities between these virtue lists and the catalogues of virtuous human qualities mentioned in the Scriptures. Given this undeniable connection, it is necessary to address these analogies when commenting on the fruit of the Spirit, but doing so can easily become a double-edged sword in that it can hijack the discussion of the topic: comparing the use of virtues in philosophical and biblical writings can affect the overall tenor of the analysis by foregrounding, if not compelling, an item-by-item analysis of the specific concepts. Such an itemised, individual virtue-centred approach, in turn, can shift the attention away from the cumulative theological purpose of the composite fruit.

(3) Not being able to see the forest for the trees. The study of the notion of the fruit of the Spirit has also been hindered by the fact that the list in Gal 5:22–23 involves as many as nine facets, each associated with rich biblical content and significant practical implications. While no real analysis of the nature of the fruit can take place without first describing the individual constituents, this initial analytical step can too easily become also the last one in a work in the sense that it takes up most of the available space and scholarly momentum.[35] In addition, the task of properly describing the individual virtues can also shift the discussion towards a largely itemised, virtue-by-virtue pattern, which—as said above—may

---

34. I.e., wisdom, courage, self-restraint, justice, and piety. For recent overviews, see Keener, "Fruit of the Spirit"; Stanley E. Porter, "Paul, Virtues, Vices, and Household Codes," in *Paul in the Greco-Roman World: A Handbook*, ed. J. Paul Sampley (London: Bloomsbury T&T Clark, 2016).

35. In the books dedicated to the fruit of the Spirit, the discussion of each facet is almost invariably covered by a full chapter, thereby constituting the bulk of the book. Most academic treatments of the fruit of the Spirit have also followed a similar virtue-by-virtue pattern of discussion due to their typical context within commentaries on Galatians: commentaries by definition provide a linear exegesis of the Scriptures and therefore they go through the nine attributes one by one.

indirectly prevent any substantial theological discussion of the fruit of the Spirit as an aggregate. Finally, producing nine separate, content-rich discussions can also give the impression that the topic has been sufficiently covered. Consequently, although Douglas Moo rightly emphasises that "the importance of this list of the fruit of the Spirit . . . lies not so much in the individual virtues as in their cumulative effect,"[36] this importance is rarely done full justice in existing discussions.

(4) Absence of an overarching theological theory of human transformation. It was mentioned earlier that the notion of being conformed to the divine image has been a familiar theme in Christian theology, as attested to by the existence of a variety of relevant theological terms ranging from justification and sanctification to deification/theosis and the union with God/ Christ. It will be shown in chapter 6 that the Bible portrays the human transformation process through a rich variety of concepts, metaphors, and images, without offering a unified specification of the economy of spiritual growth. Given that there has been no definition provided in this respect by an ecumenical council either, scholarly approaches in the area of moral/spiritual formation have displayed a great deal of diversity across different historical periods, Christian denominations, and theological schools, resulting in a rather fragmented theological landscape. The absence of a widely recognised, comprehensive theory within the theological mainstream has formed a barrier to the recognition of the significance of the fruit of the Spirit, because there has been no robust theological framework of human spiritual development that could have accommodated the fruit of the Spirit as the ultimate aspired-to end state of the process. In many ways, therefore, the key to uncovering the theological potential of the ninefold fruit lies in this domain, and we return to this question in chapter 6 to conduct a comprehensive analysis of how the fruit of the Spirit fits into the biblical portrayal of moral/spiritual formation and, more generally, into new creation and the advancement of the kingdom of God.

---

36. Douglas J. Moo, *Galatians*, BECNT (Grand Rapids: Baker Academic, 2013), 366.

2

WHAT IS THE FRUIT
OF THE SPIRIT?

L et us start the exploration of the fruit of the Spirit by examining its general properties from a number of different angles, before taking a closer look in chapter 3 at the actual virtues involved. In order to prepare the ground, we shall first seek a definition for the notion of "virtue" and then investigate the fruit of the Spirit's cultural context by analysing its relationship with the established genre of virtue list in the Greco-Roman world. Following this, we consider a fundamental aspect of the nine virtues in Gal 5:22–23—namely, that they are all mentioned elsewhere in the Bible in relation to Jesus or God the Father (or both) and can therefore be seen to reflect the divine image. Finally, we look at the "fruit" metaphor more closely, exploring what the use of this word signifies (and what it does not). The chapter will be concluded by pulling the various threads together to address the title question: What is the fruit of the Spirit?

Defining "Virtues"

The most elementary definition of the fruit of the Spirit is that it is a list made up of nine components: love, joy, peace, patience, kindness, goodness, faithfulness, gentleness, and self-control. How shall we understand the nature of these components? Are they personality traits, attitudes, emotions, habits, or behavioural practices? The most common way of referring to them in theology and philosophy has been using the term "virtue," but here we face the same question: What exactly is a virtue? Offering a definition is not merely a theoretical exercise—although the following discussion will admittedly be a bit abstract in places—as it is intended to highlight two key characteristics of the concept: on the one hand, the notion of virtue is rather *loosely defined/definable*, and on the other hand, it is rather *culture-bound*. Establishing these points with sufficient explanation will create a foundation that subsequent arguments can build on, and it will also help to prevent going off on unproductive theoretical tangents, which can be a danger when analysing complex and illusive concepts such as love or peace.

There have been a variety of definitions of "virtue" proposed in the scholarly literature, and a representative selection is presented in CONCEPT 2.1. As the list demonstrates, the various formulations tend to be complex and cover a broad range of conceptualisations *without* a dominant common theme, which explains why for example Sarah Schnitker and her colleagues refer to virtues under the noncommittal label of "hybrid personality constructs."[1] The *Catechism of the Catholic Church* sums up many of the different aspects of this construct in an extended definition: "Human virtues are firm attitudes, stable dispositions, habitual perfections of intellect and will that govern our actions, order our passions, and guide our conduct according to reason and faith."[2] There are references in this summary to virtually the whole spectrum of human psychology— cognition ("intellect"), affect/emotions ("passions"), motivation ("will"), attitudes, habits, and behaviour ("actions" and "conduct")—which reflects the gravity of the challenge to come up with a precise scientific definition of virtue.[3] Indeed, in his seminal work on Christian social ethic, Stanley

---

1. Sarah A. Schnitker et al., "The Virtue of Patience, Spirituality, and Suffering: Integrating Lessons from Positive Psychology, Psychology of Religion, and Christian Theology," *Psychology of Religion and Spirituality* 9, no. 3 (2017): 265.

2. *Catechism of the Catholic Church* #1804.

3. The challenging nature of the task is well illustrated by the fact that in a seminal paper on virtues published in the prestigious *Journal of Personality* the authors—one of the world's leading personality psychologists, Roy Baumeister, and Julie Exline—unusually recorded a question they

Hauerwas also provides a selection of different definitions of virtue and then concludes: "While this is but a random sample of definitions, little would be gained by trying to make the list more comprehensive. No such list would or could yield any satisfactory understanding. The very plurality of different notions of virtue indicates that any account of the virtues is context-dependent."[4]

Concept 2.1: Selection of Definitions of Virtue/Virtues

- "a settled and stable capacity, tendency, or propensity possessed by a person"[5]
- "a character trait that expresses some sort of excellence"[6]
- "entrenched dispositions of character (i.e., traits) which are consistently manifested in behaviour across many different types of situations"[7]
- "practical skills [that] involve knowing how to act well in particular situations"[8]

---

had been asked by a reviewer during the reviewing process concerning what the "proper unit of analysis" of their discussion was: "Is virtue a behavioural disposition, a motivational tendency, an attitude, a skill, or an ability?" The telling aspect of this question is not so much the broad variety of possible options included in it as the fact that it was asked in the first place: it indicated that the original manuscript had left the issue open, and the purpose of citing this question in the final text was clearly intended to underline the difficulty inherent to this matter. In their response, the authors offered a twofold specification, which describes the term "virtue" without really defining it in a conclusive manner: "From the community's perspective, in social functionalist terms, virtue consists of performing socially desirable actions," whereas "in terms of the inner personality processes, virtue consists of having the intention to carry out desirable actions as well as having the wherewithal to do so." Roy F. Baumeister and Julie Juola Exline, "Virtue, Personality, and Social Relations: Self-Control as the Moral Muscle," *Journal of Personality* 67, no. 6 (1999): 1170.

4. Hauerwas, *A Community of Character*, 112.

5. Philip F. Esler, *New Testament Theology: Communion and Community* (London: SPCK, 2005), 160.

6. Olli-Pekka Vainio, *Virtue: An Introduction to Theory and Practice* (Eugene, OR: Cascade Books, 2016), 8.

7. N. T. Wright, *Galatians*, Commentaries for Christian Formation (Grand Rapids: Eerdmans, 2021), 15.

8. Matthew Vess et al., "Genes and Virtue: Exploring How Heritability Beliefs Shape Conceptions of Virtue and Its Development," *Behavior Genetics* 49 (2019): 169.

- "the distinctly human (i.e., individual-level) attributes or characteristics . . . that allow people to live well together as inherently social creatures with the capacity for rationality and thus engender personal and societal well-being"[9]
- "acquired habits of excellent functioning in generic areas of human life that are challenging and important"[10]
- "an acquired human quality the possession and exercise of which tends to enable us to achieve those goods which are internal to practices and the lack of which effectively prevents us from achieving any such goods"[11]
- "habits of mind in their more general aspect"[12]

What is the cause of this general uncertainty concerning the constitution of such a salient psychological concept? Two reasons stand out in particular: the *contextual* and the *moral dependence* of the notion of virtue. Regarding the former, a recurring issue in psychology that complicates the understanding of any personality characteristics, including virtues, is the influence of contextual issues: human attributes are defined both by hereditary (i.e., genetic) and environmental factors (the "nature versus nurture" debate), and they also vary in terms of how broadly and consistently they are manifested in a person's life (the "person-situation" debate) as well as how much they fluctuate across situations (the "trait" versus "state" distinction).[13] This contextual dependency, also highlighted by

---

9. Vincent Ng and Louis Tay, "Lost in Translation: The Construct Representation of Character Virtues," *Perspectives on Psychological Science* 15, no. 2 (2020): 311.

10. W. Jay Wood, "Christian Theories of Virtue," in *The Oxford Handbook of Virtue*, ed. Nancy E. Snow (New York: Oxford University Press, 2018), 281.

11. Alasdair MacIntyre, *After Virtue: A Study in Moral Theory*, 3rd ed. (Notre Dame, IN: University of Notre Dame Press, 2007), 191.

12. Robert K. Rapa, "Galatians," in *The Expositor's Bible Commentary: Romans–Galatians*, rev. ed., ed. Tremper Longman III and David E. Garland (Grand Rapids: Zondervan, 2008), 630.

13. An example of how such variability can cause multiple understandings of a virtue is offered by Matthew Kuan Johnson concerning "joy," the second in the list of the ninefold fruit: Johnson proposes four levels of possible analysis, joy as *emotion*, joy as *mood*, joy as *disposition/trait*, and joy as *spiritual fruit* (the latter referring to a deep, spiritual sense of satisfaction). Matthew Kuan Johnson, "Joy: A Review of the Literature and Suggestions for Future Directions," *Journal of*

Hauerwas in the above quote, hampers attempts to provide a straight-forward definition. EXCURSUS 2 offers further insights into the various levels of personality analysis by introducing a relatively recent personality model by Dan McAdams, the "New Big Five" construct, which has been designed to accommodate contextual variation. (We shall return to this matter in chapter 7 when we discuss the twofold nature of the fruit of the Spirit in terms of being a function of both divine and human agency.)

The second issue that complicates the definition of the notion of virtue is that it is linked to *morality*: virtues are a special subset of person-ality characteristics that cannot be separated from the question of right or wrong because "a virtue is an habitual and firm disposition to do the *good*."[14] In other words, a virtue always has a moral value and can be thus seen as a *moral trait*. This produces considerable variability in terms of *whose* moral standards are used in defining a virtue—after all, morality is essentially *culture-dependent*. This will be evidenced in the next section, where it will be shown that Christian virtues in the NT era differed considerably from the Greco-Roman virtues of antiquity.[15]

As a result of virtue's dependency on contexts and culture-specific morality, psychological research has struggled to demonstrate sufficient consistency in people's moral behaviour; consequently, as Fleeson and his colleagues summarise in their historical overview, "The fallout was that researchers largely abandoned the study of ethics, morality, and virtue."[16] We have seen that this situation has changed over the past two decades,

---

Positive Psychology 15, no. 1 (2020): 10. It is virtually impossible to offer a unitary definition of joy that addresses all four levels in a satisfactory manner. (We shall return to this classification in chapter 3.)

14. *Catechism of the Catholic Church* #1803; emphasis added.

15. Fowers sums up this issue clearly: "Virtues are the character strengths that are necessary to pursue what is good. That means that what counts as a virtue is determined largely by what we believe to be the best, highest, most admirable, most noble aims for humans. . . . It makes a great deal of difference whether one works from an Aristotelian, Stoic, Christian, Jewish, Victorian, Buddhist, Confucian, or Lakota perspective. Each of these traditions reveres different ends or goods and consequently understands virtue in a different way. That is, they have different con-cepts of what is good for human beings and of the character strengths necessary to pursue these goods." Blaine J. Fowers, "From Continence to Virtue: Recovering Goodness, Character Unity, and Character Types for Positive Psychology," *Theory and Psychology* 18, no. 5 (2008): 630–631.

16. William R. Fleeson et al., "Personality Science and the Foundations of Character," in *Character: New Directions from Philosophy, Psychology, and Theology*, ed. Christian B. Miller et al. (Oxford: Oxford University Press, 2015), 41.

but formalising the notion of virtue in a definitive fashion remains a challenge. This explains the broad and inclusive approach taken in this book: the nine facets of the Spirit will be seen as hybrid character dispositions regulating "the lifestyle of those who are indwelt and energized by the Spirit,"[17] and they will be referred to as virtues, attributes, and dispositions in a largely interchangeable manner. More specific characterisation will be offered in chapter 3, when we consider the nine individual components of the fruit separately.

Excursus 2: McAdams's 'New Big Five' Model of Personality and the Place of Virtues in It

A major innovation in theorising the structure of personality was offered by Dan McAdams's "New Big Five" model[18] at the beginning of the new millennium. It includes five layers, of which the three middle levels constitute a three-tier framework of personality:

1. **Dispositional traits**, referring to relatively stable and decontextualised broad dimensions of individual differences.
2. **Characteristic adaptations**, referring to constructs that are highly contextualised in time, place, and/or social role, and which include "motives, goals, plans, strivings, strategies, values, virtues, schemas, self-images, mental representations of significant others, developmental tasks, and many other aspects of human individuality."[19]
3. **Integrative life narratives**, referring to "internalized and evolving life stories that reconstruct the past and imagine the

---

17. F. F. Bruce, *The Epistle to the Galatians: A Commentary on the Greek Text*, NIGTC (Grand Rapids: Eerdmans, 1982), 251.

18. Dan P. McAdams and Jennifer L. Pals, "A New Big Five: Fundamental Principles for an Integrative Science of Personality," *American Psychologist* 61, no. 3 (2006): 204–17; see also McAdams, "Psychological Science and the Nicomachean Ethics."

19. McAdams and Pals, "New Big Five," 208.

future to provide a person's life with identity (unity, purpose, meaning)."[20]

The three tiers of the model indicate that individual differences in personality occur at different levels of situatedness, which means in practical terms that a person's actions will be affected by three different sets of factors: *dispositional traits* involve stable personality dispositions that explain consistencies in behaviour across situations and over time (e.g., someone's generally anxious nature). *Characteristic adaptations* concern more situated propensities—that is, contextualised aspects of individuality that interact with specific environmental conditions (e.g., when someone is more anxious in certain situations than in others, as in stage fright) and which are therefore more malleable than dispositional traits. The real innovation of the model was the addition of a third tear, *integrative life narratives*, which concerns someone's "narrative identity": in order to make sense of their lives, people organise and understand their experiences and memories in the form of personal stories—they in effect narrate themselves into the person they become (e.g., when people produce and then internalise a strategic account of successfully conquering their anxiety). The quality of these personal life narratives constitutes a decisive aspect of why and how people differ from each other.

Thus, the three tiers in McAdams's model can be seen as three layers of description: a person's behaviour will partly respond to inherent traits, partly to situational pushes and pulls, and partly to the internalised life story that guides the person's life. An important lesson is that personality factors do not have to be assigned exclusively to one level or the other, because they can have aspects that link them to each of the three spheres of the model at the same time (as was illustrated by anxiety above).

Using this model as a theoretical framework, Schnitker and

---

20. McAdams and Pals, 212.

her colleagues have defined spiritual virtues as "hybrid personality units emerging when characteristic adaptations are given meaning by a transcendent narrative identity."[21] As they explain, in order to be virtuous, one's personal qualities that are demonstrated in concrete situations (i.e., characteristic adaptations) must be governed by a spiritual life story that promotes moral engagement—that is, "a narrative identity that values something beyond the self in a culturally appropriate manner."[22]

The Genre of Virtue List in Antiquity

The catalogue of nine attributes in Gal 5:22–23 represents a well-established literary genre in antiquity, the "virtue list," which was aimed at character building and which was highly popular in Greek ethical and philosophical writing. The most famous such list was the "catalogue of cardinal virtues" attributed to Plato—wisdom, courage, self-restraint, and justice, to which Plato later added piety[23]—which was adapted and expanded in a flexible and fluid way by other Greek philosophers without aiming for comprehensiveness or systematisation.[24] Consistent with the popularity of virtue lists in antiquity, we also find catalogues of virtues in several places in the Scriptures, with the fruit of the Spirit in Gal 5 being the most comprehensive but by no means the only one; in a comparative analysis, Dunn discussed five other listings (2 Cor 6:6; 1 Tim 4:12; 6:11; 2 Tim 2:22; 2 Pet 1:5–7),[25] and we may also add several further passages that contain catalogues of virtuous characteristics and values (e.g., Rom 12:9; 1 Cor 13:4–7; Eph 4:2–3; Phil 4:8; Col 3:12; 2 Tim

---

21. Sarah A. Schnitker, Pamela E. King, and Benjamin Houltberg, "Religion, Spirituality, and Thriving: Transcendent Narrative, Virtue, and Telos," *Journal of Research on Adolescence* 29, no. 2 (2019): 276.

22. Schnitker, King, and Houltberg, 280.

23. See e.g., Porter, "Paul, Virtues, Vices," 370.

24. Betz, *Galatians*, 281–282.

25. Dunn, *Galatians*, 309.

3:10; for a comprehensive listing see table 2 in chapter 4). These will be analysed in detail in chapter 4, but the important point to note for the current discussion is Moisés Silva's conclusion that the connection between words used for virtues in the New Testament and corresponding lists in non-Christian Greek literature is "indisputable."[26] That is, virtue lists in the Bible fitted in with the more general contemporary genre in antiquity, and all the virtue lists (including the biblical ones) shared the characteristic of having a conscious *didactic purpose*: they were intended to present the featured attributes as *models to emulate*, which was a characteristic cultural pattern of the time, consistent with the Roman practice of identifying mythical or historical figures as *exempla* in terms of their actions and attributes.[27] Virtue lists were meant to perform such a *role modelling* function, and we shall see in chapter 7, which discusses the various methods of cultivating the fruit of the Spirit, that this practice is clearly evidenced in several NT epistles.

Despite the undeniable link between Christian and secular virtue lists, New Testament commentators have been uniform in emphasising that the similarities between the virtue concepts of Hellenistic philosophy and early Christian thought were superficial, as the latter served unique Christian ecclesial purposes.[28] We saw in the previous section that virtues are *moral traits* and that the nature of this morality is inherently culture-dependent: virtues represent attributes that allow people to perform well and to achieve excellence in a specific area,[29] and for the ancient Greeks the ultimate goal to achieve was "human flourishing" in the present life, which differed in many respects from the Christian ideal.[30] N. T. Wright,

---

26. Moisés Silva, *New International Dictionary of New Testament Theology and Exegesis* (*NIDNTTE*), 2nd ed. (Grand Rapids: Zondervan, 2014), 1:390.

27. Sinclair Bell, "Role Models in the Roman World," in *Role Models in the Roman World: Identity and Assimilation*, ed. Sinclair Bell and Inge Lyse Hansen (Ann Arbor, MI: University of Michigan Press, 2008), 2.

28. See e.g., Betz, *Galatians*, 281–282; David A. deSilva, *The Letter to the Galatians*, NICNT (Grand Rapids: Eerdmans, 2018), 465; Fung, *Galatians*, 272; Porter, "Paul, Virtues, Vices," 371; N. T. Wright, *After You Believe*, 204. Indeed, Furnish categorically states, "While Gal. 5:22–23 bears certain superficial similarities to the traditional 'virtue list,' in fact it must be regarded as a genuinely Pauline creation." Victor Paul Furnish, *Theology and Ethics in Paul* (Nashville: Abingdon, 1968), 88.

29. See e.g., Hauerwas, *A Community of Character*, 111.

30. See e.g., N. T. Wright, *After You Believe*, 185–186.

for example, contrasts the Greek *exemplar* of the hero-figure who stands out of the crowd with the ideal Christian character involving a communal team spirit that enables someone to become a useful member of the body of Christ[31]—as Graham Tomlin aptly puts it, "Christian virtues are those required to live together in harmony and peace, not to win battles."[32] The difference between the Greco-Roman and Christian moral systems is perhaps best illustrated by their handling of *humility* and *pride*: within the tradition of antiquity, humility was not regarded as a virtue at all, whereas pride was held as a highly commendable personal value; in the Christian tradition this was exactly the other way round, so much so that pride was seen in fact as the paramount cardinal sin.[33]

In summary, while the Greco-Roman ethos was centred around individual success in the world, human flourishing in the Christian moral tradition was equated with community building and becoming Christlike. Accordingly, as Alasdair MacIntyre aptly points out in his seminal work on virtues, "Aristotle would certainly not have admired Jesus Christ and he would have been horrified by St Paul."[34]

Reflection of Divine Character

It was mentioned in the introduction that all the attributes listed in Gal 5:22–23 are mentioned elsewhere in the Scriptures in relation to either God the Father or the Son (or both),[35] and table 1 lists a selection of

---

31. N. T. Wright, 204.

32. Tomlin, *Spiritual Fitness*, 50.

33. For detailed discussions, see Porter, "Paul, Virtues, Vices," 375–376; Wood, "Christian Theories of Virtue," 282.

34. MacIntyre, *After Virtue*, 184. Elsewhere MacIntyre states that "the New Testament not only praises virtues of which Aristotle knows nothing—faith, hope and love—   but it praises at least one quality as a virtue which Aristotle seems to count as one of the vices relative to magnanimity, namely humility" (182). N. T. Wright (*After You Believe*, 36) adds that "Aristotle glimpsed a goal of human flourishing; so did Jesus, Paul, and the rest. But Jesus's vision of that goal was larger and richer, taking in the whole world, and putting humans not as lonely individuals developing their own moral status but as glad citizens of God's coming kingdom."

35. Because Christ is the "exact representation" of God's being (Heb 1:3) and the images of the Father and the Son are the same (2 Cor 4:4), the distinction between reflecting the Father and the Son is irrelevant.

relevant biblical passages. This indicates that the fruit of the Spirit is more than merely a commendable template for moral development, as it offers the blueprint of reproducing Christ's character in the believer through the Holy Spirit; in Keener's words, "The character of the Spirit grows in believers. . . . Those who are 'born from the Spirit' (4:29) have the Spirit's character."[36] This is consistent with a message Paul sent to the believers in Corinth: "you are a letter from Christ, the result of our ministry, written not with ink *but with the Spirit* of the living God, not on tablets of stone but *on tablets of human hearts*" (2 Cor 3:3; emphasis added).

One may wonder whether the use of the word "blueprint" was appropriate in the previous paragraph, given that it suggests an intentional design. Does Christian spiritual formation involve reproducing aspects of the divine character in the believers? Based on an analysis of the portrayal of moral/spiritual development in the Bible, chapter 6 will give an affirmative answer, and as a preliminary, it can be stated that most scholars would agree with Jennifer Herdt's summary: "A central feature of the teachings of Jesus as related in the gospels was the summons to emulate the character of God: 'Be perfect, therefore, as your heavenly Father is perfect' [Matt. 5:48]."[37] In 1 Pet 1:16, this command is paraphrased (echoing Lev 11:44, 45; 19:2) as "it is written: 'Be holy, because I am holy,'" and Derek Tidball explains that "the ancient call to 'be holy because I, the LORD your God, am holy' (Lev 19:2), updated by the new covenant . . . gives us the advantage of seeing what it means to be perfectly holy, what the unblemished image of God looks like in a human being, and so what it means to be truly human, modelled by the person of Christ. To be holy is to have the image of God, given to us at creation, restored in us. It is, therefore, to be truly human and truly Christlike."[38]

---

36. Keener, "Fruit of the Spirit," 579. C. Wright (*Cultivating the Fruit of the Spirit*, 70) argues in a similar vein: "When we talk about the fruit of the Spirit, it means that God's own character is bearing fruit in our character. The life of God is at work within our life." See also Lynn H. Cohick, "Fruit of the Spirit," in *Evangelical Dictionary of Theology*, ed. Daniel J. Treier and Walter A. Elwell (Grand Rapids: Baker Academic, 2017), 332.

37. Jennifer A. Herdt, "Frailty, Fragmentation, and Social Dependency in the Cultivation of Christian Virtue," in *Cultivating Virtue: Perspectives from Theology, Philosophy, and Psychology*, ed. Nancy E. Snow (New York: Oxford University Press, 2014), 228.

38. Derek Tidball, "Holiness: Restoring God's Image—Colossians 3:5–17," in *Sanctification: Explorations in Theology and Practice*, ed. Kelly M. Kapic (Downers Grove, IL: IVP Academic, 2014), 31.

Table 1: Examples of Biblical Passages Linking the Facets of the Fruit of the Spirit to Divine Character

	Attributed to Jesus	Attributed to God the Father
Love	John 13:1; 15:9; Eph 5:2	Exod 34:6; Num 14:18; Jonah 4:2; John 3:16; 15:9; 2 Cor 13:11; 1 John 4:8
Joy	John 15:11; 17:13	
Peace	John 14:27; Eph 2:14; Col 3:15	Rom 15:33; 16:20; 1 Cor 14:33; 2 Cor 13:11; Phil 4:7, 9; 1 Thess 5:23; Heb 13:20
Patience	1 Tim 1:16; 2 Pet 3:15	Rom 2:4; 9:22; 1 Pet 3:20
Kindness	Titus 3:4; 1 Pet 2:3	Rom 2:4; 11:22; Titus 3:4
Goodness		Pss 23:6; 25:7; 69:16; 119:68; 136:1; Jer 33:11; Nah 1:7; Mark 10:18 (and parallels)
Faithfulness	Rev 1:5	Exod 34:6; Rom 3:3; 1 Cor 1:9; 10:13
Gentleness	Matt 11:29; 21:5; 2 Cor 10:1	
Self-control[39]	"Perseverance/ steadfastness": 2 Thess 3:5; "endurance": Heb 12:2	"Slow to anger": Exod 34:6; Num 14:18; Ps 86:15; Jonah 4:2

In other words, it has been a fundamental Christian conviction that at the heart of Christian character formation is the aspiration to be conformed to the image of Jesus Christ, as believers are united with him and are adopted into the family of God.[40] Pamela King calls this goal part of the human *telos*—that is, humanity's shared inherent purpose of

---

39. As mentioned briefly in the introduction (to be elaborated on in chapter 3), there are few biblical occurrences of the specific Greek term (or its derivatives) used for self-control in Gal 5:23; however, the broader semantic domain of self-discipline/self-mastery is well represented in the Scriptures, and several examples of this representation are associated with Jesus or God the Father.

40. For a summary, see Ray S. Yeo, "Christian Character Formation and the Infusion of Grace," in *Character: New Directions from Philosophy, Psychology, and Theology*, ed. Christian B. Miller et al. (New York: Oxford University Press, 2015), 546.

growing towards the character of Christ,[41] and chapter 6 will argue that the fruit of the Spirit offers the most detailed and specific outline of this aspired-to *telos*.

The Meaning of "Fruit" in Galatians 5:22

The phrase "fruit of the Spirit" is unique in Gal 5 in the sense that it is not used by any other NT author, and neither does it occur elsewhere in Paul's epistles. There are two close parallels to it—"fruit of righteousness" (Phil 1:11) and "fruit of the light" (Eph 5:9)—but these are not considered theological concepts in their own right, which raises the question of why the "fruit of the Spirit" is different in this respect. Let us explore this issue first by examining whether it is scripturally warranted to use "fruit of the Spirit" as a set phrase and a label, and then whether it is legitimate to read into the interpretation of this phrase several biblical echoes and allusions associated with the word "fruit" (as has often been done in commentaries). Finally, we shall address briefly the oft-discussed question as to whether it has any special significance that the "fruit" in Gal 5:22 is in the singular even though it refers to nine virtues.

Is "the Fruit of the Spirit" a Genuine Scriptural Label?

There is no doubt that in Christian parlance the phrase "fruit of the Spirit" has been used as a fixed expression serving as a descriptive label for the set of virtues listed in Gal 5:22–23. One may wonder, however, whether the text in v. 22 was written with such an intent, or whether

---

41. As King argues, "The Bible declares that Christ is the perfect image of God. Becoming like Christ is part of our *telos*. Being conformed to the likeness of the image of God in Christ is a shared *telos* amongst humans. Thus, we take on the ways of Christ and grow towards the character of Christ. Believers are to take Jesus' command to his disciples to 'Follow me' literally." Pamela Ebstyne King, "The Reciprocating Self: Trinitarian and Christological Anthropologies of Being and Becoming," *Journal of Psychology and Christianity* 35, no. 3 (2016): 220. Likewise, Samra submits that "for Paul Christ paradigmatically exemplified the character all believers should aspire to and thus is the standard of maturity for believers." James George Samra, *Being Conformed to Christ in Community: A Study of Maturity, Maturation and the Local Church in the Undisputed Pauline Epistles* (London: T&T Clark, 2006), 76.

what we consider a set phrase was merely part of an ordinary, nonidiomatic grammatical construction meaning "the outcome/consequence of the Spirit's impact."[42] This latter reading is supported by the fact that the word "fruit" (*karpos*) is frequently employed in the Scriptures in a figurative sense meaning "result" or "product" (e.g., Matt 3:8; 7:16, 20; Eph 5:9; Phil 1:11; Heb 12:11; 13:15; Jas 3:17, 18), both in relation to good and bad activities; for example, Rom 7:4–5 includes both the positive sense ("we might bear fruit for God") and the negative one ("we bore fruit for death"), and in Rom 6:21–22, *karpos* is again used in both senses: "But what fruit were you getting at that time from the things of which you are now ashamed? For the end of those things is death. But now that you have been set free from sin and have become slaves of God, the fruit you get leads to sanctification and its end, eternal life" (ESV).

In fact, although in a few cases *karpos* is used in the Bible in its original meaning of an actual fruit (e.g., Luke 13:6; 1 Cor 9:7) or, more generally, crop (e.g., Matt 13:8, 23), the vast majority of its occurrences are figurative, indicating the consequence/result of actions and lives. This would suggest that in Gal 5:22 Paul may have used "fruit" simply as a synonym for "consequence," which in turn implies that "the fruit of the Spirit" is not a phrase that Paul specifically coined to serve as a descriptive label for a collection of Christlike virtues. Of course, we cannot know the apostle's exact intentions, and therefore the real question for the current discussion is whether it is consistent with Paul's message in Gal 5 that the phrase has been added to the Christian theological register.

To start with, the word "fruit" has a definite moral connotation in the Bible, with "bearing/producing fruit" indicating righteous living[43]: we are told, for example, that "the gospel is bearing fruit" (Col 1:6) and that "the kingdom of God will be . . . given to a people who will produce its fruit" (Matt 21:43); in contrast, fruitlessness is associated with darkness (Eph 5:11) as well as with heresy and death (Jude 12). Keener therefore

---

42. I.e., a prepositional phrase that functions as a "periphrastic possessive/genitive," indicating origin.

43. See e.g., Frank J. Matera, *Galatians*, SP 9 (Collegeville, MN: Liturgical Press, 2007), 202–203; Philip Graham Ryken, *Galatians*, Reformed Expository Commentary (Phillipsburg, NJ: P&R, 2005), 310–311.

concludes that the metaphor of moral fruit is an established semantic unit in Scripture.[44] Accordingly, the fact that such a morally loaded metaphor is used in Gal 5:22–23 to precede the most detailed list of virtues in the biblical canon may explain partly why the phrase "fruit of the Spirit" has become increasingly conventionalised in association with Christlike personality features. And given the fact that—as will be argued in chapter 4—the nine virtues in the Galatian passage can be viewed to represent a coherent, composite character, the position taken in this book is that using "the fruit of the Spirit" as a formulaic descriptor for this character is not inconsistent with Paul's message, irrespective of whether the apostle intended to coin it as a label or not.

The Fruit Motif

With the phrase "fruit of the Spirit" becoming an established label for Gal 5:22–23, it was inevitable that the motif of "fruit" would start playing a role in the interpretation of the virtues contained in the passage. There have indeed been several parallels drawn between the growing of fruit and the Spirit's work in producing the nine virtues in believers. For example, along with other commentators, Tidball has characterised the *timescale* of human spiritual formation on the basis of the fruit metaphor: "The mature fruit we long to produce is likely to take time to grow and unlikely to develop overnight. Consequently, we need patience with ourselves and with others to allow the crop to ripen."[45] N. T. Wright referred to growing actual fruit in order to emphasise the importance of *human agency* in developing it: "The point of using the term 'fruit,' after all, is that these are things which grow from within rather than being imposed from without. . . . The common misperception [is] that, if it is fruit, it ought to happen without our making any effort."[46] In addition to drawing on such biological analogies, scholars have also identified intertextual links

---

44. Keener, "Fruit of the Spirit," 578. In fact, Dunn (*Galatians*, 308) explains that the moral-metaphorical meaning of *karpos* was so salient in NT times that it became proverbial that the fruit was a manifestation of the nature of the tree which bore it (see e.g., Matt 7:16; Luke 6:43).

45. Derek Tidball, *The Message of Holiness: Restoring God's Masterpiece* (Nottingham: Inter-Varsity, 2010), 209.

46. N. T. Wright, *After You Believe*, 206.

between the fruit of the Spirit and occurrences of the "fruit" motif else-where in the Bible, thereby enriching the interpretation of Gal 5. The most obvious parallel of this kind is Jesus's final "I am" saying in the Gospel of John concerning the vine and the branches (John 15:1–17), because it contains the word "fruit" no fewer than eight times.[47] John Walvoord's exposition represents a common approach to utilise this link: "This fruit of the Spirit is also related to the vital union of a believer in Christ, as illustrated in Christ's discourse on the vine and the branches (John 15). Believers, because of their relationship to Christ as well as to the Holy Spirit, are able to bear fruit, but as the dependence of the branch upon the vine illustrates, they are at the same time dependent upon the Holy Spirit for the manifestation of any evidences of sanctification in their lives."[48]

The motif of the "firstfruit" (Rom 8:23; 1 Cor 15:20) is a further obvious parallel, with the *Catechism of the Catholic Church* describing the connection as follows: "The *fruits* of the Spirit are perfections that the Holy Spirit forms in us as the first fruits of eternal glory."[49] The fruit motif is also prominent in the Old Testament, as Israel is often compared to a fruit-bearing tree or vineyard.[50] Beale draws specific attention to Isaiah's prophecies about Israel's fruitfulness in the new creation, high-lighting the role of the Spirit "as the producer of new-creational ethical fruit."[51] In the oracle in Isa 32:15–20, the fruit is specifically connected to the outpouring of the Holy Spirit,[52] and Beale underlines the fact that Isa 57:15–19 (in the Septuagint translation) and Gal 5:22 are the only two

---

47. "I am the true vine, and my Father is the gardener. He cuts off every branch in me that bears no fruit, while every branch that does bear fruit he prunes so that it will be even more fruit-ful. . . . No branch can bear fruit by itself; it must remain in the vine. Neither can you bear fruit unless you remain in me. . . . If you remain in me and I in you, you will bear much fruit; apart from me you can do nothing. . . . This is to my Father's glory, that you bear much fruit. . . . You did not choose me, but I chose you and appointed you so that you might go and bear fruit—fruit that will last" (John 15:1–16).

48. John F. Walvoord, "The Augustinian Dispensational Perspective," in *Five Views on Sanctification*, ed. Stanley N. Gundry (Grand Rapids: Zondervan, 1987), 221.

49. *Catechism of the Catholic Church* #1832.

50. See D. S. Dockery, "Fruit of the Spirit," in *Dictionary of Paul and His Letters*, ed. Gerald F. Hawthorne and Ralph P. Martin (Downers Grove, IL: InterVarsity, 1993), 317.

51. G. K. Beale, *A New Testament Biblical Theology: The Unfolding of the Old Testament in the New* (Grand Rapids: Baker Academic, 2011), 583.

52. Beale, 305.

passages in the Bible where the combination of the five Greek words for "Spirit," "fruit," "peace," "patience," and "joy" occurs.[53] Accordingly, he concludes, "That this is not merely a formal parallel but rather a material one is also borne out by the observation that the notion of the Spirit creating fruit that is spiritual in character is unique to the book of Isaiah in the OT and to Gal. 5 in the NT."[54]

We have to ask at this point whether all these similarities could simply be a coincidence; that is, did the apostle have in mind all the scriptural allusions and links as well as the various properties of an actual fruit when he selected the word for Gal 5:22? On the one hand, John Barclay, for example, argues for consciousness in Paul's word choice: "By choosing a word with these rich associations, Paul is able to provide his appeal with further support."[55] On the other hand, we have also seen above that Paul frequently employs the word fruit as a synonym for "outcome/result" in different contexts and combinations, and it is unlikely that all the biological and intertextual echoes were meant to be heard in all those occurrences. Yet, the fact remains that the word "fruit" has a range of biblical and nonbiblical connotations, and some of these will undoubtedly resonate in the reader of Gal 5:22–23, either on the conscious or the unconscious level.

Fruit or Fruits?

A recurring point in commentaries about Gal 5 is to contrast the fact that the list of vices is referred to by a plural word (the "works/acts" of the flesh), whereas the subsequent virtues are introduced by a singular word ("fruit" of the Spirit), implying that the fruit of the Spirit is singularly one.[56] The point is clearly made by Ben Witherington: "I would suggest that the singular here suggests the unity and unifying

---

53. Beale, 586.
54. Beale, 587.
55. John M. G. Barclay, *Obeying the Truth: A Study of Paul's Ethics in Galatians* (Edinburgh: T&T Clark, 1988), 121.
56. E.g., Betz, *Galatians*, 286; Cohick, "Fruit of the Spirit," 332; Fung, *Galatians*, 262; Wesley L. Gerig, "Fruit of the Spirit," in *Baker Encyclopedia of the Bible*, ed. Walter A. Elwell and Barry J. Beitzel (Grand Rapids: Baker, 1988), 819; Matera, *Galatians*, 202; Porter, "Paul, Virtues, Vices," 375; Rapa, "Galatians," 608.

nature of these qualities as opposed to the divisive effects of the traits listed in the vice list. The singular also suggests that Paul expects all of these traits to be manifested not only in any Christian community but in any Christian life, not love in one person, peace in another and so on."[57]

Despite the marked plural/singular contrast between the "works of the flesh" and the "fruit of the Spirit" in Gal 5, linguistically speaking, this argument cannot be seen as conclusive. Although the position taken in this book agrees with the view that the fruit is one composite entity with nine different facets (see chapter 4), Gordon Fee, amongst others, rightly points out that *karpos* can function in Greek as a collective singular, very much as the word "fruit" does in English.[58] In fact, elsewhere in his letters Paul always uses this singular form when the word is used in a figurative sense,[59] which would suggest that the singular has no marked meaning but is merely a stylistic preference.[60] On the other hand, it is worth noting here that if Paul had wanted to underline the multiplicity of the parts, he could have easily used a different word instead of "fruit."

Summary: What Is the Fruit of the Spirit?

Having examined some of the basic properties of the fruit of the Spirit, let us return to the question in the title of this chapter: What is the fruit of the Spirit? We can arrive at an answer by pulling together several threads from the previous discussion:

---

57. Ben Witherington III, *Grace in Galatia: A Commentary on St. Paul's Letter to the Galatians* (Grand Rapids: Eerdmans, 1998), 408.

58. Gordon D. Fee, *God's Empowering Presence: The Holy Spirit in the Letters of Paul* (Peabody, MA: Hendrickson, 1994), 444; as he explains, "In both Greek and English one would refer to 'the fruit in the bowl,' whether 'they' are all of one kind or of several."

59. As Keener ("Fruit of the Spirit," 581–582) summarises, the term appears in the Pauline corpus eleven times in the singular and only once in the plural (2 Tim 2:6), but in the latter case it refers to actual agricultural products.

60. See e.g., Martinus C. de Boer, *Galatians: A Commentary*, NTL (Louisville: Westminster John Knox, 2011), 362; deSilva, *Galatians*, 465; Keener, *Galatians*, 518; Moo, *Galatians*, 363.

- First, the nine attributes in Gal 5:22–23 relate to virtues that reflect divine character, and therefore the list concerns some kind of an ideal for Christians to strive for—that is, aspects of an *ideal Christlike character.*
- Second, the word "fruit" in the descriptive label preceding the nine attributes is telling in that both its literal meaning (i.e., "fruit," which develops gradually from the ovary of a flowering plant) and its metaphorical meaning (i.e., "outcome" or "result" of a process) suggest that the listed attributes are to be understood as the product of some kind of a *process of transformation*; for example, Keener explains that "Paul emphasizes here that the solution to the passions of the flesh is not more laws, but rather the Spirit, who *transforms* from within."[61]
- Third, the specific mention of the "Spirit" in the phrase qualifies the transformation process in an important way in that it links it to *divine involvement*; as Thomas Schreiner puts it, the "new quality of life (5:22–23) is the result of the Spirit's work."[62]

Taking the three points together, the fruit of the Spirit will be understood in the current work as *the ideal outcome of a divinely orchestrated transformation process to produce a Christlike character in the believer.* Bruce Longenecker's summary echoes this view when he talks about Paul presenting "a charter and blueprint for social relationships within the eschatological community in which the sovereign creator is transforming people in conformity with the character of the loving and self-giving Son."[63]

---

61. Keener, *Galatians*, 490; emphasis added.
62. Schreiner, *Galatians*, 352.
63. Bruce W. Longenecker, *The Triumph of Abraham's God: The Transformation of Identity in Galatians* (Edinburgh: T&T Clark, 1998), 72.

3

THE NINE FACETS OF THE FRUIT OF THE SPIRIT

It was argued in chapter 1 that the significance of the fruit of the Spirit is not limited solely to offering a list of nine independent virtuous attributes, because the aggregate of these virtues can be seen as a representation of an ideal, Christlike character. This, however, does not reduce the value of the nine individual virtues—after all, those include such core Christian concepts as love, peace, and self-control—and any systematic account of the fruit of the Spirit requires an exegesis of the terms listed in Gal 5:22–23. This chapter presents a discussion of the nine attributes in a manner like the traditional itemised approach to the fruit—that is, by treating the virtues largely independently from each other. The focus of this survey will be on two analytical aspects: First, it will be shown that the seemingly straightforward English labels for the nine virtues hide several ambiguities in the translation of the specific Greek words used, and in some cases the meaning of the original terms does not coincide exactly with the semantic domain that the English rendering suggests. Second, in order to explore the full content of the nine virtues, the discussion will combine theological insights with relevant findings from the fields of personality and positive psychology.

Love (*Agapē*)

The word 'love' requires little introduction to Christian readers, as it is one of the central concepts in the Bible—after all, "God is love" (1 John 4:8) and Jesus affirmed that the greatest commandments are "Love the Lord your God with all your heart and with all your soul and with all your mind" and "Love your neighbour as yourself" (Matt 22:37, 39 and parallels). Furthermore, not only has the subject of love been addressed by countless sermons and treatises over the centuries, but we also find detailed explanations about its nature in the Scriptures themselves, most notably in Matt 5:43–48; Rom 12:9–21; 1 Cor 13; and 1 John 4:7–21. In light of this, it is rather surprising how difficult it is to define what "love" actually means. In chapter 2 we characterised virtues as hybrid personality constructs, and we shall see below that this mixed nature is particularly true of love: it covers several diverse areas, from emotions and attitudes to compassion and action. Scott Peck speaks for many when he submits that "One result of the mysterious nature of love is that no one has ever, to my knowledge, arrived at a truly satisfactory definition of love."[1] In order to uncover some of the complex layers of the meaning of this virtue, let us examine the concept from a number of different angles, starting with the semantic reference of the Greek term, *agapē*, that is used in Gal 5:22.

The Meaning of *Agapē*

The Greek word for love that Paul uses in the description of the fruit of the Spirit is *agapē*, a term that has attained considerable fame over the centuries and which has not only entered the English Christian lexicon but also the psychological one, as scholars sometimes talk about "agape love" as a technical term (see below). It is one of the four main words used in classical Greek for the semantic domain that is covered by the English word "love"; two of these—*erōs* (romantic/sexual love) and *storgē* (love between family members)—do not occur in the New

---

1. M. Scott Peck, *The Road Less Travelled: A New Psychology of Love, Traditional Values and Spiritual Growth*, 25th anniversary ed. (London: Rider Books, 2003), 6.

Testament, while the third, *philia* (a general word for tender love in secular Greek), occurs in the New Testament some twenty-five times in a similar meaning as *agapē*, sometimes interchangeably with it.[2] However, for NT writers the word of choice for love was *agapē*, which occurs (along with its cognates) over 300 times in a variety of senses. This high frequency of the biblical occurrence of *agapē* is in stark contrast with the relative rarity of the same word in the secular Greek of the time,[3] which has led many scholars to conclude that *agapē* "seems to have been patented by the writers of the New Testament,"[4] a point made by N. T. Wright expressively: "The early Christians, in fact, did with the word *agapē* pretty much what they did with the ancient notion of virtue. They picked it up, soaked it in the message and achievement of Jesus, and gave it a new life, a new sort of life."[5]

However, the fact that the word was favoured and appropriated by Christian writers does not necessarily mean that its specific semantic content was linked exclusively to "Christian love." Granted, it is used in the Scriptures for the love between the believers and also in association with the Father, the Son, and the Spirit, but in other places the word concerns neutral issues (e.g., the Pharisees' love for the most important seats in the synagogues; Luke 11:43) and sometimes even moral darkness ("people loved darkness instead of light"; John 3:19). Therefore, Moo rightly submits that the distinctive Christian flavour of the word derives not so much from its semantic properties as from the unique Christian focus on the subject of love with which *agapē* was associated.[6]

---

2. E.g., as Beasley-Murray summarises, "In John's Gospel the two terms are used as synonyms [e.g., both terms are used for the Father's love for the Son (3:35; 5:20), Jesus' love for humans (11:5; 11:3), and the love of humans for Jesus (8:42; 16:27)]. A distinction has sometimes been made in the use of the two terms in the well-known scene when Jesus reinstates Peter (John 21:15–19), but most exegetes now reject this view." George R. Beasley-Murray, *John*, rev. ed. (Dallas: Word, 1999), 394.

3. In secular Greek the other three Greek words for love were more common, although the verb form of *agapē* (*agapaō*) was relatively frequent; see e.g., Keener, *Galatians*, 460; R. N. Longenecker, *Galatians*, 260; Moo, *Galatians*, 364.

4. Ryken, *Galatians*, 232.

5. N. T. Wright, *After You Believe*, 183–184.

6. Moo, *Galatians*, 364.

What Is "Love"?

First Corinthians 13:1–3 speaks about love as something one can "have" (see also John 5:42; 15:13), which suggests that it is a distinct entity whose presence or absence is discernible. However, the subsequent passage in the same epistle, which details what love is like and how it acts (1 Cor 13:4–8), does not specify the nature of this entity, and Paul simply describes it as "the most excellent way" (12:31). What exactly is this "most excellent way"? CONCEPT 3.1 presents a selection of definitions for love taken both from theology and psychology, which illustrate well the complex, hybrid nature of the concept: the four primary categories for classifying any construct in psychology are cognitive, affective (i.e., related to emotion), motivational, and behavioural; and the list in CONCEPT 3.1 includes elements of all four: *cognitive*: "discernment" and "knowledge"; *affective*: "emotion"; *motivational*: "will"; *behavioural*: "action."

Concept 3.1: A Selection of Definitions of Love

- "Many love scholars define love as an *attitude*—or a predisposition to think, feel, and behave in positive ways toward another . . . As opposed to an attitude, most laypersons and some love scholars prefer to think of love as an *emotion*."[7]
- "Love is that outgoing, self-giving kind of *action*, not necessarily emotion, that characterized God himself when he loved the world so much that he gave his only Son (Jn 3:16)."[8]
- "I define love thus: The *will* to extend one's self for the purpose of nurturing one's own or another's spiritual growth."[9]

---

7. Ellen Berscheid, "Love in the Fourth Dimension," *Annual Review of Psychology* 51 (2010): 8; emphasis added.

8. Gerig, "Fruit of the Spirit," in *Baker Encyclopedia*, 818; emphasis added.

9. Peck, *The Road Less Travelled*, 69; emphasis added.

- "Love, in the Christian sense, does not mean an emotion. It is a *state* not of the feelings but *of the will*."[10]
- "Love is the *atmosphere* of the Christian life."[11]
- "The working definition of compassionate love includes both the *attitudes* and *actions* related to giving of self for the good of the other. . . . But at the core of the construct are *motivation* and *discernment*, facets of free choice to stretch and to give."[12]
- "And this is my prayer: that your love may abound more and more in *knowledge* and *depth of insight*, so that you may be able to *discern* what is best" (Phil 1:9–10, emphasis added).

Significantly, some definitions combine more than one of these categories, while some others use even broader descriptors such as "atmosphere" or "state" to avoid any reduction of meaning. It seems therefore that such a forensic analysis does not take us very far in trying to pin down what love is beyond identifying it as a selfless desire for the good of another person, which is not dissimilar to the way Aristotle captured the notion.[13] We shall return to this matter when we survey the relevant psychological research below; at this stage we may have a better chance of capturing the essence of this "most excellent way" by focusing on four salient aspects of biblical love, namely that it is *self-giving*, *active*, *strategic*, and *communal*.

---

10. C. S. Lewis, *Christian Behaviour* (London: William Collins, [1943] 2016), 129; emphasis added.

11. William Barclay, *Flesh and Spirit: An Examination of Galatians 5.19–23* (London: SCM, 1962), 71; emphasis added.

12. Lynn G. Underwood, "Compassionate Love: A Framework for Research," in *The Science of Compassionate Love: Theory, Research, and Applications*, ed. Beverley Fehr, Susan Sprecher, and Lynn G. Underwood (Malden, MA: Wiley-Blackwell, 2009), 4; emphasis added.

13. In *Eudemian Ethics* (EE VII 6 1240a23–b9) Aristotle writes, "A friend is someone who wishes good things (or the sort of things he thinks are good) for someone, not for his own sake but for that person's sake. In another way, one would most be thought to love a person if one wishes that he should exist, for his sake and not one's own, even if one doesn't confer goods on him, let alone existence." Cited in Corinne A. Gartner, "Aristotle on Love and Friendship," in *The Cambridge Companion to Ancient Ethics*, ed. Christopher Bobonich (Cambridge: Cambridge University Press, 2017), 147.

Love Is Self-Giving

Love is a central attribute of God (1 John 4:8, 16), and as is well known, this love is characterised in Scripture as *sacrificial*: "He gave his one and only Son" (John 3:16). The sacrificial, self-giving nature of love is also emphasised by Jesus when he declares, "Greater love has no one than this: to lay down one's life for one's friends" (John 15:13), and 1 John 3:16 calls all believers to "lay down our lives for our brothers and sisters." Paul, too, set this self-giving quality as a standard for all Christian disciples: "For Christ's love compels us, because . . . he died for all, [so] that those who live should no longer live for themselves" (2 Cor 5:14–15), and in Gal 5:13 he explicitly calls believers to "serve one another humbly in love," before reminding them of Jesus's command in the next verse, "Love your neighbour as yourself" (v. 14). Accordingly, Richard Longenecker concludes that "the self-giving of Christ through death on a cross is the central soteriological theme of Galatians (cf., 1:4; 3:1, 13; 6:12, 14), just as it was the focus of early Christian preaching (cf., the sermons recorded in Acts and the passion narratives of the Gospels)."[14] The other-centred, self-giving love that Christ displayed and that the disciples were called to imitate as a governing principle in their everyday conduct was an altogether unique and novel quality in that it introduced into the world, in N. T. Wright's words, "a different way to be human"[15]—in fact, as he continues, "Nobody had ever thought of living like that before."[16]

Love Is Active

Several definitions in CONCEPT 3.1 reflect the fact that love lends itself to being described not so much in terms of its internal, emotional side as through what it leads people to *do*.[17] We find a similar emphasis

---

14. R. N. Longenecker, *Galatians*, 264.
15. N. T. Wright, *After You Believe*, 236.
16. N. T. Wright, 236.
17. Peck (*The Road Less Travelled*, 104–105) elaborates on this point as follows: "I have said that love is an action, an activity. This leads to the final major misconception of love which needs to be addressed. Love is not a feeling. Many, many people possessing a feeling of love and even acting in response to that feeling act in all manner of unloving and destructive ways. A genuinely loving individual will often take loving and constructive action toward a person he or

in the Bible: as we saw above, in John 3:16, God's love is characterised by specifying what he did ("gave his one and only Son"), and in John 15:13 ultimate love is described through the deed it results in ("to lay down one's life for one's friend"). The link between love and its outworking is also illustrated in the parable of the good Samaritan (Luke 10:25–37): when a teacher of the law asked Jesus about the greatest commandments, Jesus did not engage in a theological discussion but characterised the essence of loving one's neighbour by means of the Samaritan's actions. Thus, love and *acting on love* go hand in hand—as Peck has succinctly put it, "Love is as love does."[18] This principle is expressed particularly clearly in 1 John 3:18, "Dear children, let us not love with words or speech but with actions and in truth."

The active element of love is also a defining aspect of Paul's exposition of the concept. Werner Jeanrond refers to this active construal of love as "praxis," arguing that in Paul's epistles love is not an idea or an abstraction, and it "neither moralizes, nor sentimentalizes, nor psychologizes."[19] Instead, love is foregrounded in its human embodiment—that is, in the way it is manifested in people's actions. For example, the thirty illustrations of "sincere love in action" in Rom 12:9–21 embrace a wide range of aspects of Christian conduct, from how to relate to each other to practicing hospitality,[20] and the notion of active love is beautifully recapped in Paul's praise of love in 1 Cor 13:4–8: "Love is patient, love is kind. It does not envy, it does not boast, it is not proud. It does not dishonour others, it is not self-seeking, it is not easily angered, it keeps no record of wrongs. Love does not delight in evil but rejoices with the truth. It always protects, always trusts, always hopes, always perseveres. Love never fails."

---

she consciously dislikes, actually feeling no love toward the person at the time and perhaps even finding the person repugnant in some way."

18. Peck, 108.

19. Werner G. Jeanrond, *A Theology of Love* (London: T&T Clark, 2010), 38. B. W. Longenecker (*The Triumph of Abraham's God*, 73) concurs: "When he [Paul] speaks of 'love' . . . the emotional connotations of this word are far overshadowed by the practical, concrete aspect whereby 'love' becomes realised in action."

20. See Esler, *New Testament Theology*, 281.

Love Is Strategic

Several of the definitions in CONCEPT 3.1 portray love as a conscious, strategic product of one's will rather than an emotion one comes to feel. This volitional aspect is evident in Jesus's famous teaching in the Sermon on the Mount that urges believers to love their enemies rather than only those who love them (Matt 5:44–46), because "if you love those who love you, what reward will you get?" (v. 46). What Jesus called for was something that goes against the grain of most people's instincts and can only be achieved through the active involvement of the mind. The need for a fusion of love and cognition is also underlined in Phil 1:9–10, where Paul prays "that your love may abound more and more in knowledge and depth of insight, so that you may be able to discern what is best." This prayer highlights the fact that making the right kind of loving decision requires cognitive appraisal and strategic judgment. All this, however, raises the question of why one needs to involve the mind in a domain that is usually associated with the heart. We can think of several reasons:

- One reason for the necessary involvement of conscious strategic thinking in love concerns the *inevitable cost* of maintaining a compassionate loving relationship: self-giving requires conscious commitment that needs to be considered (a topic that we shall address in detail in the next chapter when we look at the interdependence of love and self-control).
- A second reason, mentioned by Peck, is the fact that the human capacity to love is limited, and therefore people must make a conscious and informed *choice* about the person towards whom they will direct their love.[21]
- Conscious discernment is also needed to determine what will *genuinely benefit* the loved one, given that well-intentioned actions can sometimes turn out to cause harm in some way.[22]
- Finally and related to the previous points, conscious strategic thinking is required in cases when love leads to potential *goal*

---

21. Peck, *The Road Less Travelled*, 107.
22. Underwood, "Compassionate Love," 15.

conflict, for example when people have to juggle between several help-related actions that require prioritisation (for a famous experiment at Princeton Theological Seminary that illustrates this point, see CONCEPT 3.2).

Concept 3.2: "From Jerusalem to Jericho": Exploring the Psychology of Helping[23]

In a famous experiment in the 1970s, John Darley and Daniel Batson asked a group of students at Princeton Theological Seminary to go to another building on campus to give a short talk, some on the parable of the good Samaritan, some on a non-help-related topic. The participants were divided into three groups according to how much they were asked to hurry because someone depended on their speedy arrival (i.e., low-hurry, intermediate-hurry, and high-hurry groups). On the way to the venue, they all encountered a shabbily dressed person slumped by the side of the road—who was positioned there by the experimenters—and it was found that 37% of the low-hurry group, 55% of the immediate-hurry group, and 90% of the high-hurry group did *not* stop to offer help. Interestingly, whether they were to give a speech on the topic of the good Samaritan or not did not significantly affect their helping behaviour! These results showed unambiguously that the knowledge that someone required their assistance increasingly caused the participants to neglect to offer help to someone else.

Thus, to love and to love well requires the involvement of the mind. Indeed, in a study of love amongst Trappist monks, Lynn Underwood

---

23. John M. Darley and C. Daniel Batson, "'From Jerusalem to Jericho': A Study of Situational and Dispositional Variables in Helping Behavior," *Journal of Personality and Social Psychology* 27, no. 1 (1973): 100–108.

found that her participants were fully aware of the fact that loving action required "a clear picture of reality that is shaped by experience and insight over time,"[24] and that some of the monks tended to be "quite analytical about their choices to give of self for the good of the other, weighing various articulated factors."[25] We may thus conclude with Peck that "true love is not a feeling by which we are overwhelmed. It is a committed, thoughtful decision."[26]

Love Is Communal

In Gal 5:13, Paul appeals to the readers that they should "through love become slaves to one another" (NRSVA), thereby highlighting the communal nature of love; and in order to make sure that the message that love is a *social* construct is fully understood, Paul adds in the next verse: "For the whole law is summed up in a single commandment, 'You shall love your neighbour as yourself'" (v. 14 NRSVA). Similarly, we read in 1 John 3:16 that believers should lay down their lives for one another in love, and here again, in order to avoid any misunderstanding, the next verse reiterates the message: "If anyone has material possessions and sees a brother or sister in need but has no pity on them, how can the love of God be in that person?" (v. 17). Loving compassion for others is indeed at the heart of Scripture: The Gospels include multiple references to Jesus's compassion (e.g., "When he saw the crowds, he had compassion on them, because they were harassed and helpless, like sheep without a shepherd" [Matt 9:36][27]) and Winward rightly concludes that "with few exceptions, his mighty deeds were works of mercy; he was motivated by compassion."[28] The significance of loving care for the community is also reflected by the fact that in a virtue list in Col 3:12–14, which closely parallels the fruit of the Spirit, "compassion" is mentioned in the first place. This emphasis is not limited to the New Testament; compassion

---

24. Lynn G. Underwood, "Interviews with Trappist Monks as a Contribution to Research Methodology in the Investigation of Compassionate Love," *Journal for the Theory of Social Behaviour* 35, no. 3 (2005): 293.

25. Underwood, "Compassionate Love," 15.

26. Peck, *The Road Less Travelled*, 107.

27. Other examples include Matt 14:14; 15:32; 20:34; Mark 6:34; 8:2; Luke 7:13.

28. Winward, *Fruit of the Spirit*, 43.

and mercy are abiding attributes of God in the Old Testament, and in King David's psalms they are often directly linked to love; for example, "Have mercy on me, O God, according to your unfailing love; according to your great compassion" (Ps 51:1; see also 25:6; 145:8).[29]

In summary, caring for one's neighbours and reaching out to others is a central ingredient of love, and when we consider psychological research on love in a separate section below, we shall see that compassion and a "prosocial orientation" have also emerged there as defining elements of a loving disposition. Accordingly, *loving compassion* will be introduced in chapter 5 as one of the three central dimensions of the fruit of the Spirit.

Love as the Supreme Virtue

Love is the first in the list of virtues in Gal 5:22–23, which reflects a unique position in the fruit of the Spirit. The paramount importance of love was already signalled earlier in Paul's letter (5:6, 13), and in v. 14 the apostle declares that "the entire law is fulfilled in keeping this one command: 'Love your neighbour as yourself.'" This message about the capability of love to accomplish God's commandments is reiterated elsewhere in the New Testament (Matt 22:40; Rom 13:10), and we also read that "love covers over a multitude of sins" (1 Pet 4:8; see also Prov 10:12). This being the case, Luther rightly suggests about the fruit of the Spirit that "it would have sufficed to list only love, for this expands into all of the fruit of the Spirit."[30] Yet, as we know, Paul did not stop here but added as many as eight other virtues. Why? And how is love related to the other virtues?

CONCEPT 3.3 lists a selection of proposals for how love may be connected to the subsequent virtues in the fruit of the Spirit, with the last two definitions (by Fung and Schreiner) drawing on Col 3:14, where a catalogue of virtues is concluded by the statement, "And over all these

---

29. For an overview of mercy and compassion, see John Frederick, "Mercy and Compassion," in *Lexham Theological Wordbook*, ed. D. Mangum et al. (Bellingham, WA: Lexham, 2014).

30. *Luther's Works*, vol. 27, p. 93, cited by George, who agrees: "Paul might well have placed a period after love and moved on into the conclusion of his letter." Timothy George, *Galatians* (Nashville: Broadman & Holman, 1994), 400.

virtues put on love, which *binds them all together in perfect unity*" (emphasis added). This is an unambiguous indication that love is in some way a higher-order virtue that acts like a cohesive force connecting the various attributes in a unity. Such an integrated interrelationship of virtues in general (without, however, specifying love's role in it) has been, in fact, a well-known tenet of ancient Greek ethics, and in chapter 4 we shall discuss further the "unity of virtues" thesis. For the purpose of the current discussion, let us return to the question of why Paul included an extended list of virtues when outlining the fruit of the Spirit rather than using the supreme virtue of love as meaningful shorthand. The large number of the fruit's facets in Gal 5:22–23 suggests that the list was meant to be a detailed character sketch, aimed at clarifying the question of what exactly being loving involves: Paul's answer is that a loving disposition at its best means being joyful, peaceful, and patient, acting in a good, kind, and gentle manner, and exercising steadfastness and self-control. The verbs describing the relationship between love and the other virtues in CONCEPT 3.3—"include," "define," "flow from," "enable," "sustain," "express," and "bind"—suggest a dynamic, often two-way link, and it will be shown in the next chapter that indeed, all these facets are aligned to serve together the same purpose of loving compassion within the composite fruit.

Concept 3.3: Relationships between Love and the Subsequent Virtues in the Fruit of the Spirit

- All the other virtues are included in love and flow from it.[31]
- They define love and flow from it.[32]
- They are expressions of love.[33]

---

31. Rapa, "Galatians," 630.
32. G. Walter Hansen, *Galatians*, IVP New Testament Commentary Series (Downers Grove, IL: InterVarsity, 1994).
33. Dunn, *Galatians*, 309.

- They are specifications or aspects of love.[34]
- The list is a description of the concrete ways in which love is expressed.[35]
- Love enables the other virtues, and they in turn sustain it.[36]
- Love is not one virtue among a list of virtues, but the sum and substance of what it means to be a Christian.[37]
- Love is "the bond of perfectness"[38] or "the bond that holds all the virtues together."[39]

Love in Psychology

In 1954, renowned psychologist Abraham Maslow expressed his amasement about the paucity of research in psychology on the subject of love,[40] but after a slow start the situation began to change dramatically, and currently love psychology is a vibrant specialisation area.[41] The discussion of love in the previous sections indicated the complexity of the subject in the sense that in order to talk about it meaningfully, it is necessary to integrate cognitive, emotional, motivational, and behavioural matters, which is not something that psychologists are naturally inclined to do.[42] Indeed, an increase in love-related psychological research only

---

34. de Boer, *Galatians*, 362.
35. Furnish, *Theology and Ethics in Paul*, 88.
36. N. T. Wright, *After You Believe*, 254.
37. Charles B. Cousar, *Galatians*, Interpretation (Louisville: John Knox, 1982), 131.
38. Fung, *Galatians*, 263.
39. Schreiner, *Galatians*, 349.
40. Maslow states, "It is amazing how little the empirical sciences have to offer on the subject of love. Particularly strange is the silence of the psychologists, for one might think this to be their particular obligation." Abraham H. Maslow, *Motivation and Personality* (New York: Harper and Row, 1954), 235.
41. For good overviews, see Berscheid, "Love"; Beverley Fehr, "The Social Psychology of Love," in *The Oxford Handbook of Close Relationships*, ed. Jeffry A. Simpson and Lorne Campbell (Oxford: Oxford University Press, 2013); Beverley Fehr, Susan Sprecher, and Lynn G. Underwood, eds., *The Science of Compassionate Love: Theory, Research, and Applications* (Malden, MA: Wiley-Blackwell, 2009); Karin Sternberg, *Psychology of Love 101* (New York: Springer, 2014).
42. One reason for this reluctance is that the measurement traditions in the various subfields are often difficult to integrate.

began after scholars had started to break down the rather unmanageable entity of "love" into distinct subcategories, thereby allowing for more rigorous investigation. The first such division involved in the 1970s differentiating "romantic/passionate love" (a widely emotional state involving sexual arousal, experienced for a single target) from "companionate love" (a deep, friendship-like attachment, experienced for a number of significant people in one's life).[43] This initial step was followed by a surge of models of love being proposed from the 1980s onwards, with an emphasis on the most popular love area, romantic/passionate love. The current situation is still somewhat unsettled, with several coexisting definitions, taxonomies, and paradigms; in her authoritative overview in the *Annual Review of Psychology*, Ellen Berscheid highlights the fact that the failure to delineate the love construct sufficiently constitutes a major obstacle to the study of the love phenomenon.[44]

On the positive side, Berscheid's review establishes four major types of love that have emerged from previous taxonomic and psychometric efforts, and which are assumed to subsume all the different varieties of love: the traditional categories of *romantic* and *companionate love*, complemented by two new love types, *compassionate love* and *attachment love*. The former refers to selfless, altruistic love involving communal responsiveness, the latter to a strong affectional bond with an attachment figure (e.g., someone who offers security and comfort, such as a parent or caregiver). The similarity of the first three categories to the ancient Greek/biblical division discussed earlier is striking: as Fehr summarises,[45] romantic love corresponds to *erōs*, companionate love to *storgē*, and compassionate love to *agapē*; the fourth category, attachment love, originates in contemporary psychological research, more specifically in the study of children forming attachments as part of their social development.[46] For

---

43. Fehr, "Social Psychology of Love," 202.
44. Berscheid, "Love," 1.
45. Beverley Fehr, "Everyday Conceptions of Love," in *The New Psychology of Love*, ed. Robert J. Sternberg and Karin Sternberg (Cambridge: Cambridge University Press, 2019), 155–156.
46. E.g., John Bowlby, *Attachment*, vol. 1 of *Attachment and Loss* (New York: Basic Books, 1969).

the purpose of the current book, compassionate love is our primary interest, because—as shown by its association with *agapē*—it closely follows the biblical connotation of love.

Research on compassionate love is a recent development, as the actual label only emerged in 2006 at a meeting of the World Health Organisation when participants tried to find a name for a facet of "quality of life" characterised by loving-kindness and love for others (with "altruistic love" being a close second option in the rank list).[47] The concept's link with corresponding notions in many religious traditions was of course noted, but psychology did more than merely summarise existing knowledge under a new rubric: once the construct had been defined, it became the subject of extensive empirical assessment, resulting in insights into the construct's causal conditions, antecedents, relationships with other constructs, and behavioural outcomes. According to Fehr and Sprecher, the main findings confirm that compassionate love correlates with other prosocial factors such as empathy and sympathy, and that altruistic concerns are prime motivators of compassionate love, which in turns leads to behavioural manifestations related to offering social support, caregiving, helpfulness, volunteering, giving, and self-sacrifice.[48] We shall further elaborate on these factors in chapter 5.

Joy (*Chara*)

Similar to love, joy is a familiar concept to modern readers, but as we shall see below, just like *agapē*, the Greek word used in the fruit of the Spirit, *chara*, only refers to a segment of the semantic domain of its English translation. *Chara* was a popular noun in the Greco-Roman world—it was even used as a proper name, like Joy in English[49]—but its typical secular usage differed from how it was employed in the Scriptures. In the everyday Greek

---

47. Underwood, "Compassionate Love," 8.
48. Beverley Fehr and Susan Sprecher, "Compassionate Love: What We Know So Far," in *Positive Psychology of Love*, ed. Mahzad Hojjat and Duncan Cramer (New York: Oxford University Press, 2013), 113.
49. Longenecker, *Galatians*, 261.

language the term mainly referred to pleasure,[50] whereas this connotation is completely absent in the NT. This raises the question of why Paul selected this particular word for the description of the fruit of the Spirit rather than opting for a seemingly more obvious candidate, *eudaimonia*, which was the established term for happiness in ancient virtue ethics.[51] Interestingly, it was the very ethical connotation of the term—referring to happiness as the highest human good—that made *eudaimonia* inappropriate for Christian use, because, as Keener points out, "most biblical ethics' goal was oriented toward God's pleasure rather than that of mortals."[52] Thus, Paul—along with every other NT author—avoided *eudaimonia* completely and substituted it with the alternative word *chara*. This was a highly marked decision, particularly in view of how widespread the notion of joy is in the Bible, a point Karl Barth commented on: "It is astonishing, and certainly does not need to be verified by quotations, how many references there are in the Old and New Testaments to delight, joy, bliss, exultation, merry-making and rejoicing, and how emphatically these are demanded from the Book of Psalms to the Epistle to the Philippians."[53]

Joy is frequently mentioned in the Old Testament to characterise the exuberant aspects of Israel's life and worship, well illustrated by Stephen Smalley when highlighting a passage in the Book of Zephaniah (3:14–17), which contains as many as eight different words for joy and the act of rejoicing.[54] Regarding the New Testament, we find well over 300 instances of several Greek terms related to various aspects of joy and delight,[55] of which *chara* and its cognates are by far the most com-

---

50. Moo, *Galatians*, 364.

51. As Keener ("Fruit of the Spirit," 583) explains, *eudaimonia* was emphasised in Greek philosophy as the chief goal of moral formation, responsible for human flourishing and welfare.

52. Keener, 583.

53. Karl Barth, *Church Dogmatics IV/3.4: The Doctrine of Creation* (Edinburgh: T&T Clark, 1961), 375.

54. Zephaniah 3:14–17: "Sing, Daughter Zion; shout aloud, Israel! Be glad and rejoice with all your heart, Daughter Jerusalem! . . . The Lord your God is with you, the Mighty Warrior who saves. He will take great delight in you; in his love he will no longer rebuke you, but will rejoice over you with singing." See Stephen S. Smalley, "Joy," in *New Dictionary of Biblical Theology*, ed. T. Desmond Alexander and Brian S. Rosner (Leicester: Inter-Varsity, 2000), 608.

55. See William G. Morrice, *Joy in the New Testament* (Exeter: Paternoster, 1984), 70; Leland Ryken, James C. Wilhoit, and Tremper Longman III, *Dictionary of Biblical Imagery* (Downers Grove, IL: InterVarsity, 1998), 464–465. As Green explains, the wide array of terms used to

mon (141 occurrences), used most frequently by Paul (64 times).[56] Indeed, N. T. Wright states that in Paul's letters "joy" takes second place only to "love," which reflects the fact, as Wright argues, that joy was a critical aspect—the "dominant note"—in the worldview of early Christians.[57] The emphasis on joy is well illustrated by Phil 4:4, which urges believers that they should "rejoice in the Lord always. I will say it again: Rejoice!"[58] and also by 1 Thess 5:16–18, which reiterates, "Rejoice always, pray continually, give thanks in all circumstances; for this is God's will for you in Christ Jesus." Jürgen Moltmann goes as far as calling Christianity "a unique religion of joy."[59]

What Is "Joy"?

It is easier to specify the nature of "joy" than that of love, because joy can be categorised as an affective state—that is, an emotion proper. It is conceptually related to other positive emotions such as gladness, elation, amusement, and especially happiness, but it differs from the latter in an important way: happiness is defined in psychology as referring "to a general sense of well-being and to a cognitive evaluation of one's life as a whole,"[60] and as such, it concerns a broader and more cognitive attribution, whereas joy is a momentary emotion; as Patty Van Cappellen succinctly puts it, "joy is the brief, at the moment, version of happiness."[61] However, the biblical usage of the term *chara* in the fruit of the Spirit deviates somewhat from this general psychological

---

signify "joy" includes *chara* ("joy"), *chairō* ("to rejoice"), *sunchairō* ("to rejoice with"), *agalliaō* ("to be overjoyed"), *galleas* ("great joy"), *skirtaō* ("to leap with joy"), *makarios* ("happy," often translated as "blessed"), and *makarizō* ("to be regarded as happy or blessed"). Joel B. Green, "Joy," in *Dictionary of Jesus and the Gospels*, 2nd ed., ed. Joel B. Green, Jeannine K. Brown, and Nicholas Perrin (Downers Grove, IL: InterVarsity, 2013), 448.

56. Morrice, *Joy*, 70.

57. N. T. Wright, "Joy: Some New Testament Perspectives and Questions," in *Joy and Human Flourishing: Essays on Theology, Culture, and the Good Life*, ed. Miroslav Volf and Justin E. Crisp (Minneapolis: Fortress, 2015), 46–47.

58. Winward, *Fruit of the Spirit*, 91.

59. Jürgen Moltmann, "Christianity: A Religion of Joy," in *Joy and Human Flourishing: Essays on Theology, Culture, and the Good Life*, ed. Miroslav Volf and Justin E. Crisp (Minneapolis: Fortress, 2015), 6.

60. Patty Van Cappellen, "The Emotion of Joy: Commentary on Johnson," *Journal of Positive Psychology* 15, no. 1 (2020): 40.

61. Van Cappellen, 40.

characterisation, because for most of the Christian writers joy signified something more profound than mere gaiety and delight: it involved a deep spiritual sense, rooted in faith and in a mindset of peace.[62] Some commentators underline in this respect the fact that it may not be a coincidence that the Greek words for joy (*chara*) and grace (*charis*) are linked to the same root (*char-*).[63] Indeed, there is an ongoing association between joy and the Spirit in the Scriptures: in 1 Thess 1:6 joy is "given by the Holy Spirit"; in Acts 13:52 we read that "the disciples were filled with joy and with the Holy Spirit"; and Paul's famous prayer in Rom 15:13 declares, "May the God of hope fill you with all joy and peace as you trust in him, so that you may overflow with hope by the power of the Holy Spirit."

Besides stating that God can fill us with joy, Rom 15:13 also high-lights an important link between joy and *hope*, which is reiterated in Rom 12:12: "Be joyful in hope." This connection is not a coincidence; as Barth explains, along with many others, most joy is *anticipatory* in nature,[64] and for example Timothy George concludes that hope is "that element of Christian joy that differentiates it from secular happiness."[65] Interestingly, psychological research also offers some support to this claim: Watkins and his colleagues point out that receiving good news constitutes an archetypical context for people experiencing joy, particularly news that one has been waiting for. As they explain, "The news is good because it in some way fulfils the individual's hope. . . . We experience joy when we are longing for something and we finally receive news that it's coming to be."[66] In the light of biblical joy being associated with receiving the good

---

62. Gerald F. Hawthorne, "Joy," in *Dictionary of the Later New Testament and Its Developments*, ed. Ralph P. Martin and Peter H. Davids (Downers Grove, IL: InterVarsity, 1997), 604.

63. E.g., George, *Galatians*, 401; William G. Morrice, "Joy," in *Dictionary of Paul and His Letters*, ed. Gerald F. Hawthorne and Ralph P. Martin (Downers Grove, IL: InterVarsity, 1993), 512. We should note, however, that N. T. Wright ("Joy," 47) advises caution in this respect because the New Testament writers do not explicitly acknowledge this link, and therefore it may not have played a role in their word choice.

64. Barth, *Church Dogmatics IV/3.4*, 375.

65. George, *Galatians*, 401.

66. Philip C. Watkins et al., "Joy Is a Distinct Positive Emotion: Assessment of Joy and Relationship to Gratitude and Well-Being," *Journal of Positive Psychology* 13, no. 5 (2018): 523.

news (e.g., Luke 2:10), the term is undoubtedly appropriate for referring to Christian spiritual delight.

The association between joy and hope can also explain the paradox that joy can be present even at times of suffering, affliction, and trouble. Jesus declares in the Sermon on the Mount that people who are insulted and persecuted should "rejoice and be glad, because great is your reward in heaven" (Matt 5:12), and the apostles did indeed rejoice after being flogged for teaching about Jesus "because they had been counted worthy of suffering disgrace for the Name" (Acts 5:41). In a similar vein, Paul also affirms that "in all our troubles my joy knows no bounds" (2 Cor 7:4), and Clinton Arnold comments that suffering is prominent in the background to the statements concerning joy in 1 Peter and Hebrews, arguing that "Eschatological anticipation . . . provided incentive for rejoicing even when one's personal property was plundered (Heb 10:34) or when one faced persecution (1 Pet 4:13)."[67] (We shall come back to the relationship between hope and the fruit of the Spirit in chapter 4, when addressing the absence of this famous virtue from the facets of the fruit.)

Joy as Communal Activity

So far we have talked about joy only as an internal emotional response, but this is only part of the complete picture. Upon experiencing joy, people's first reaction is typically the desire to communicate the good news with someone else and to celebrate with others.[68] There is also a common urge in many to express the joy in collective action such as clapping, singing, shouting (with joy), jumping about, or dancing. Indeed, N. T. Wright emphasises the "robustly physical nature of 'joy' in the Hebrew scriptures"[69] and reminds us that the idea of a great feast is one of the central channels of joy throughout the whole Bible, always involving the community. In fact, Deut 16:14 lists the full range of people to participate in the festivals, as if to make sure that nobody in the community is left out:

---

67. Clinton E. Arnold, "Joy," in *ABD*, ed. David Noel Freedman (New York: Doubleday, 1992), 3:1023; see also Barclay, *Flesh and Spirit*, 80.

68. Watkins et al., "Joy," 524.

69. N. T. Wright, "Joy," 42.

"Be joyful at your festival—you, your sons and daughters, your male and female servants, and the Levites, the foreigners, the fatherless and the widows who live in your towns." In the New Testament Paul echoes the communal aspect of joy by urging the believers to "Rejoice with those who rejoice" (Rom 12:15), because "if one part is honoured, every part rejoices with it" (1 Cor 12:26).

Thus, the biblical message is consistent: joy is to be shared with others in fellowship, as it is a quality of communal life.[70] Miroslav Volf sums this up perfectly in three words: "Joy seeks company."[71] Indeed, in his commentary on Gal 5:22, Calvin specifically emphasises the ethical dimension of joy as "cheerfulness toward our fellow human beings,"[72] a perspective shared by Barth when he states, "What is really demanded is that I ask myself from the standpoint of the other what will give him joy, and that I then consider this and put it into effect. Joy shared with another, or with a company which aims at mutual enjoyment, is a costly matter, and upon this depends the secret of a successful festival as a genuinely joyous occasion."[73]

Joy in Psychology

The study of joy has had a chequered history in psychology. Traditionally, joy has been one of the least studied human emotions,[74] initially eclipsed by negative emotions (e.g., anxiety), which used to be the targets of most research in this area, and recently also by happiness, which has become a central theme in positive psychology over the past two decades. As a result, the existing research on joy has been rather disjointed, with the construct defined in several different ways, often

---

70. See e.g., Creath Davis, "Joy," in *Evangelical Dictionary of Theology*, ed. Daniel J. Treier and Walter A. Elwell (Grand Rapids: Baker Academic, 2017), 451; Fee, *God's Empowering Presence*, 447.

71. Miroslav Volf, "The Crown of the Good Life: A Hypothesis," in *Joy and Human Flourishing: Essays on Theology, Culture, and the Good Life*, ed. Miroslav Volf and Justin E. Crisp (Minneapolis: Fortress, 2015), 132.

72. Gerald L. Bray, ed., *Galatians, Ephesians*, Reformation Commentary on Scripture, New Testament 10 (Downers Grove, IL: IVP Academic, 2011), 198.

73. Barth, *Church Dogmatics IV/3.4*, 380.

74. See Robert A. Emmons, "Joy: An Introduction to This Special Issue," *Journal of Positive Psychology* 15, no. 1 (2020): 1.

in a conflicting manner.[75] The situation, however, has taken a positive turn over the past ten years, partly as the outcome of a large-scale interdisciplinary project at Yale University entitled the "Theology of Joy and the Good Life project,"[76] sponsored by the Templeton foundation.[77] In order to produce a unified theoretical base, this project brought together a group of eminent psychologists, philosophers, and theologians with the explicit objective of boosting research on joy and promoting a dialogue amongst the various research strands. Two salient fruits of this ambitious enterprise have been an anthology on *Joy and Human Flourishing: Essays on Theology, Culture, and the Good Life*, edited by Miroslav Volf and Justin Crisp,[78] and a special issue of the *Journal of Positive Psychology* on "Joy and Positive Psychology," edited by Robert Emmons.[79] This special issue includes a comprehensive review article of the subject by Matthew Kuan Johnson,[80] followed by over ten short commentary papers authored by some of the leading experts in the field (including Pamela King, Robert Roberts, Sarah Schnittker, Lynn Underwood, Patty Van Cappellen, and Philip Watkins). Several contributions to these two works have already been cited earlier.

From a psychological perspective, arguably the most important achievement of the project was the proposal of a unified construal of joy: Johnson outlined four levels of analysis, which resonate closely with the multilevel conception of virtues discussed in chapter 2: (1) joy as emotion; (2) joy as mood; (3) joy as disposition/trait; and (4) joy as spiritual fruit. Needless to say, for the current book the most relevant level is the last one, which has been defined as "a disposition to experience the emotional state of joy" combined with "a deep, spiritual sense of satisfaction, confidence, or gratitude, even in the midst of severe persecution, suffering, or sorrow."[81]

---

75. Johnson, "Joy," 5.

76. https://faith.yale.edu/legacy-projects/theology-of-joy; for an overview, see Matthew Kuan Johnson, "Chasing Joy: A Retrospective Analysis of the Theology of Joy and the Good Life Project," *Journal of Psychology and Christianity* 39, no. 3 (2019): 166–71.

77. https://www.templeton.org/grant/theology-of-joy-and-the-good-life-2.

78. Miroslav Volf and Justin E. Crisp, eds., *Joy and Human Flourishing: Essays on Theology, Culture, and the Good Life* (Minneapolis: Fortress, 2015).

79. Emmons, "Joy."

80. Johnson, "Joy."

81. Johnson, 10.

In commenting on this operationalisation, Schnitker and colleagues suggested framing joy more consciously as a virtue—that is, as a combination of a characteristic adaptation and a transcendent narrative identity[82] (see Excursus 2 in chapter 2). They also proposed that joy might be seen as the outcome of virtuous life in general,[83] which according to King has the additional benefit of foregrounding "the moral component of joy, . . . including individual, social, and ecological flourishing."[84]

Peace (*Eirēnē*)

We saw in the previous section that the difference between "joy" and "happiness" in psychology is usually related to viewing happiness as a more enduring state than joy, involving a general sense of well-being and satisfaction with life as a whole. The definition of "peace"—*šālôm* in the Old Testament and *eirēnē* in the New—typically includes similar characteristics and indeed, peace can be seen in many ways as the Christian equivalent of happiness, almost like an extended version of spiritual joy. The English term "peace" covers a relatively wide range of meanings, from internal serenity to the lack of war, but the semantic range of biblical "peace" is even broader than the absence of mental turmoil or interpersonal strife—it is "one of those huge words in the Bible,"[85] as reflected by the fact that it occurs in the two Testaments over 330 times.[86] This prominence is ultimately rooted in the spiritual dimension of the term, one's harmony with God, which offers therefore an appropriate starting point for unpacking the nature of biblical peace.

---

82. Sarah A. Schnitker, Juliette L. Ratchford, and Rosemond T. Lorona, "How Can Joy Escape Jingle-Jangle? Virtue and Telos Conceptualizations as Alternative Approaches to the Scientific Study of Joy," *Journal of Positive Psychology* 15, no. 1 (2020): 45; see further discussion of this proposal by Pamela Ebstyne King, "Joy Distinguished: Teleological Perspectives on Joy as a Virtue," *Journal of Positive Psychology* 15, no. 1 (2020): 34–35.

83. Schnitker, Ratchford, and Lorona, "How Can Joy Escape Jingle-Jangle?," 46.

84. King, "Joy Distinguished," 36–37.

85. C. Wright, *Cultivating the Fruit of the Spirit*, 55.

86. *Šālôm* occurs over 230 times and *eirēnē* about 100 times; see Willard M. Swartley, "Peace," in *Dictionary of Scripture and Ethics*, ed. Joel B. Green (Grand Rapids: Baker Academic, 2011), 583.

Harmony with God

We have seen in chapter 2 (table 1) that peace is a central feature of the divine character: in the New Testament God is called "the God of peace" no fewer than six times[87] and Eph 2:14–17 affirms that Jesus "is our peace" and that he was "making peace" and "preached peace."[88] Indeed, in one of the best-known passages in Isaiah, the oracle foretells Jesus, the Prince of Peace, administering peace to the world[89]:

> And he will be called
>> Wonderful Counsellor, Mighty God,
>> Everlasting Father, Prince of Peace.
> Of the greatness of his government and peace
>> there will be no end. (9:6–7)

The same message is reiterated in Zechariah's prophecy about the role of Jesus "to guide our feet into the path of peace" (Luke 1:79),[90] and elsewhere the Bible speaks of the "gospel of peace" (Eph 6:15; cf. Acts 10:36). The close association between peace and the core biblical message is also testified by Paul when he declares that "the kingdom of God is not a matter of eating and drinking, but of righteousness, peace and joy in the Holy Spirit" (Rom 14:17).

The unique spiritual character of peace derives from a close harmony with God—as F. F. Bruce summarises, "Those who are at peace with God receive something of the 'peace of God.'"[91] This harmony explains why the new covenant prophesied by Ezekiel is referred to as the "covenant of

---

87. Rom 15:33; 16:20; 2 Cor 13:11; Phil 4:9; 1 Thess 5:23; Heb 13:20; also, "Lord of peace": 2 Thess 3:16.

88. Erich Dinkler, "Eirene: The Early Christian Concept of Peace," in *The Meaning of Peace: Biblical Studies*, ed. Perry B. Yoder and Willard M. Swartley, trans. Walter Sawatsky (Louisville: Westminster John Knox, 1992), 181.

89. J. Alec Motyer, *Isaiah: An Introduction and Commentary*, TOTC (Nottingham: Inter-Varsity, 1999), 102.

90. Bock also submits that in the Gospel of Luke, salvation is often described in terms of peace. Darrell L. Bock, *Luke: 1:1–9:50*, BECNT (Grand Rapids: Baker Academic, 1994), 193–194.

91. Bruce, *Galatians*, 252. Moo's (*Galatians*, 364–365) conclusion is similar: "Peace can mean 'peace with God': the objective state that follows our deliverance from the hostility that characterizes our natural relationship with God because of sin (Rom. 5:1; Eph. 2:17; probably both other occurrences in Galatians: 1:3; 6:16)."

peace" (Ezek 34:25; 37:26; see also Isa 54:10), and in a similar vein, Rom 5:1 declares that "since we are justified by faith, we have peace with God through our Lord Jesus Christ" (NRSVA).[92] Finally, Paul states in Rom 8:6 that "the mind governed by the Spirit is life and peace," and in addressing the question of what Paul means by "peace" in this verse, Keener submits, "Most obviously, he means 'peace with God'—reconciliation that ends one's enmity in relation to God (Rom 5:1, 10-11)."[93]

Shalom

In order to uncover further layers of the complex meaning of biblical peace, let us look at the grand notion of "shalom" in the Old Testament. The Hebrew word *šālôm* (usually transcribed in English as "shalom") refers to general well-being, prosperity, peace, and harmony, both at the individual and social levels (e.g., internal serenity and political peace). In his analysis of shalom, Claus Westermann explains that the notion concerns something "elemental" about being human: "To have shalom has obviously been essential for human existence throughout all the ages, through all the manner and forms of existence. It has remained the same in its essential thread of meaning in a way similar to that of 'life' or 'thirst' or 'joy.'"[94]

Besides its more abstract connotation, shalom may also refer to material prosperity (Ps 37:11: "the meek will inherit the land and enjoy peace and prosperity [*šālôm*]"), personal security (1 Sam 20:21: "you are safe [*šālôm*]; there is no danger"), and as Willard Swartley emphasises, even to physical well-being—that is, health[95] (Ps 38:3: "There is no health in

---

92. According to Grever, "It is only in the inauguration of the new covenant that this lasting peace with God and one another is achieved, and thus this new covenant is called a 'covenant of peace,' a covenant that assuages divine wrath (Isa 54:10; Ezek 34:25; 37:26; compare Num 25:12; Mal 2:5)." Joshua M. Grever, "Peace," in *The Lexham Bible Dictionary*, ed. John D. Barry et al. (Bellingham, WA: Lexham, 2016). For a similar view, see also Matera, *Galatians*, 203.

93. Craig S. Keener, *The Mind of the Spirit: Paul's Approach to Transformed Thinking* (Grand Rapids: Baker Academic, 2016), 135.

94. Claus Westermann, "Peace (Shalom) in the Old Testament," in *The Meaning of Peace: Biblical Studies*, ed. Perry B. Yoder and Willard M. Swartley, trans. Walter Sawatsky (Louisville: Westminster John Knox, 1992), 20–21.

95. Swartley, "Peace," 583; in fact, Swartley points out that a cognate of shalom, *šālēm*, is best translated as "health."

my body; there is no soundness [šālôm] in my bones"). Significantly, shalom also refers to well-being in a community, characterised by beneficial relationships and the cohesiveness of communal ties,[96] and Walter Brueggemann explains in this respect that in the "covenant of shalom" (Ezek 34:25) people are not only bound to God but also to one another "in a caring, sharing, rejoicing community with none to make them afraid."[97] Finally, the general positive content of shalom has also been conventionalised in greetings, for example in 1 Sam 25:6: "Say to him: 'Long life [šālôm] to you! Good health [šālôm] to you and your household! And good health [šālôm] to all that is yours!'"

Shalom was such a prominent concept in NT Judaism that the meaning of the Greek term used for peace in the Bible, eirēnē, was more influenced by shalom than by the word's use in nonbiblical Greek. This Hebrew association was further reinforced by the fact that in the Greek version of the Hebrew Bible, the Septuagint, shalom is almost invariably translated as eirēnē.[98] A good reflection of the Hebrew impact is offered by the adoption of eirēnē for greeting purposes at the beginning or end of all the NT epistles (except James and 1 John): as William Barclay explains, the standard greeting in secular Greek letters was chaire (usually translated as "Greetings!" or "Hail!"), and this form of salutation was merged with the Jewish greeting of shalom by replacing chaire with eirēnē.[99]

Individual versus Communal Peace

Just like peace in English, eirēnē refers both to the inner harmony of the individual and the lack of hostility in the community. While most scholars maintain that the latter meaning is more pronounced in the

---

96. See e.g., Ryan S. Schellenberg, "Peace," in *Dictionary of Jesus and the Gospels*, 2nd ed., ed. Joel B. Green, Jeannine K. Brown, and Nicholas Perrin (Downers Grove, IL: IVP Academic, 2013), 667.

97. Walter Brueggemann, *Peace* (St. Louis: Chalice, 2001), 15.

98. Ronald F. Youngblood, "Peace," in *The International Standard Bible Encyclopedia*, rev. ed., ed. Geoffrey W. Bromiley (Grand Rapids: Eerdmans, 1988), 3:733.

99. Barclay, *Flesh and Spirit*, 86. The fusion is particularly clear in the greetings where "grace" is added to peace (e.g., "Grace and peace to you from God our Father and from the Lord Jesus Christ" [Rom 1:7]), because the words *charis* ("grace") and *chaire* have the same root.

Bible,[100] this does not mean that references to individual tranquillity are completely absent from Scripture. The fourth century Latin translator of the Vulgate, Jerome, for example argued, "We should not suppose that peace is limited to not quarrelling with others. Rather the peace of Christ—that is, our inheritance—is with us when the mind is at peace and undisturbed by conflicting emotions."[101] A case in point is Phil 4:7, "And the peace of God, which transcends all understanding, will guard your hearts and your minds in Christ Jesus." And inner peace is also probably meant in Paul's famous prayer, "May the God of hope fill you with all joy and peace as you trust in him" (Rom 15:13).[102]

Inner peacefulness goes hand in hand with peace in the community (see CONCEPT 3.4) because, as Kenneson rightly points out, peace is not something "confined within one's psyche; instead, peace is a way of life."[103] Jesus calls his disciples to be at peace with one another in no uncertain terms—"be at peace with each other" (Mark 9:50)—and in the Sermon on the Mount he reiterates, "Blessed are the peacemakers, for they will be called children of God" (Matt 5:9). Paul's exhortations in Romans could not have been any clearer in this respect: "If it is possible, as far as it depends on you, live at peace with everyone" (12:18), and "let us therefore make every effort to do what leads to peace and to mutual edification" (14:19). Indeed, promoting communal peace in different forms is a recurring instruction in the Bible,[104] which is not only a mark of the significance of this issue but which also signals that it is particularly difficult for people to maintain communal peace in the world (hence the need to remind them again and again). Regarding

---

100. See e.g., Keener, *The Mind of the Spirit*, 135.

101. Jerome, *Commentary on the Epistle to the Galatians* 3.5.2, in Mark J. Edwards, ed., *Galatians, Ephesians, Philippians*, ACCNT 8 (Downers Grove, IL: InterVarsity, 1999), 85.

102. Grever ("Peace") argues that Jesus also refers to this subjective, inner sense of peace, security, and tranquillity when he states in his farewell discourse to the disciples, "Peace I leave with you; my peace I give you" (John 14:27).

103. Kenneson, *Life on the Vine*, 83. Dunn (*Galatians*, 310) argues in a similar way: "In Jewish thought 'peace' was not reducible to an individualistic inner tranquillity, but included also a corporate dimension, all that makes for social well-being and harmonious relationships."

104. E.g., Ps 34:14; 37:37; Prov 12:20; 2 Cor 13:11; Eph 4:3; Col 3:15; Heb 12:14; Jas 3:18; 1 Pet 3:11.

the virtue of peace within the fruit of the Spirit, Keener highlights the communal implication of the term (i.e., peace with others) as it offers a natural contrast to "biting and devouring" one another, mentioned earlier in 5:15, as well as to eight of the works of the flesh in 5:20–21 ("hatred, discord, jealousy, fits of rage, selfish ambition, dissensions, factions, and envy").[105]

Concept 3.4: The Dynamic Link between "Inner" and "Outer" Peace

Several scholars emphasise that separating "inner" and "outer" peace is not compatible with the more integrated biblical worldview; for example, Westermann states that "if there is an outer struggle but there is peace within or an inner peace, then this is not shalom."[106] The connection between individual and communal peace is also mentioned in Jer 29:7, as highlighted in Brueggemann's translation: "But seek the shalom of the city where I have sent you into exile, and pray to the Lord on its behalf, for in its shalom you will find your shalom."[107]

The link between "inner" and "outer" peace is not unidirectional but dynamic, because not only can a peaceful environment contribute to a peaceful mindset but it can also happen the other way round: Gordon Fee is right that it is unrealistic to expect peace in a community where God's people know little peace individually,[108] and in his review of psychological research on peace, Linden

---

105. Keener, *Galatians*, 520.
106. Westermann, "Peace," 20. In a similar vein, Luz submits that "the 'inner' and the 'outer' are modern points of contrast, whereas in biblical anthropology they are integrated." Ulrich Luz, "The Significance of the Biblical Witnesses for Church Peace Action," trans. Walter Sawatsky, in *The Meaning of Peace: Biblical Studies*, ed. Perry B. Yoder and Willard M. Swartley (Louisville: Westminster John Knox, 1992), 237.
107. Brueggemann, *Peace*, 22.
108. Fee, *God's Empowering Presence*, 449.

Nelson confirms that "people who experience relatively more inner peace tend to be more peaceful toward others, and people who are peaceful toward others tend to be more peaceful within themselves."[109] It stands to reason that a peaceful mindset characterised by serenity and security allows a person to pay more attention to the concerns of others, and indeed, several experimental studies have shown that cultivating positive feelings in someone promotes interpersonal peacefulness.[110]

Finally, we should note that the ultimate biblical imperative to implement God's peace in the believer's everyday communal lives was a major departure from the Greco-Roman worldview, which did not share this priority.[111] This is why F. F. Bruce underlines that peace is one of the defining marks of the children of God, and it should therefore characterise every aspect of the saints' lives, from home to church.[112]

Peace in Psychology

Peace is a topic targeted by a great deal of psychological research, and "peace psychology" is a recognised scholarly subfield. It is represented within the American Psychological Association by a separate division (APA Division 48, "Society for the Study of Peace, Conflict, and Violence: Peace Psychology Division") and it has its own journal (*Peace and Conflict: Journal of Peace Psychology*), a three-volume encyclopaedia,[113] and a book series.[114] According to Christie and his colleagues,

---

109. Linden L. Nelson, "Peacefulness as a Personality Trait," in *Personal Peacefulness: Psychological Perspectives*, ed. Gregory K. Sims et al. (New York: Springer, 2014), 28.

110. Linden L. Nelson, "Peaceful Personality: Psychological Dynamics and Core Factors," in *Personal Peacefulness: Psychological Perspectives*, ed. Gregory K. Sims, Linden L. Nelson, and Mindy R. Puopolo (New York: Springer, 2014), 72.

111. See William Klassen, "Peace: New Testament," in *ABD*, ed. David Noel Freedman (New York: Doubleday, 1992), 210.

112. Bruce, *Galatians*, 252.

113. Daniel J. Christie, ed., *The Encyclopedia of Peace Psychology*, 3 vols. (Malden, MA: Wiley-Blackwell, 2012).

114. Springer Peace Psychology Book Series, https://www.springer.com/series/7298.

the purpose of the field is to "develop theories and practices aimed at the prevention and mitigation of direct and structural violence. Framed positively, peace psychology promotes the nonviolent management of conflict and the pursuit of social justice, what we refer to as peacemaking and peacebuilding, respectively."[115]

This definition demonstrates that the field has an overt political agenda, and indeed, peace psychology as a whole has shown little consideration of peace as a personality attribute or virtue. However, there have been some valuable exceptions to this trend: peace psychology's intersection with positive psychology has got some helpful insights to offer on community peace[116] (which we shall refer to in chapter 5 when discussing communal harmony), and the study of a peaceful mindset has been summarised in a volume on *Personal Peacefulness: Psychological Perspectives*.[117] Two chapters in the volume by Nelson (already mentioned) provide a thorough overview of the research literature on the intersection of inner peace and peace with others,[118] and a chapter by Dale Floody surveys the various perspectives on serenity and inner peace.[119] In this latter chapter the author follows an avenue similar to theologians who consider the virtue of peace to be "a way of life" (discussed above): "Serenity can be thought of as a personal and unique way of living which includes behavioural and cognitive components that are associated with feeling calm, peaceful, and untroubled. Synonyms for serenity may include inner peacefulness, peace of mind, tranquillity, contentment, equanimity, and 'cool.'"[120]

This definition of serenity is useful to illustrate the multifaceted nature of the concept, and a recent paper by Berenbaum and colleagues

---

115. Daniel J. Christie, Richard V. Wagner, and Deborah D. Winter, "Introduction to Peace Psychology," in *Peace, Conflict, and Violence: Peace Psychology for the 21st Century*, ed. Daniel J. Christie, Richard V. Wagner, and Deborah D. Winter (Upper Saddle River, NJ: Prentice Hall, 2001), 7.

116. See J. Christopher Cohrs et al., "Contributions of Positive Psychology to Peace: Toward Global Well-Being and Resilience," *American Psychologist* 68, no. 7 (2013): 590–600.

117. Gregory K. Sims, Linden L. Nelson, and Mindy R. Puopolo, eds., *Personal Peacefulness: Psychological Perspectives* (New York: Springer, 2014).

118. Nelson, "Peacefulness"; "Peaceful Personality."

119. Dale R. Floody, "Serenity and Inner Peace: Positive Perspectives," in *Personal Peacefulness: Psychological Perspectives*, ed. Gregory K. Sims, Linden L. Nelson, and Mindy R. Puopolo (New York: Springer, 2014).

120. Floody, "Serenity and Inner Peace," 107.

has examined the relationship between two of the most important facets of inner peace: contentment and tranquillity.[121] We are thus facing a personality dimension that has been captured through a variety of interrelated concepts, and Nelson further characterises the dimension of intrapersonal peacefulness at three different levels (in line with our previous multilevel understanding of virtues): (1) a disposition for self-acceptance and self-compassion, (2) a relatively enduring state of harmony between aspects of self, and (3) a disposition for emotional states that support peaceful relationships and/or are associated with experiencing harmony.[122] Significantly for our current discussion, Nelson demonstrates that the empirical assessments of these different layers correlate with each other, thereby implying the existence of a more general underlying disposition. We shall draw on this finding in chapter 5 when proposing a "spiritual contentment" dimension for the fruit of the Spirit.

Patience (*Makrothymia*)

Although the notion of patience appears to be straightforward, deciphering the exact meaning of the Greek word used in Gal 5:22, *makrothymia*, is not unproblematic. An indication of the semantic complexity involved is offered by the fact that the NIV chose to render it into "forbearance" rather than "patience," and that Bruce felt the need to coin a new term to translate it: "long-tempered."[123] These versions indicate that *makrothymia* also embraces an element of steadfastness and staying power, which is clearly expressed by James in his epistle to the believers, urging them as follows: "Be patient, then, brothers and sisters, until the Lord's coming. See how the farmer waits for the land to yield its valuable crop, patiently waiting for the autumn and spring rains. You too, be patient and stand firm, because the Lord's coming is near. . . . Brothers and sisters, as an

---

121. Howard Berenbaum, Alice B. Huang, and Luis E. Flores, "Contentment and Tranquillity: Exploring Their Similarities and Differences," *Journal of Positive Psychology* 14, no. 2 (2019): 252–59.
122. Nelson, "Peacefulness," 12.
123. Bruce, *Galatians*, 253.

example of patience in the face of suffering, take the prophets who spoke in the name of the Lord" (Jas 5:7–8, 10).

Thus, the term has a strong flavour of "patient endurance" of something that someone needs to "put up with,"[124] and accordingly, some commentators have also suggested the now somewhat old-fashioned word "long-suffering" as a possible way of rendering it.[125] We may therefore conclude that *makrothymia* incorporates two fairly distinct meanings, one relating to waiting for something calmly (e.g., in a queue), the other relating to putting up with something frustrating (e.g., a person or situation) or even suffering. That is, as Schnitker helpfully summarises, "Although it often involves a temporal or waiting component, patience is also called forth in situations with no direct focus on time (e.g., dealing with a difficult person)."[126] Interestingly, the two meanings of the term sometime occur in the Bible within the same passage (e.g., Jas 5:7–10 above, where the two instances in v. 7 clearly concern time, while the occurrence in v. 10 concerns suffering). While this twofold meaning is also true to some extent of the English word "patience," Fee highlights a major difference: "patience" is used in English only for enduring lesser difficulties (e.g., daily hassles), whereas *makrothymia* also covers more serious hardships and suffering (e.g., Jas 5:10).

We need to also recognise the communal nature of patience. *Makrothymia* in the New Testament is predominantly not about resisting impatience in order to sustain one's own peace of mind but rather to build up a harmonious community. In 1 Thess 5:14, Paul urges the believers to "be patient with everyone," and Eph 4:2 combines patience with love ("be patient, bearing with one another in love") in the same way as 1 Cor 13:4 does: "love is patient." Finally, Col 3:12–13 also emphasises the need to forgive: "Clothe yourselves with . . . patience. Bear with each other and forgive one another if any of you has a grievance against someone." Winward

---

124. See e.g., Fee, *God's Empowering Presence*, 450.

125. E.g., Barclay, *Flesh and Spirit*, 91; R. N. Longenecker, *Galatians*, 261; Fung, *Galatians*, 267. Charles R. Pinches, "Patience," in *Dictionary of Scripture and Ethics*, ed. Joel B. Green (Grand Rapids: Baker Academic, 2011), 582; *NIDNTTE* 2:61.

126. Sarah A. Schnitker, "An Examination of Patience and Well-Being," *Journal of Positive Psychology* 7, no. 4 (2012): 263.

captures the essence of such forbearance well when he considers it "an aspect of caring; it's one of the colours in the spectrum of love. It's the way in which a loving person responds to, and deals with, trying and difficult people."[127]

The Spiritual Dimension of Biblical Patience

Similar to the other facets of the fruit of the Spirit, patience is also rooted in divine forbearance (see table 1 in chapter 2), and an important purpose for humans to exercise this virtue is to ensure their redemption: Heb 6:12 urges believers to "imitate those who through faith and patience inherit what has been promised," and Jas 5:7 calls them to "be patient, then, brothers and sisters, until the Lord's coming"; the importance of this latter call is affirmed by its repetition in the next verse: "Be patient and stand firm, because the Lord's coming is near."[128] The apostle Paul underlines the importance of *hope* with regard to waiting patiently when he states in Rom 8:25, "If we hope for what we do not yet have, we wait for it patiently," and in his seminal work on virtues, Hauerwas explains that hope and patience are inextricably bound: "The hope necessary to initiate us into the adventure must be schooled by patience if the adventure is to be sustained. . . . Yet patience equally requires hope, for without hope patience too easily accepts the world and the self for what it is rather than what it can or should be."[129]

A further spiritual requirement for the ability to be patient is *trust*, which is highlighted in Ps 37. Goldingay and Payne explain that if we read the famous line "be still before the LORD and wait patiently for him" (v. 7) in the context of the whole psalm, it becomes clear that it refers to a "suggestive expression of trust" implying "a willingness to submit to Yhwh."[130] Indeed, just before this appeal, the psalm specifically calls the reader to "trust in the LORD" (v. 3) and then elaborates on the rewards of this trust as follows:

---

127. Winward, *Fruit of the Spirit*, 124.

128. Schnitker et al. ("The Virtue of Patience, Spirituality, and Suffering," 268) conclude that patience in the Christian tradition has strong redemptive elements: "Patience is not just the acceptance of present reality, but also includes hope for some future state where things are redeemed."

129. Hauerwas, *A Community of Character*, 127–128.

130. John Goldingay and David Payne, *A Critical and Exegetical Commentary on Isaiah 40–55* (London: T&T Clark, 2006), 2:521.

> Commit your way to the LORD;
>> trust in him and he will do this:
> He will make your righteous reward shine like the dawn,
>> your vindication like the noonday sun. (vv. 5–6)

The reward of trusting the Lord is stated in v. 9: "Those who hope in the LORD will inherit the land," to be repeated in v. 34: "Hope in the LORD and keep his way. He will exalt you to inherit the land." Although written at a time when Jesus Christ and the good news had not been revealed to the world yet, the psalm's message is not dissimilar to that of James: "Be patient and stand firm, because the Lord's coming is near" (5:8).

Patience in Psychology

The treatment of patience in psychology has been curious: although it has always been regarded as an important trait, it had not received any focused attention as a topic of empirical research until about fifteen years ago.[131] Before that, patience-related research tended to be framed in self-regulation-centred paradigms such as "delayed gratification" (to be discussed below when describing self-control). Even the emerging emphasis in positive psychology on virtues at the beginning of the new millennium initially overlooked patience, because Peterson and Seligman did not include it in their list of primary character strengths; they considered patience an amalgam of self-regulation, persistence, and open-mindedness.[132] It was the dedicated research initiative of Sarah Schnitker and her colleagues that provided evidence that patience represented more than the sum of various attributes and would thus qualify as a distinct virtue.[133] Similar to how virtues have been conceptualised in general, these scholars defined patience as a hybrid personality construct, in which emotion regulation strategies are

---

131. See Schnitker, "Patience and Well-Being," 263.

132. Peterson and Seligman, *Character Strengths and Virtues*, 24.

133. This was evidenced by the fact that empirical research found only small correlations between patience and the three strengths; see Schnitker et al., "The Virtue of Patience, Spirituality, and Suffering," 265.

coupled with a transcendent narrative.[134] The latter is a central aspect of patience as it ascribes meaning to any affliction involved—that is, it explains why suffering is something one needs to put up with—and Schnitker and Emmons stress that people's faith can offer appropriate spiritual narratives to promote patient endurance: "One essential feature to narratives that value suffering is their transcendent elements, pointing the individual to something bigger than the self and the present circumstances."[135]

More specifically, through assessing various patient responses to what people perceived as negative circumstances, Schnitker et al. identified three types of patience: (1) *interpersonal patience*, which involves a calm response to people who are regarded as frustrating; (2) *life hardships patience*, which concerns a tolerance for adverse conditions (e.g., health-related or financial); and (3) *daily hassles patience*, which involves a calm response to the difficulties accompanying everyday living.[136] To deal with any potential impatience, people need to employ emotion regulation strategies, and Schnitker et al. argue that this practice amounts to a virtue proper if it is utilised to benefit the larger community and if it follows a sufficiently internalised transcendent narrative that presents the affliction as meaningful.[137]

Kindness (*Chrēstotēs*)

The word "kindness" (*chrēstotēs*) and its cognates occur eighteen times in the Bible, once in its secular meaning of "good quality" regarding food and drinks (Luke 5:39), the other times referring to an attribute of both God and humans. In the Septuagint the word group is used most frequently of God, usually connoting kindness but sometimes also translated into English as "good"—for example, Ps 34:8 states, "Taste and see that the LORD is good," which is cited by 1 Pet 2:3 ("now that you have

---

134. Schnitker et al., 264.
135. Schnitker and Emmons, "The Psychology of Virtue," 240.
136. Schnitker et al., "The Virtue of Patience, Spirituality, and Suffering," 265.
137. Schnitker et al., 266.

tasted that the Lord is good"), with both the Septuagint and the New Testament using the word *chrēstos*. This is an illustration of the fact that the word's semantic range considerably overlaps with that of "goodness" (*agathōsynē*), which is the next facet of the fruit of the Spirit, to be discussed below.

Although in popular parlance being kind is sometimes used in the sense of a "nice" or "pleasant" interpersonal style, kindness proper concerns a consideration for others and a readiness to help them through specific actions of caring. Silva emphasises that it is this active aspect of the word that defines its true meaning,[138] a connotation modelled by divine example: Eph 2:7 declares that God's grace is "expressed in his kindness to us in Christ Jesus"—that is, God's kindness was expressed through sending his Son to us.[139] In this sense *chrēstotēs* can be understood as a concrete outworking of love, and this "love in action" quality makes kindness the most recognisable characteristic of the fruit of the Spirit.[140] It is also a "universal language," understood by all people, whether Christian or not,[141] and similar to how kindness is valued today, it was regarded as laudable by the whole spectrum of society in antiquity, from philosophers to average people.[142] Interestingly, the similarity between the Greek word for Christ (*Christos*) and kindness (*chrēstos*) often confused people in NT times, and Christians were referred to as the latter, because they were seen as kind.[143]

Kindness in Psychology

Psychology has little to say specifically about kindness, not because this caring human orientation has not been of scholarly interest, but because the relevant human quality has typically been discussed under the rubrics of altruism and compassion (see chapter 5). In addition, kind actions have also been investigated under different labels, for example

---

138. *NIDNTTE* 4:687–688.
139. See e.g., Fee, *God's Empowering Presence*, 450–451.
140. Kenneson, *Life on the Vine*, 136–137.
141. Winward, *Fruit of the Spirit*, 144.
142. Tina Malti, "Kindness: A Perspective from Developmental Psychology," *European Journal of Developmental Psychology* 18 (2021): 631.
143. See e.g., Kenneson, *Life on the Vine*, 137.

"prosocial behaviours" and "doing good." The specific measurement of kindness as a distinct attribute has only begun over the past decade,[144] but recent research has shown promise. For example, in order to offer an accurate representation, Tina Malti separates three components of kindness: *kind emotions* (e.g., other-oriented emotions such as empathy and sympathy), *kind cognitions* (e.g., efforts to actively understand other perspectives and integrate them into one's own), and *kind actions* (e.g., helping, cooperating, or comforting behaviours). Even more importantly, she highlighted the fact that the gentleness and benevolence of kindness can be directed not only towards others but also towards oneself,[145] and argued that for maximum effectiveness the two aspects need to be balanced; that is, one can best reach out to others from a stable base of internal stability and harmony. In this way, kindness fits into the overall pattern of the other facets of the fruit of the Spirit by having an internal and a communal angle.

Finally, Canter and his colleagues have recently developed a forty-item questionnaire to assess various aspects of kindness, and the statistical analysis of the results give rise to three aspects of a broad kindness construct: (1) *benign tolerance*, which concerns "permissive humanity revealed in an everyday courteousness, acceptance and love of one's fellows"; (2) empathetic *responsivity*, which concerns a more personalised consideration of the specific feelings of other particular individuals; and (3) *principled proaction*, which is about behaving honourably towards others and being proactive rather than reactive in an altruistic sense.[146] Underlying these facets of kindness, they also identified a more fundamental form of kindness that they termed *core kindness* and which they conceived as an important aspect of personality in general.[147]

---

144. See David Canter, Donna Youngs, and Miroslava Yaneva, "Towards a Measure of Kindness: An Exploration of a Neglected Interpersonal Trait," *Personality and Individual Differences* 106 (2017): 15–20.

145. Malti, "Kindness," 629.

146. Canter, Youngs, and Yaneva, "Kindness," 16–17.

147. Canter, Youngs, and Yaneva, 17–18.

Goodness (*Agathōsynē*)

We need to begin the examination of the virtue of goodness by addressing a seeming contradiction: both Mark and Luke record an episode when a rich young man addresses Jesus as "Good Teacher" and then asks him: "What must I do to inherit eternal life?" In response, Jesus rebukes him by declaring, "Why do you call me good? . . . No one is good—except God alone" (Mark 10:17–18; Luke 18:18–19). If indeed only God is good, why does Paul write in Gal 5:22 that the fruit of the Spirit includes goodness, or in Rom 15:14 that "I myself am convinced, my brothers and sisters, that you yourselves are full of goodness"? Is "goodness" purely a divine attribute, or is it something that humans can also aspire to?

Commentators of these Gospel passages agree that the phrase "Good Teacher" is rather unusual and has no previous biblical or Jewish precedents.[148] This suggests that it is not a formulaic salutation but rather a way for the rich young man to specifically honour Jesus by calling him "good" (which is further confirmed by the fact that he—again unusually—kneels before Jesus). The reason for Jesus's initial rebuff is not explained in the text, which has allowed for several different explanations over the centuries.[149] One possible reading is that Jesus's response anticipates the rich young man's subsequent claim that he has kept all the commandments since his childhood. This claim implies that the young man believes that his past achievements have made him "good," and he addresses Jesus as a "good" teacher on similar achievement-based grounds as an acknowledgment that Jesus has earned this title through the quality of his past teaching.[150] According to this reading, therefore, Jesus's rebuke is meant

---

148. Craig A. Evans, *Mark 8:27–16:20*, WBC 34b (Nashville: Thomas Nelson, 2001), 95.

149. See, e.g., Evans, 95–96; Robert H. Stein, *Mark*, BECNT (Grand Rapids: Baker Academic, 2008), 468.

150. See Mark L. Strauss, *Mark*, Zondervan Exegetical Commentary on the New Testament (Grand Rapids: Zondervan, 2014), 440; William L. Lane, *The Gospel of Mark*, NICNT (Grand Rapids: Eerdmans, 1974), 365; Walter W. Wessel and Mark L. Strauss, "Mark," in *The Expositor's Bible Commentary: Matthew–Mark*, rev. ed., ed. Tremper Longman III and David E. Garland (Grand Rapids: Zondervan, 2010), 864.

to signal that one cannot earn goodness merely through human deeds such as observing regulations.[151]

This qualification offers us an important clue about the spiritually construed meaning of goodness, and such a clue is particularly welcome because there is otherwise little to go on in the Scriptures to clarify the exact meaning of this virtue: goodness as a noun does not appear in secular Greek, and there are only three other occurrences of it in the New Testament, none of which shed any particular light on its content. Therefore, interpretations need to rely on the meaning of the adjective "good" (*agathos*) from which the noun is formed, but here we have the opposite problem: this adjective—similar to "good" in English—was very common in classic Greek and has one hundred occurrences in the New Testament, with a wide range of meanings.[152] The dialogue between Jesus and the rich young man indicates that when "good" is used in a moral sense, it has a prominent spiritual connotation as it refers to an essential aspect of the image of God, and indeed, variations of the phrase "God is good" are very common in the Old Testament (e.g., in the Psalms: "The LORD is good and his love endures for ever" [100:5]; "Praise the LORD, for the LORD is good" [135:3]). In a similar vein, Jas 1:17 declares, "Every good and perfect gift is from above, coming down from the Father of the heavenly lights." This, in turn, justifies why "goodness" can be part of the fruit of the Spirit: exactly because it is of the Spirit.

The spiritual connotation of "good" is also present when it is used to refer to a human being, as illustrated by the description of Barnabas, "a good man, full of the Holy Spirit and faith" (Acts 11:24); and it needs to be noted that in such cases the "good" quality goes beyond the moral aspect of righteousness in its spiritual intensity, as indicated by Rom 5:7: "Very rarely will anyone die for a righteous person, though for a good person someone might possibly dare to die." Finally, an indirect but powerful pointer to the spiritual quality of "good" is that Jesus uses it as the

---

151. This reading is supported by the fact that the word order in Jesus's follow-up question places the emphasis on "me" ("Why *me* do you call good?") rather than on "good."

152. As Barclay (*Flesh and Spirit*, 103) summarises, it can describe excellence in several spheres, ranging from a tree or fertile ground to gifts, deeds, and human conscience.

opposite of evil: "Make a tree good and its fruit will be good, or make a tree bad and its fruit will be bad, for a tree is recognised by its fruit. You brood of vipers, how can you who are evil say anything good? For the mouth speaks what the heart is full of. A good man brings good things out of the good stored up in him, and an evil man brings evil things out of the evil stored up in him" (Matt 12:33–35).

Generosity

Curiously, the Latin translation of the Bible, the Vulgate, tradition-ally included twelve rather than nine virtues in Gal 5:22–23. A closer look at the additional three virtues—generosity, modesty, and chasti-ty[153]—as well as manuscript details over the centuries[154] reveal that the most likely explanation for these additions is that the early Latin trans-lators (as this part of the Vulgate was not translated by Jerome himself) included more than one word when the original Greek term had several meanings: *agathōsynē* was rendered into goodness and generosity, while *enkrateia* into self-control and chastity (and possibly *prautēs* into gentle-ness and modesty). That the meaning of *agathōsynē* does include a sense of generosity is also attested to in the parable of the workers in the vine-yard, where the landowner asks the workers (Matt 20:15): "Don't I have the right to do what I want with my own money? Or are you envious because I am generous [*agathos*]?" Commentators therefore agree that both translations (i.e., goodness and generosity) are possible,[155] and the close association between the two senses has been highlighted in ethics: as Lester Hunt explains, a necessary condition for true generosity is that it is a voluntary act: "One gives, not from duty, but from the *goodness of one's heart.*"[156]

---

153. *Catechism of the Catholic Church* #1832.

154. James Snapp, "Galatians 5:22–23: Have We Lost Some Fruit?," *The Text of the Gospels* (blog), 4 July 2019, https://www.thetextofthegospels.com/2019/07/galatians-522-23-have-we-lost-some-fruit.html.

155. E.g., R. Alan Cole, *Galatians: An Introduction and Commentary*, TNTC 9 (Downers Grove, IL: InterVarsity, 1989), 221; deSilva, *Galatians*, 467; Rapa, "Galatians," 631; C. Wright, *Cultivating the Fruit of the Spirit*, 97.

156. Lester H. Hunt, "Generosity," in *International Encyclopedia of Ethics* (online), ed. Hugh LaFollette (Hoboken, NJ: John Wiley & Sons, 2019), 2; emphasis added.

Goodness in Psychology

It was argued in chapter 2 that the notion of virtue is inherently linked to morality, because virtues are by definition personality dispositions underpinning the pursuit of what is good. Because of its generic reference to what is ethically good,[157] the moral connotation of "goodness" is particularly strong, which has made the notion unattractive for contemporary research psychologists, who typically follow a value-neutral approach. Blaine Fowers summarises this traditional averseness as follows: "The reason why psychologists of all kinds are so reluctant to focus on substantive goods is that defining what is good substantively requires a commitment to a particular understanding of worthiness. This sounds risky. Moreover, social scientists and professional practitioners rightly worry about prescribing how individuals should live. They are concerned about bias, ideological distortion, and value imposition."[158]

Indeed, McAdams adds that many psychologists "may have worried that venturing into the virtue domain might compromise their scientific objectivity."[159] Curiously, even positive psychologists have had little to say about goodness, even though part of their stated agenda has been to explore the psychological factors that lead to a "good life."[160] Fowers explains this by the fact that they have found the notion of goodness too broad, and as such it did not facilitate the general thrust of positive psychology of linking virtues with *particular* goods. Also, while there is a great deal said about positive *feelings* in this domain, feeling good is different from *being* good.[161]

On the other hand, one would expect the other meaning of *agathōsynē*, generosity, to have fared better in positive psychology as it is related to a more specific quality of selfless giving. However, in their original classification, Peterson and Seligman clustered generosity together with

---

157. Keener, *Galatians*, 521.
158. Fowers, "From Continence to Virtue," 636.
159. McAdams, "Psychological Science and the Nicomachean Ethics," 307.
160. See e.g., Brian P. Cole, "Good Life," in *The Encyclopedia of Positive Psychology*, ed. S. J. Lopez (Chichester, UK: Wiley-Blackwell, 2009), 438; Brent Dean Robbins, "What Is the Good Life? Positive Psychology and the Renaissance of Humanistic Psychology," *Humanistic Psychologist* 36 (2008): 101.
161. Fowers, "From Continence to Virtue," 635.

several other virtues (nurturance, care, compassion, altruistic love, nice-ness) under the rubric of "kindness," referring to the tendency to be "nice to other people—to be compassionate and concerned about their wel-fare, to do favours for them, to perform good deeds, and to take care of them"[162] (we shall return to this cluster in chapter 5 when discussing the underlying dimensions of the fruit of the Spirit). This being the case, generosity received little individual attention.

The only area of psychological research where goodness has featured prominently is a line of inquiry focusing on "doing good."[163] This is also a featured biblical theme, as for example Peter described to Cornelius how Jesus "went around doing good" (Acts 10:38), and Paul also high-lighted it in Gal 6:9–10: "Let us not become weary in doing good . . . as we have opportunity, let us do good to all people, especially to those who belong to the family of believers." However, the primary focus of the psychological investigations on doing good has not concerned what "good" entails but rather the personal consequences of good deeds in the actor, exploring the common observation that positive acts can set into motion a cycle of kindness and happiness.[164] C. S. Lewis summarised this process concerning loving actions (i.e., kindness) as follows: "The rule for all of us is perfectly simple. Do not waste time bothering whether you 'love' your neighbour; act as if you did. As soon as we do this we find one of the great secrets. When you are behaving as if you loved someone, you will presently come to love him. If you injure someone you dislike, you will find yourself disliking him more. If you do him a good turn, you will find yourself disliking him less."[165] We shall further investigate this "do-good-and-become-good" cycle in chapter 7 when discussing methods of cultivating the fruit of the Spirit.

---

162. Peterson and Seligman, *Character Strengths and Virtues*, 296.
163. See e.g., Klodiana Lanaj, Russell E. Johnson, and Mo Wang, "When Lending a Hand Depletes the Will: The Daily Costs and Benefits of Helping," *Journal of Applied Psychology* 101, no. 8 (2016): 1097–1110; Kristin Layous et al., "What Triggers Prosocial Effort? A Positive Feedback Loop between Positive Activities, Kindness, and Well-Being," *Journal of Positive Psychology* 12, no. 4 (2017): 385–98; Ben. M. Tappin and Valerio Capraro, "Doing Good vs. Avoiding Bad in Prosocial Choice: A Refined Test and Extension of the Morality Preference Hypothesis," *Journal of Experimental Social Psychology* 79 (2018): 64–70.
164. E.g., Layous et al. "Prosocial Effort," 396.
165. Lewis, *Christian Behaviour*, 131.

Faithfulness (*Pistis*)

The Greek word *pistis* in Gal 5:22 can have two senses, "faith" and "faithfulness." In most cases "faith" is a better translation in the New Testament, although whether or not this heavily loaded English theological term expresses Paul's meaning appropriately has been the subject of considerable discussion in Pauline studies.[166] However, most commentators agree that the virtue in the Galatian passage is better denoted by "faithfulness."[167] Indeed, similar to all other virtues in Gal 5:22–23, *pistis* is also used for God (e.g., Rom 3:3), and it is difficult to see how spiritual faith (rather than faithfulness) would be relevant to God; this link with the divine also excludes sexual faithfulness, which is the most common understanding of the word in English. Instead, faithfulness as a biblical virtue refers to consistent trustworthiness and dependability—something one can count on. We find a particularly clear example of this in the parable of the shrewd manager, where the *pistis* word group appears as many as five times, always translated by the "trust" word group: "Whoever can be trusted with very little can also be trusted with much, and whoever is dishonest with very little will also be dishonest with much. So if you have not been trustworthy in handling worldly wealth, who will trust you with true riches? And if you have not been trustworthy with someone else's property, who will give you property of your own?" (Luke 16:10–12). Thus, "faithfulness" in Gal 5:22 concerns the believer's relationships with others, which fits in well with Paul's focus in the fruit of the Spirit on the relational aspect of the ideal Christlike character. Tidball captures this aspect well: "Faithfulness is not so much faithfulness to the truth as trustworthiness in general, and reliability in all relationships and commitments."[168]

The quality of faithfulness also includes integrity, which, according to Lynne McFall, requires that a person subscribes to a set of principles or commitments and upholds these in the face of temptation and challenge

---

166. See e.g., Varghese P. Chiraparamban, "The Translation of Πίστις and Its Cognates in the Pauline Epistles," *Bible Translator* 66, no. 2 (2015): 185–86; Peter Oakes, "*Pistis* as Relational Way of Life in Galatians," *Journal for the Study of the New Testament* 40, no. 3 (2018): 255.

167. E.g., Keener, *Galatians*, 522; R. N. Longenecker, *Galatians*, 262; Moo, *Galatians*, 365.

168. Tidball, *The Message of Holiness*, 211.

"for what the agent takes to be the right reasons."[169] Accordingly, faithfulness as personal integrity is determined by someone following a certain set of principles, and this understanding creates a meaningful link between the two readings of *pistis*, "faith" and "faithfulness": following Jesus Christ provides believers with the standards to stand by and at the same time it also fortifies their faithfulness to stand firm. Related to this, C. Wright highlights the temporal element in faithfulness—namely, that "faithfulness also includes *long-term, steady, dependable, lifelong commitment*."[170]

Faithfulness in Psychology

The term "faithfulness" is used in psychology largely to refer to marital/sexual fidelity, which is not relevant to the current discussion. However, the notions of "trust" and "trustworthiness" have been subject to a reasonable amount of psychological research in the past. Having said that, Levine and her colleagues rightly point out that most investigations on trust have disproportionately focused on what makes people more or less trusting (i.e., trusting others), rather than trustworthy (i.e., deserving trust),[171] and we find only a handful of studies on the latter aspect. The traditional understanding of trustworthiness has involved three underlying mechanisms: ability, integrity, and benevolence.[172] The first component is logical and makes sense as it refers to competence and expertise; the second is in line with the content of faithfulness discussed above; but the third determinant, *benevolence*, adds an interesting novel element to the understanding of the notion. Mayer and his colleagues define benevolence as "the extent to which a trustee is believed to want to do good to the trustor, aside from an egocentric profit motive," which is a quality that has also been labelled as "unconditional kindness."[173]

---

169. Lynne McFall, "Integrity," *Ethics* 98, no. 1 (1987): 9.

170. C. Wright, *Cultivating the Fruit of the Spirit*, 124; emphasis original.

171. Emma E. Levine et al., "Who Is Trustworthy? Predicting Trustworthy Intentions and Behavior," *Journal of Personality and Social Psychology* 115, no. 3 (2018): 468.

172. Roger C. Mayer, James H. Davis, and F. David Schoorman, "An Integrative Model of Organisational Trust," *Academy of Management Review* 20, no. 3 (1995): 717.

173. E.g., Isabel Thielmann and Benjamin E. Hilbig, "The Traits One Can Trust: Dissecting Reciprocity and Kindness as Determinants of Trustworthy Behavior," *Personality and Social Psychology Bulletin* 41, no. 11 (2015): 1524.

It is reflected, for example, in the relationship between a mentor and a protégé when there is no extrinsic reward for the mentor. Thus, a pillar of trustworthiness is the person's selfless benevolent compassion for others, which creates an obvious link with compassionate love.

Research conducted by Levine and her colleagues has further enriched the understanding of trustworthiness in a way relevant to biblical faithfulness. They have found that the best predictor of the notion in their study was "guilt-proneness"—that is, "the individual difference that captures the *anticipation* of guilt over wrongdoing."[174] In an article analysing the relationship between guilt-proneness and moral character, Cohen and her colleagues describe this character trait as "indicative of a predisposition to experience negative feelings about personal wrongdoing, even when the wrongdoing is private. It is characterized by the anticipation of feeling bad about committing transgressions rather than by guilty feelings in a particular moment."[175] Thus, the Christian awareness of one's own sinful nature is undoubtedly related to this attribute, and indeed, Cohen and her colleagues report studies that found that people scoring high on guilt-proneness behaved more ethically in a range of spheres (from business decisions to criminal behaviours).[176] In the study of Levine et al., people high in guilt-proneness were found to be more likely to behave in interpersonally sensitive ways when they were responsible for others' outcomes.[177] This creates a meaningful mediating link between guilt-proneness and trustworthiness, and it also helps us to fit trustworthiness in the ideal Christian character. Peter Oakes submits that in NT times faithfulness was "the fundamental virtue of relationship" because "trust, loyalty and/or trustworthiness was a virtue expected in every proper relationship."[178] It was thus a virtue concerning "a relational way of life,"[179] and emerging research in psychology appears to corroborate this conclusion.

---

174. Levine et al., "Who Is Trustworthy?," 471.

175. Taya R. Cohen, A. T. Panter, and Nazli Turan, "Guilt Proneness and Moral Character," *Current Directions in Psychological Science* 21, no. 5 (2012): 355.

176. Cohen, Panter, and Turan, 357–58.

177. Levine et al., "Who Is Trustworthy?," 468.

178. Oakes, "*Pistis*," 264.

179. Oakes, 255.

Gentleness (*Prautēs*)

The Greek word translated as "gentleness" in Gal 5:23, *prautēs*, is also translated elsewhere in the Bible as "meekness" (e.g., "Blessed are the meek" [Matt 5:5]) and "humility" (e.g., "by deeds done in the humility that comes from wisdom" [Jas 3:13]), although the latter meaning, humility, is primarily expressed by a different word group, *tapeino-phrosynē/tapeinos*. The semantic overlap between gentleness and humility is further reflected by the fact that in the three places in the Scriptures where *prautēs* and *tapeinophrosynē* (or their cognates) occur together (Matt 11:29; 2 Cor 10:1; Eph 4:2), only twice do they follow the expected translation pattern. In the third case (2 Cor 10:1), the NIV renders *prautēs* into "humility" (rather than gentleness), *tapeino-phrosynē* into "timidity" (rather than humility), and uses "gentleness" as the translation of a third word, *epieikeias*: "By the humility [*prautētos*] and gentleness [*epieikeias*] of Christ, I appeal to you—I, Paul, who am 'timid' [*tapeinos*] when face to face with you, but 'bold' towards you when away!"[180]

These variations indicate that, as Fee concludes (amongst others), this facet of the fruit of the Spirit is arguably the hardest to find an adequate English word for.[181] Indeed, Winward points out that gentleness, meekness, and humility are inappropriate renderings of the Greek term, because in English these attributes suggest a certain amount of weakness, which is not true about *prautēs*,[182] and Tidball also adds the warning that gentleness should not be confused with "spinelessness."[183] To realise that weakness and spinelessness have nothing to do with gentleness, one only needs to think of Moses and Jesus, both of whom

---

180. Moreover, in one of the key OT verses concerning humility ("Now Moses was a very humble man, more humble than anyone else on the face of the earth" [Num 12:3]), the Septuagint translates the Hebrew word for "humble," *'ānāyw*, as *praus*. On the other hand, in arguably the most famous NT verse concerning humility ("And being found in appearance as a man, he [Jesus] humbled himself by becoming obedient to death—even death on a cross!" [Phil 2:8]), the Greek word for "humbled" is *etapeinōsen*, the verb form of *tapeinophrosynē*.

181. Fee, *God's Empowering Presence*, 452.

182. Winward, *Fruit of the Spirit*, 173–74.

183. Tidball, *The Message of Holiness*, 211.

have been described as "gentle" in the Scriptures;[184] however, their gentleness involved great strength that we could describe as "strength under control."[185]

The involvement of a degree of self-control in gentleness is also suggested by Aristotle, who defines it as the mean between the extremes of "excessive anger" and the "inability to be angry"[186] with regard to dealing with other people, which suggests a certain amount of self-discipline. In his commentary on Gal 5:23, Martin Luther describes gentleness in a similar vein as "the virtue that is not provoked to anger and does not take vengeance."[187] Bruce further submits that not only does gentleness imply self-control, but it also has a lot in common with patience, and in Eph 4:2 and Col 3:12 the two virtues (gentleness and patience) are listed alongside each other.[188]

Taking the various facets of gentleness together, we may conclude that the virtue refers to a calm, considerate, tender, and measured disposition towards others, the type of conduct that Paul considers vital in assisting other people: "If someone is caught in a sin, you who live by the Spirit should restore that person gently" (Gal 6:1), and "opponents must be gently instructed" (2 Tim 2:25)—indeed, Paul's general rule is "always to be gentle towards everyone" (Titus 3:2).[189] Barclay illustrates this virtue expressively: "It is when we have *prautēs* that we treat all men with perfect courtesy, that we can rebuke without rancour, that we can argue without intolerance, that we can face the truth without resentment, that we can be angry and yet sin not, that we can be gentle and yet not weak. *Prautēs* is the virtue in which our relationships both with ourselves and our fellowmen become perfect and complete."[190]

---

184. Num 12:3 and Matt 11:29, respectively.

185. Keener (*Galatians*, 522) confirms that in the antiquity *prautēs* was also applied to leaders and was "understood not as weakness but rather as mercy or compassion."

186. See R. N. Longenecker, *Galatians*, 262.

187. In Bray, *Galatians, Ephesians*, 199.

188. Bruce, *Galatians*, 255. In a similar vein, C. Wright (*Cultivating the Fruit of the Spirit*, 127) argues, "Gentleness is very close to patience. . . . If patience is the ability to endure hostility and criticism without anger, then gentleness is the ability to endure such things without aggression."

189. See also Moo, *Galatians*, 365–366.

190. Barclay, *Flesh and Spirit*, 121.

Gentleness in Psychology

The notion of gentleness has been ambiguously represented in psychology. There are virtually no in-depth analyses of the disposition, but it is included in high-profile contemporary personality constructs as a lower-level (i.e., facet-level) constituent of larger dimensions. For example, the most famous personality model currently, the Big Five,[191] includes "agreeableness" as one of its five major dimensions, and one of the facets of this dimension is "tender-mindedness," which appears close to gentleness in content. However, because the main emphasis in such broad personality structures is to *reduce* the great number of individual differences into a parsimonious set, most of the analysis concerns the higher-order components only rather than the facets; consequently, even a paper entitled "Facet Scales for Agreeableness and Conscientiousness" only offers the following brief description: "Tender-Mindedness refers to the tendency to be guided by feelings, particularly those of sympathy, in making judgments and forming attitudes."[192]

A recent personality model, the HEXACO Model of personality structure,[193] offers more promise in this respect: it also contains agreeableness as a basic dimension, and one of the four components of this factor is specifically labelled "gentleness." However, even in a dedicated paper entitled "The HEXACO Honesty-Humility, Agreeableness, and Emotionality Factors: A Review of Research and Theory," we only find the following short specification: "The Gentleness scale assesses a tendency to be mild and lenient in dealings with other people. Low scorers tend to be critical in their evaluations of others, whereas high scorers

---

191. E.g., Paul T. Costa Jr. and Robert R. McCrae, "The Revised Neo Personality Inventory (Neo-Pi-R)," in *Personality Measurement and Testing*, vol. 2 of *The SAGE Handbook of Personality Theory and Assessment*, ed. Gregory J. Boyle, Gerald Matthews, and Donald H. Saklofske (London: Sage, 2008).

192. Paul T. Costa Jr., Robert R. McCrae, and David A. Dye, "Facet Scales for Agreeableness and Conscientiousness: A Revision of the Neo Personality Inventory," *Personality and Individual Differences* 12, no. 9 (1991): 889.

193. Michael C. Ashton and Kibeom Lee, "The HEXACO Model of Personality Structure," in *Personality Measurement and Testing*, vol. 2 of *The SAGE Handbook of Personality Theory and Assessment*, ed. Gregory J. Boyle, Gerald Matthews, and Donald H. Saklofske (London: Sage, 2008).

are reluctant to judge others harshly."[194] Finally, not even a recent theo-retical paper focusing on the comparative analysis of the composition of agreeableness in various personality inventories (including the Big Five and HEXACO) turns out to be more helpful, as it covers gentleness only in two short bracketed descriptors: "agreeable, amiable vs. harsh, antagonistic, combative" and "interpersonal lenience or reluctance to judge others harshly."[195] This is in some ways a good news / bad news scenario: the good news is that gentleness is recognised as an important psychological element; the bad news is partly that its content is assumed to be unproblematic enough to warrant only shorthand descriptors and partly that psychological investigations have only focused on higher levels of the composite models of which gentleness is a part. Unfortunately, therefore, psychological research at the moment has little to contribute to the understanding of the ambiguous nature of gentleness indicated in the virtue literature.

Self-Control (*Enkrateia*)

The Greek word for self-control in Gal 5:23, *enkrateia*, derives from the word "power" (*kratos*) and thus refers to having power/mastery over one's emotions, passions, and desires.[196] The term was often used with a sexual connotation, but we should note that Paul applies it in a more general sense, as evidenced by his statement that "athletes exercise self-control *in all things*" (1 Cor 9:25 NRSVA; emphasis added), referring to one's overall self-mastery and discipline. It was mentioned in the discussion of goodness that the Vulgate traditionally included twelve rather than nine virtues in Gal 5:22–23, because the Latin translators used more than one word when the original Greek term had several

---

194. Michael C. Ashton, Kibeom Lee, and Reinout E. de Vries, "The HEXACO Honesty-Humility, Agreeableness, and Emotionality Factors: A Review of Research and Theory," *Personality and Social Psychology Review* 18, no. 2 (2014): 142.

195. Michael L. Crowe, Donald R. Lynam, and Joshua D. Miller, "Uncovering the Structure of Agreeableness from Self-Report Measures," *Journal of Personality* 86 (2018): 772.

196. See e.g., *NIDNTTE* 2:83.

meanings, and for *enkrateia* they included both self-control and chastity, which confirms the broad semantic domain of the NT usage of *enkrateia*. One way of illustrating the range of meanings that this mastery over one's impulses and faculties subsumes is to think of the notion as the opposite of indulgence: its content can refer to anything one may indulge in, including as diverse things as a vice, lavish opulence, or idle thoughts.

Although the current discussion largely focuses on self-control in the New Testament, we should also recognise its importance in the Old Testament: self-discipline appears right at the beginning of Genesis when the Lord says to Cain in Gen 4:7, "sin is lurking at the door; its desire is for you, but you must *master it*" (NRSVA; emphasis added), and self-controlled restraint is mentioned in the OT wisdom literature as a vital aspect of being victorious (e.g., Prov 16:32). It is emphasised that the absence of self-control can ruin a person: "For lack of discipline they [the wicked] will die, led astray by their own great folly" (Prov 5:23; see also 25:28).

Enkrateia was also a well-known concept in antiquity in general, as it was considered a principal virtue by Greek philosophers such as Socrates, Plato, Aristotle, and the Stoics[197]—in fact, Keener explains that of all the constituents of the fruit of the Spirit, this was probably the virtue most often emphasised in the Galatians' Hellenistic environment.[198] It was also appreciated in popular culture as a requirement for an athlete's training, and we find several references to the imagery of an athlete running the race to the end in the New Testament,[199] implying that believers should become "Christ's athletes."[200] Interestingly, as Kenneson reminds us, athletics seems to be still one of the few areas in our contemporary society where we honour self-discipline and self-control.[201]

---

197. See e.g., Betz, *Galatians*, 288; Bruce, *Galatians*, 255; B. W. Longenecker, *The Triumph of Abraham's God*, 263;

198. Keener, *Galatians*, 522–523.

199. E.g., Acts 20:24; 1 Cor 9:24–27; 2 Tim 4:7; Heb 12:1; see also Gal 5:7; Phil 3:14.

200. Winward, *Fruit of the Spirit*, 189.

201. Kenneson, *Life on the Vine*, 223.

Foundational Virtue

Taking the final position in the list of the facets of the fruit of the Spirit, self-control has a privileged place, because the final position in a Greek structure implies special emphasis.[202] Most commentators agree with Betz that this conspicuous placement was intentional, putting self-control in juxtaposition to love at the other end of the list.[203] We shall explore the specific connection between love and self-control in the next chapter, when we discuss the interrelated nature of the nine facets of the fruit, but it is important to underline here the foundational nature of self-control as a virtue. This is a point where ancient philosophy and modern psychology come to full agreement. A good illustration of the high esteem attributed to self-control in antiquity is Xenophon's summary of the views of his teacher, Socrates: "Shall not every man hold self-control to be the foundation of all virtue, and first lay this foundation firmly in his soul? For who without this can learn any good or practice it worthily?"[204] Very similar thoughts have been expressed in a seminal paper on the psychology of virtues by Baumeister and Exline, who argue that self-control is centrally involved in most virtues and can be understood as a kind of "moral muscle."[205] As they conclude, "Morality is a set of rules that enable people to live together in harmony, and virtue involves internalizing those rules. Insofar as virtue depends on overcoming selfish or antisocial impulses for the sake of what is best for the group or collective, self-control can be said to be the master virtue."[206]

The central role of self-control is also confirmed by a point that Paul makes in Galatians immediately after describing the fruit of the Spirit. In Gal 5:24 he declares that "those who belong to Christ Jesus have crucified the flesh with its passions and desires." The phrase "crucifying one's passions and desires" is an expressive synonym for exercising total self-control over the temptations of vices, and the fact that Paul singled

---

202. E.g., Hays, "Galatians," 328; R. N. Longenecker, *Galatians*, 260.
203. Betz, *Galatians*, 288.
204. Xenophon, *Memorabilia* 1.5.4–5, cited in Kenneson, *Life on the Vine*, 224.
205. Baumeister and Exline, "Virtue," 1165.
206. Baumeister and Exline, 1165.

out this particular virtue as a mark of being a follower of Christ highlights its critical nature.

The general significance attached to the concept of self-control, however, appears to be at odds with the rather low frequency of the term in
the NT corpus: *enkrateia* and its cognates[207] only occur seven times, and
even the inclusion of the related terms "persevere," "perseverance," and
"lack of self-restraint," (through the common root of *kratos*, "power"[208])
adds only four further occurrences. This relatively restricted distribution
has prompted several commentators to call *enkrateia* "a rare word in the
NT,"[209] which plays only a "minor role."[210] What causes this seeming
contradiction? The reason lies in the practice of labelling various closely
related aspects of self-control differently; let us have a look at this issue
more closely, particularly because it will shed further light on the nature
of self-regulation in general.

The Labelling and Frequency of Self-Control

Titus 1:8 has been translated by the NIV as "he [an elder] must be
hospitable, one who loves what is good, who is self-controlled, upright,
holy and disciplined." Interestingly, the Greek word for "self-controlled"
here is not the adjective form of *enkrateia* (*enkratēs*), but a different word,
sōphrōn, even though *enkratēs* does appear in the verse but is rendered
"disciplined." This example illustrates a broader issue underlying the
ambiguous labelling of various, rather similar aspects of self-control. In
this case, for example, what is the difference between "self-controlled"
and "disciplined"? We would be hard pressed to identify any, because
the two terms are more or less interchangeable, and we find a similar
fluid situation in the psychological literature in general regarding the
notion of self-control/self-discipline: personality psychology accom-
modates a wide range of concepts of self-control with definitions that

---

207. *Enkrateuomai* ("to exercise self-control") and *enkratēs* ("self-controlled").
208. *Akrasia* ("incontinence/lack of self-control"), *karvtereō* ("to persevere/be steadfast"),
proskarterēsis ("perseverance").
209. Schreiner, *Galatians*, 350; for similar views, see e.g., Betz, *Galatians*, 288; Moo, *Galatians*,
360; *NIDNTTE* 2:84.
210. Matera, *Galatians*, 204.

overlap considerably, for example, self-regulation, self-mastery, grit, resilience, coping capacity, hardiness, buoyancy, conscientiousness, mental toughness, persistence, perseverance, tenacity, and stamina.[211] This large variety of interrelated concepts is not used consistently, and even when they are distinguished from each other, they display considerably overlapping meaning with only relatively subtle dissimilarities, as all of them concern, one way or another, the human capacity to resist temptations, to control one's impulses, and to persevere in the face of distractions or adversity. This proliferation of self-control-related constructs has been regarded as a growing problem in the field of psychology,[212] as most leading scholars acknowledge that the various proposed new terms correlate with each other strongly.[213] The absence of firm category boundaries regarding this concept is not an accident; the fact is that there are numerous variations of human functioning in how people navigate temptations and stand firm in the face of challenges or disrupting impulses, and it is not a straightforward task in many cases to unambiguously match these comparable strategic behaviours with distinct theoretical categories.

When we approach the Scriptures with such an awareness, we find that the broad notion of "self-control/self-mastery" appears in the New Testament in several different forms, thereby resulting in a much larger corpus of biblical examples: we find seven relevant word groups[214] with a

---

211. See Zoltán Dörnyei, *Innovations and Challenges in Language Learning Motivation* (London: Routledge, 2020), 154.

212. E.g., Angela L. Duckworth et al., "Self-Control and Academic Achievement," *Annual Review of Psychology* 70 (2019): 375; Matt C. Howard and Matthew P. Crayne, "Persistence: Defining the Multidimensional Construct and Creating a Measure," *Personality and Individual Differences* 139 (2019): 77; Kennon M. Sheldon et al., "Personality, Effective Goal-Striving, and Enhanced Well-Being: Comparing 10 Candidate Personality Strengths," *Personality and Social Psychology Bulletin* 41, no. 4 (2015): 577.

213. E.g., "The terms *self-control* and *self-regulation* are sometimes used interchangeably" (Baumeister and Exline, "Virtue," 1171); or "We use the terms perseverance and persistence interchangeably, as have most previous researchers" (Peterson and Seligman, *Character Strengths and Virtues*, 230); or "It is perhaps no wonder that self-control and grit are often used interchangeably by laypeople and scientists alike. These two determinants of success are highly correlated" (Angela L. Duckworth and James J. Gross, "Self-Control and Grit: Related but Separable Determinants of Success," *Current Directions in Psychological Science* 23, no. 5 [2014]: 320).

214. Besides *enkrateia* and its cognates, there is *sōphronismos* ("self-discipline") and its cognates; *nēphalios* ("temperate") and its cognates; *hypomonē* ("steadfastness") and its cognates; *anechomai* ("to endure, bear") and its cognates; *chalinagōgeō* ("to bridle, hold in check"); *stegō* ("to endure"). Moreover, as Bruce (*Galatians*, 254–255) explains, even "gentleness" (*prautēs*) shares something in

total frequency of over ninety. This figure reflects a salient presence and is in accordance with the theoretical importance attached to the notion of self-control earlier. The ambiguous labelling practice is also the reason why it is sometimes claimed that self-control is the only facet of the fruit of the Spirit that is not mentioned elsewhere in the Scriptures in relation to either God the Father or the Son.[215] While this claim is true of the term *enkrateia*, other aspects of the broader semantic domain of self-mastery do show divine links: as shown in table 1 (chapter 2), "perseverance" and "endurance" are associated with Jesus (2 Thess 3:5 and Heb 12:2, respectively)—which stands to reason, given that Jesus is described in the Gospels as having to resist temptations several times—and we also read about God the Father repeatedly in the Old Testament that he is "slow to anger" (e.g., Ex 34:6; Num 14:18; Ps 86:15; Jonah 4:2), which reflects temperance.

The Communal Aspect of Self-Control

In a comprehensive analysis of the letters of Paul, Gordon Fee submits that self-control is "the one virtue in the list [i.e., the fruit of the Spirit] that is clearly aimed at the individual believer. This is not something one does in community; it is a general stance toward excesses of various kinds."[216] In stark contrast, another prominent expert of Paul, James Dunn, argues that "it is not as an ideal in itself that Paul lauds 'self-control', but because of its importance in *community relations*, in contrast to the unrestrained emphasis placed on the flesh."[217] The contradiction stems partly from the labelling ambiguities discussed above: associating self-control solely with the capacity to resist (mainly physical) temptation often creates an individual emphasis (e.g., when one needs to stop using harmful substances), but the broader semantic domain of self-discipline is linked to communal aspects: passions need to be curbed, the tongue restrained, and one's anger contained in order to foster and maintain harmonious relationships. In

---

common with self-control as it refers to a restrained temperament between proneness to rage and incapacity for anger.

215. E.g., C. Wright, *Cultivating the Fruit of the Spirit*, 143.

216. Fee, *God's Empowering Presence*, 452.

217. Dunn, *Galatians*, 313; emphasis added.

other words, self-control by definition concerns forgoing an immediate desire in order to reach a more coveted state in the future, and while the sought-after future purpose/goal sometimes serves individual well-being (such as health), many of people's most valued enduring goals concern some aspects of interpersonal harmony. In fact, even self-control (or the lack of it) related to lust can have community bearings, as evidenced by several OT stories where sexual sin leads to serious communal consequences.[218]

The communal aspect of self-control makes this virtue fully compatible with all the other facets of the fruit of the Spirit in this respect, in line with N. T. Wright's claim that the notion of "virtue" has an inherent communal dimension: "To speak of 'virtue' is indeed to say that we are concerned with the moral growth, the habits of the heart, of every single individual."[219] Psychologists Baumeister and Exline echo this claim: "As has been recognized by ancient philosophers, medieval theologians, and modern therapists, virtue involves overcoming one's own undesirable dispositions in order to act in ways that will *benefit others*. The processes by which people alter their own behaviour so as to behave *in socially desirable ways* can be studied objectively, and indeed the study of these processes holds a promising key to major features of human personality."[220]

These latter scholars highlight the role of self-control in particular for the purpose of community building, because one often faces a choice "between acting for oneself in some antisocial manner—or overriding one's own motivations and doing what is best for the group (or broader society). The latter is the course of virtue, but by definition overriding one's impulses requires self-control."[221] Indeed, it has been widely recognised in psychology that self-regulatory failure is a core feature of many social problems.[222]

---

218. E.g., in Gen 34:1–31 the rape of Jacob's daughter, Dinah, leads to Simeon and Levi taking revenge by plundering a Canaan city and killing all the males, thereby creating an ethnic conflict with the Canaanites and the Perizzites.

219. N. T. Wright, *After You Believe*, 204.

220. Baumeister and Exline, "Virtue," 1189–1190; emphases added.

221. Baumeister and Exline, 1175–1176.

222. See e.g., Todd F. Heatherton and Dylan D. Wagner, "Cognitive Neuroscience of Self-Regulation Failure," *Trends in Cognitive Sciences* 15, no. 3 (2011): 132.

Self-Control in Psychology

Of all the virtues making up the fruit of the Spirit, self-control has received the most attention in psychological research. The notion of "self-regulation" has been one of the grand themes in psychology over the past fifteen years,[223] and self-control is an important aspect of this domain, generating dozens of papers every year. In the previous sections several relevant psychological findings have already been mentioned (e.g., concerning the overlapping nature of concepts with different labels or self-control being a foundational virtue); the following discussion addresses two additional aspects of self-control that are pertinent to the fruit of the Spirit: the intriguing phenomenon of "ego depletion" and the question as to whether self-control is a personality trait or a set of strategic behaviours.

Ego Depletion

We know that exerting physical energy leads to fatigue, but recent research has found that exhaustion is not limited to the physical domain, because exercising self-control will equally lead to mental fatigue. In other words, it appears that a person's self-control capacity might be a limited resource that can be exhausted. The phenomenon whereby one's self-regulatory resource pool has been drained has been referred to as *ego depletion*, defined by Baumeister and Vohs as follows: "*Ego depletion* refers to a state in which the self does not have all the resources it has normally. We shall suggest that self's executive function, which includes self-regulation as well as effortful choice and active initiative, depends on a limited resource that is consumed during such activities. Ego depletion renders the self temporarily less able and less willing to function normally or optimally."[224]

The ego depletion paradigm therefore suggests a resource model whereby self-control relies on some mental fuel that can run out through continuous use. In practical terms this would mean, for example, that the

---

223. A high-profile handbook on the subject is already on its third edition: Kathleen D. Vohs and Roy F. Baumeister, eds., *Handbook of Self-Regulation: Research, Theory, and Applications*, 3rd ed. (New York: Guilford, 2016).

224. Roy F. Baumeister and Kathleen D. Vohs, "Self-Regulation, Ego Depletion, and Motivation," *Social and Personality Psychology Compass* 1, no. 1 (2007): 116.

longer we have to resist something, the weaker our resistance becomes. This scenario would be familiar to many, and the existence of a limited pool of ego strength has also been implicit in the traditional concept of *willpower*.[225] It is, however, not at all clear what substance is actually depleted by mental engagement, and this uncertainty about the nature of the mental pool that is drained has caused controversy and debate in psychology regarding the notion of ego depletion.[226] Notwithstanding any outstanding issues, Seligman and Peterson's conclusion about the essence of ego depletion still holds: "Regulating the self or making a decision temporarily depletes some crucial resource of the self, so that the self is less able to perform another act of self-regulation or volition."[227] Given that, as we have seen above, self-control is a foundational virtue that acts as a "spiritual muscle" for all the other facets of the ninefold fruit of the Spirit, ego depletion has a critical bearing on one's capacity to be virtuous: according to the theory, the extent of exercising loving compassion and other aspects of community outreach will be dependent, at least partly, on one's available mental strength. We shall address how to regenerate this resource pool in chapter 7 when we discuss methods of cultivating the fruit of the Spirit.

Personality Trait or Strategic Behaviour?

We have seen above that the differently labelled self-control-related constructs show considerable overlap, but this is not the only source of uncertainty concerning self-control capacity in psychology. In accordance with the hybrid nature of virtues discussed in chapter 2, the capability to exercise self-control appears to depend on a variety of diverse factors such as inherent personality traits (because some people are simply more disciplined by nature) and specific learned skills to process temptations and distractions (because people have a better chance to exercise self-control if they are equipped with some personalised techniques). Because

---

225. Mark Muraven, Dianne M. Tice, and Roy F. Baumeister, "Self-Control as Limited Resource: Regulatory Depletion Patterns," *Journal of Personality and Social Psychology* 74, no. 3 (1998): 774.

226. For a review, see Michael Inzlicht and Malte Friese, "The Past, Present, and Future of Ego Depletion," *Social Psychology* 50, no. 5–6 (2019): 370–78.

227. Peterson and Seligman, *Character Strengths and Virtues*, 510.

resilience-boosting and goal-protective factors operate at various levels, it is virtually impossible to determine whether self-control capacity is primarily trait-like or is based on strategic behaviour.[228] The twofold nature of the virtue has been best illustrated by the famous "marshmallow test," which assessed children's ability to resist temptation in relation to their future achievements as adults (see CONCEPT 3.5). On the one hand, the fact that the degree of self-control a child displayed at an early age predicted positive outcomes decades later points to the trait-like nature of self-control; on the other hand, the researchers also identified certain strategies whose effective use helped the participants to persist: (1) actively reminding themselves of their chosen goal on a continual basis; (2) monitoring their goal progress and making necessary corrections by flexibly shifting their attention and cognitions between goal-oriented thoughts and temptation-reducing techniques; and (3) inhibiting impulsive responses such as thinking about the appealing nature of temptation. Accordingly, the principal investigator of the marshmallow test, Walter Mischel, has concluded that "self-control skills, both cognitive and emotional, can be learned, enhanced, and harnessed so that they become automatically activated when you need them."[229] The twofold nature of self-control—having both trait-like and skill-like characteristics—will be helpful in explaining (in chapter 7) the paradox of the fruit of the Spirit as being a function of both divine and human agency.

Concept 3.5: The Marshmallow Test

"The marshmallow test" is an umbrella term for a series of experiments in the late 1960s and early 1970s at Stanford University led

---

228. See Christophe Leys et al., "Perspectives on Resilience: Personality Trait or Skill?," *European Journal of Trauma & Dissociation* 4, no. 2 (2020): 5. Howard and Crayne's ("Persistence," 78) conclusion summarises the duality well: "Although persistence is often discussed as state-level motivation towards a particular goal, researchers have also observed people for whom persistence appears habitual and is applied in the pursuit of all goals broadly. The latter observation prompted the notion of the persistent person, and the idea that persistence may also manifest as a distinct trait."

229. Walter Mischel, *The Marshmallow Test: Understanding Self-Control and How to Master It* (London: Corgi, 2014), 230.

by Walter Mischel on "delayed gratification,"[230] which is the ability to resist the temptation of an immediate reward in preference for a later reward. Participating preschool children were offered a simple choice: they could receive one small reward (e.g., one marshmallow) immediately or two small rewards (e.g., two marshmallows) if they waited for a short period, approximately fifteen minutes. The children varied in their choices and also in how long they were able to persist if they chose to wait (which was agonising for some with the goodies in sight). The astonishing subsequent discovery came when follow-up studies unambiguously showed that children who were able to wait longer tended to have better life outcomes as *adults*; as Mischel recounts, "Around age twenty-five to thirty, those who had delayed longer in preschool self-reported that they were more able to pursue and reach long-term goals, used risky drugs less, had reached higher educational levels, and had a significantly lower body mass index. They were also more resilient and adaptive in coping with interpersonal problems and better at maintaining close relationships."[231] The remarkable finding that effective self-control at an early age can predict positive outcomes in adulthood was replicated in many studies over the subsequent decades, pointing to the stable, trait-like nature of self-control.

Summary: The Fruit of the Spirit and Christian Conduct

This chapter has followed the traditional approach of exploring the fruit of the Spirit by discussing each facet separately. Without wanting to preempt the content of the following chapters, which will focus on the composite fruit, the description of the nine virtues offers some more

---

230. For an overview, see Mischel, *Marshmallow Test*.
231. Mischel, *Marshmallow Test*, 24–25.

general implications: all the attributes reflect an ideal way of Christian conduct that applies both to the life of the individual believer and to the believer's community. This is consistent with the core characteristic of the new covenant: although God's laws are to govern the whole society of God's human stewards, they have been written on individual hearts, which means that they need to be personally internalised.

It is noteworthy to consider the personal characteristics that are conspicuous by their absence from the Gal 5 list, most notably aspects of individual talent such as intelligence and aptitude/ability. These are highly prized endowments according to contemporary standards because they lead to heightened individual achievement. Their absence from Gal 5:22–23 indicates that the biblical ideal is first and foremost related to the quality of social life rather than generating products of individual excellence such as scientific discoveries or works of art (which does not mean that the latter are not valuable). The fruit of the Spirit describes a character that enables one to become primarily a citizen of the kingdom of God rather than a hero, a renowned philosopher or scholar, or indeed any kind of celebrity.

The survey of the nine virtues demonstrates that the two attributes occupying prominent positions in the list (i.e., beginning and end)—love and self-control—are indeed "supreme" or "foundational" in some respects. A picture has begun to emerge in which compassionate love qualitatively defines and self-control upholds the Christian ideal of virtuous living, with the other virtues seen as the necessary ingredients complementing and adding flavour to the divine recipe. This aspect will be further developed in the next chapter, when we start focusing on the larger picture outlined by the composite fruit.

Finally, it is interesting to observe the fluctuating quality of the contribution that psychological research can offer to the examined areas. Given that the nine facets of the fruit of the Spirit constitute some highly salient aspects of human personality, it is noteworthy that modern psychology has struggled in several cases (e.g., regarding kindness, goodness, or gentleness) to provide substantial insights, partly impeded by the field's ambiguous approach to dealing with the moral aspect of virtue. Nonetheless, the perspective of psychology has been useful in highlighting several noteworthy issues and removing some blind spots. Moreover, we shall see in the final chapter of this book that psychological research will come into its strength when addressing how the human attributes making up the ninefold fruit can be cultivated.

4

The Composite Fruit

The previous chapter considered the nine facets of the fruit of the Spirit separately, exploring the nature of the individual virtues listed by Paul. This was an indispensable first step of the investigation to uncover the nuances of the semantic range of the Greek terms used in Gal 5:22–23. However, it was only the first step, because the key assumption underlying the current book is that the catalogue of virtuous attributes was also intended to convey a more general message related to the composite fruit. Considering the fruit to be of a unitary nature has been an established position in past scholarship, and by way of illustration CONCEPT 4.1 presents six representative quotes expressing such a unified understanding.[1] This chapter addresses the question as to whether this view is justifiable. We have seen earlier that the fact that Paul used the singular form of the Greek word for "fruit" when referring to the nine virtues comprising the fruit of the Spirit is not conclusive, because the Greek collective noun for "fruit," *karpos*, can be used both in singular and plural, and Paul's stylistic preference in his epistles was the singular form. However, there are at least four other points that can be made to justify a collective, unified understanding of the notion:

---

1. See also Gerig, "Fruit of the Spirit," in *Evangelical Dictionary*, 275; Martyn, *Galatians*, 498; Witherington, *Grace in Galatia*, 408.

a. the function of the nine attributes in Gal 5:22–23 is not merely (or not even primarily) to offer specific virtues for Christians to emulate but to paint a *larger picture*;

b. the list of attributes comprising the fruit of the Spirit is not *ad hoc* but *comprehensive* in the sense that it includes all the major aspects of biblical virtue mentioned in the NT;

c. the nine facets of the fruit of the Spirit form a coherent whole by being *interrelated*;

d. the *unity of virtues* is an established maxim in virtue ethics.

Concept 4.1: The Unitary Nature of the Fruit of the Spirit

- "These qualities are a unity, all present to some degree in the life of each believer."[2]
- "It is certainly with intention that the open-ended and unstructured list of vices is contrasted by a *unity* called 'the fruit of the Spirit.'"[3]
- "It is not as if the Spirit in one individual creates love, in another joy, and in a third gentleness. . . . The fruit of the Spirit is one and thus the list indivisible."[4]
- "All the traits should be taken together as a single call to moral transformation. Thus, for example, one cannot merely desire peace and kindness while putting aside patience."[5]
- "All the graces of the Spirit belong together. . . . The fruit of the Spirit is one whole spiritual life that is rooted in the one Spirit of God. To change the image for a moment, these virtues are

2. Rapa, "Galatians," 626.
3. Betz, *Galatians*, 286.
4. Cousar, *Galatians*, 139.
5. Cohick, "Fruit of the Spirit," 332.

> not nine different gems, but nine different facets of the same dazzling jewel."[6]
>
> - "The 'fruit,' singular, comes as a package. One may not plead the necessity of specialization—selecting, say, 'kindness' and 'gentleness' while leaving faithfulness and self-control to others."[7] "Paul does not envisage that someone might cultivate one or two of these characteristics and reckon that she had enough of an orchard to be going on with. No: when the Spirit is at work, you will see all nine varieties of this fruit."[8]

The Function of the Attributes in Galatians 5:22–23

In his commentary on Galatians, Richard Hays makes the point about the fruit of the Spirit that "Paul is not directly exhorting the Galatians to cultivate these qualities. Rather, he is speaking descriptively, *painting a picture* of the harvest the Spirit produces."[9] That is, unlike most other catalogues of virtues in the Bible, the primary function of the list in Gal 5 is not so much to present normative standards to be approximated in believers' lives. Of course, the mere act of listing the nine virtues inevitably represents a great deal of normative force—and elsewhere in the Scriptures all the listed attributes are highlighted as models for Christian conduct—but the apostle's main purpose in this particular passage appears to be to paint a larger picture of some kind. Regarding the nature of this picture, the juxtaposition of the nine virtues and the previous list of vices (vv. 16–21) leaves no doubt that the Galatians passage was to highlight the radical difference between what the flesh

---

6. Ryken, *Galatians*, 234.
7. N. T. Wright, *Galatians*, 335.
8. N. T. Wright, *After You Believe*, 195.
9. Hays, "Galatians," 328; emphasis added.

and the Spirit represent—that is, to offer an expressive description of a Spirit-led alternative to the vice-ridden pursuit of gratifying the flesh; in David deSilva's words, "The contrasting pictures underscore the incompatibility of 'what the flesh desires' and 'what the Spirit desires' and why these two cannot coexist."[10] Furnish rightly points out that Paul identifies the nine virtues collectively and "avoids speaking of them as separate, individual traits of character."[11] In other words, the list in Gal 5:22–23 is to operate cumulatively, as a collective portrayal of the Spirit-led believer, rather than as a list of items in a menu to choose from.

This reading is in accordance with how the fruit of the Spirit was defined at the end of chapter 2, as the ideal outcome of a divinely orchestrated transformation process to produce a Christlike character in the believer. Let us leave aside for the moment the transformation part of this characterization—it will be explored in chapter 6 in detail—and focus here on the "ideal outcome." The obvious feature of Gal 5:22–23 is that this aggregate outcome is sketched out vividly, as Paul includes as many as nine elements, thereby making it the longest virtue list in the Scriptures. It will be argued below that these elements together delineate—or "exemplify," to use Dunn's wording[12]—a rounded Christlike character, and Ryken emphasises that "the point is not so much the specific character traits as it is the entire lifestyle they represent."[13] C. Wright offers a good summary of this reading: "The fruit of the Spirit is a single character package. The fruit of the Spirit is not like the gifts of the Spirit, which are distributed among God's people, some to some people, others to other people, all within the body of Christ (1 Cor 12:4–11). The fruit of the Spirit grows all together within a Christian's life, with a unity, wholeness, and balance. All the pieces of the one fruit work together and strengthen each other."[14]

---

10. deSilva, *Galatians*, 464.
11. Furnish, *Theology and Ethics in Paul*, 87.
12. Dunn, *Galatians*, 338.
13. Ryken, *Galatians*, 234.
14. C. Wright, *Cultivating the Fruit of the Spirit*, 155–156.

The Question of Comprehensiveness

How comprehensive is the list of attributes in Gal 5:22–23? Can it be really taken as an outline of a rounded character, or is it, as some scholars believe, merely a relatively *ad hoc* list of commendable character features that Paul wanted to draw the Galatian readers' attention to? After all, Paul's epistles in the New Testament are not theological treatises but rather letters written to specific church communities, addressing concrete matters (usually problems)—an aspect that has been referred to as the "problem of their particularity."[15] Accordingly, one may rightly argue that Paul only included those attributes in the list in Gal 5:22–23 that were specifically relevant to the Galatian readers; Douglas Moo for example summarises this view clearly: "Paul has chosen the particular virtues he includes here with an eye on the apparently quarrelsome Galatians. Hence his list of the fruit of the Spirit might have looked a bit different if it had come in a different context."[16]

While this observation is true of much of Paul's writing, it may be less relevant to the Gal 5 passage given that, as argued above, the apostle's immediate concern here was not so much to offer ethical exhortations concerning the Galatian believers' conduct—which would have been tailored to their specific problems and needs—as to paint a larger and more generic picture of the Spirit-led human character. Having said that, if we found that the description of the fruit of the Spirit omitted some key virtues that are highlighted elsewhere in the Scriptures, this would undoubtedly weaken the proposal that Paul's list was intended to serve as the portrayal of the ideal Christian character. In order to examine this matter systematically, an extensive survey of the virtues mentioned in the New Testament will be presented below. Although

---

15. See e.g., L. Ann Jervis, "Paul the Theologian," in *The Oxford Handbook of Pauline Studies* (online), ed. Matthew V. Novenson and R. Barry Matlock (Oxford: Oxford University Press, 2017), 3.

16. Moo, *Galatians*, 366.

there is an inevitable subjective element in the following analysis, and there will undoubtedly be cases that could or should have been classified differently, on balance the exercise will show that the vast majority of the NT virtues are covered to some extent by the fruit of the Spirit. Furthermore, as was already mentioned in chapter 1, if we view Gal 5:22–23 as a character sketch of the Christlike personality, the issue of comprehensiveness loses a great deal of its importance, because when we describe someone's character, we can do it focusing on a few key features or elaborating on several details, and yet the personality in question remains the same.

An Analysis of the Virtues Mentioned in the New Testament

Table 2 presents the summary of a survey of the virtues mentioned in the New Testament. Because of the inherent difficulty of producing a comprehensive catalogue of this sort, the list should not be seen as exhaustive. To mention but two challenges, some virtuous characteristics are not described in the Scriptures by a specific attribute but rather by an action (e.g., "They must keep hold of the deep truths of the faith with a clear conscience" [1 Tim 3:9]) or by the negative of an

Table 2: New Testament Virtues[17] and the Corresponding Greek Lemmas

Matt 5:5–10	meek (*praus*), righteousness (*dikaiosynē*), merciful (*eleēmōn*), peacemaker (*eirēnopoios*)
Rom 12:9–13; 14:17; 15:13	love (*agapē*), spiritually enthusiastic (*zeō*), joy/joyful (*chara, chairō*), hope (*elpis*), patient (*hypomenō*), faithful (*proskantereō*), hospitality (*philoxenia*), righteousness (*dikaiosynē*), peace (*eirēnē*)
1 Cor 13:4–7	love (*agapē*), patient (*makrothymeō*), kind (*chrēsteuomai*), hopes (*elpizō*), perseveres (*hypomenō*), rejoices (*synchairō*), believes (*pisteuō*), endures (*stegō*)

---

17. The list contains the English forms of the specific virtuous characteristics in the way they occur in the NIVUK.

2 Cor 6:6–10	purity (*hagnotēs*), understanding/knowledge (*gnōsis*), patience (*makrothymia*), kindness (*chrēstotēs*), love (*agapē*), truthful (*alētheia*), righteousness (*dikaiosynē*), genuine (*alēthēs*), rejoicing (*chairō*)
Gal 5:22–23	love (*agapē*), joy (*chara*), peace (*eirēnē*), patience (*makrothymia*), kindness (*chrēstotēs*), goodness (*agathōsynē*), faithfulness (*pistis*), gentleness (*prautēs*), self-control (*enkrateia*)
Eph 4:2–3; 4:32–5:2; 5:9	humble (*tapeinophrosynē*), gentle (*prautēs*), patient (*makrothymia*), bearing with one another (*anechomai*), love (*agapē*), peace (*eirēnē*), kind (*chrēstos*), compassionate (*eusplanchnos*), forgiving (*charizomai*), goodness (*agathōsynē*), righteousness (*dikaiosynē*), truth (*alētheia*)
Col 3:12–15	compassion (*splanchnon*), kindness (*chrēstotēs*), humility (*tapeinophrosynē*), gentleness (*prautēs*), patience (*makrothymia*), bear with each other (*anechomai*), forgive (*charizomai*), love (*agapē*), peace (*eirēnē*)
1 Tim 3:2–4, 8–12; 4:12; 6:6, 11, 18	above reproach (*anepilēmptos*), temperate (*nēphalios*), self-controlled (*sōphrōn*), respectable (*kosmios*), hospitable (*philoxenos*), able to teach (*didaktikos*), gentle (*epieikēs*), worthy of respect (*semnotēs, semnos*), faith/trustworthy (*pistis, pistos*), love (*agapē*), purity (*hagneia*), righteousness (*dikaiosynē*), godliness (*eusebeia*), endurance (*hypomonē*), gentleness (*praupathia*), good (*agathoergeō*), generous (*eumetadotos*)
2 Tim 2:22–24; 3:10	righteousness (*dikaiosynē*), faith (*pistis*), love (*agapē*), peace (*eirēnē*), kind (*ēpios*), able to teach (*didaktikos*), patience (*makrothymia*), endurance (*hypomonē*)
Titus 1:8; 2:2–7, 12; 3:1–2	hospitable (*philoxenos*), loves what is good (*philagathos*), self-controlled (*sōphrōn*), upright (*dikaios*), holy (*hosios*), disciplined (*enkratēs*), temperate (*nēphalios*), worthy of respect (*semnos*), sound in faith (*pistis*), love (*agapē*), endurance (*hypomonē*), reverent (*hieroprepēs*), pure (*hagnos*), kind (*agathos*), godly (*eusebōs*), obedient (*peitharcheō*), peaceable (*amachos*), considerate (*epieikēs*), gentle (*prautēs*)
Heb 6:11–12	diligence (*spoudē*), faith (*pistis*), patience (*makrothymia*)

Jas 3:13, 17–18	humility (*prautēs*), pure (*hagnos*), peace/peace-loving (*eirēnē, eirēnikos*), considerate (*epieikēs*), submissive (*eupeithēs*), mercy (*eleos*), impartial (*adiakritos*), sincere (*anypokritos*), righteousness (*dikaiosynē*)
1 Pet 3:8	like-minded (*homophrōn*), sympathetic (*sympathēs*), love (*agapē*), compassionate (*eusplanchnos*), humble (*tapeinophrōn*)
2 Pet 1:5–7	faith (*pistis*), goodness (*aretē*), knowledge (*gnōsis*), self-control (*enkrateia*), perseverance (*hypomonē*), godliness (*eusebeia*), mutual affection (*philadelphia*), love (*agapē*)
Jude 2	mercy (*eleos*), peace (*eirēnē*), love (*agapē*)

antonym (e.g., "not quarrelsome" [1 Tim 3:3]), and such cases have not been included in the table. Yet the list is representative in the sense that it covers the whole breadth of the virtues mentioned in the New Testament, without leaving out any prominent ones that have been highlighted by the Scriptures themselves or by commentators over the centuries. The table contains a total of forty-six relevant word groups, and if we compare this figure to Furnish's estimate that Paul used fewer than twenty terms relating to sixteen distinct virtues,[18] we can see that the list is more inclusive, which is partly due to the fact that the table also draws on non-Pauline sources.

Of the forty-six different virtues included in table 2, nine are the actual facets of the fruit of the Spirit (i.e., love, joy, etc.), and many others are synonyms or closely associated with these (i.e., tapping into the semantic domain of one of the facets of the fruit of the Spirit).[19] This, however, still leaves sixteen virtues unaccounted for,[20] and CONCEPT 4.2 presents a further analysis of this latter cluster. Although it must

---

18. Furnish, *Theology and Ethics in Paul*, 86.

19. LOVE: mutual affection (*philadelphia*), compassion (*splanchnon*), merciful (*eleēmōn*), sympathetic (*sympathēs*); PEACE: peaceable (*amachos*), like-minded (*homophrōn*); KINDNESS: kind (*ēpios*), considerate (*epieikēs*), hospitality (*philoxenia*); GOODNESS: goodness (*aretē*), generous (*eumetadotos*); FAITHFULNESS: spiritually enthusiastic (*zeō*), faithful (*proskartereō*), godliness (*eusebeia*), reverent (*hieroprepēs*); GENTLENESS: gentle (*epieikēs*); SELF-CONTROL: self-controlled (*sōphrōn*), temperate (*nēphalios*), perseveres (*hypomenō*), endures (*stegō*), bearing with one another (*anechomai*).

20. Able to teach (*didaktikos*), above reproach (*anepilēmptos*), diligence (*spoudē*), forgiving (*charizomai*), holy (*hosios*), hope (*elpis*), humble (*tapeinophrosynē*), impartial (*adiakritos*), obedient

be reiterated that this analysis is admittedly subjective to some extent, it offers a good indication that most of the unaccounted-for attributes in table 2 are either not virtues in the strict sense or are sufficiently covered by some facets of the fruit of the Spirit. After the elimination process described in CONCEPT 4.2, only two prominent virtues are left still unaccounted for: humility (*tapeinophrosynē*) and hope (*elpis*). Given that these are unquestionably central aspects of the Christian character, let us examine their relationship to the fruit of the Spirit in more detail. It will be argued below that although they are not specifically listed as part of the fruit of the Spirit, their essence is represented by several facets of the fruit.

Concept 4.2: Sixteen NT Virtues That Are Not Accounted For by the Fruit of the Spirit

- The largest subset of the fifteen unaccounted-for virtues concerns general moral integrity, honesty, and uprightness: righteousness (*dikaiosynē*), holy (*hosios*), purity (*hagnotēs*), sincere (*anypokritos*), truthful (*alētheia*), above reproach (*anepilēmptos*), and impartial (*adiakritos*). Given the significance repeatedly attached to such qualities in the Bible, it is curious that Gal 5:22–23 does not include any of them. There may be two possible explanations for this omission. First, righteousness is a holistic quality of personal integrity, and one may argue that the nine facets of the fruit are more specific attributes that cumulatively produce such spiritual purity. Second, there are some grounds for believing that righteousness is at least partly covered by the biblical meaning of peace/shalom. Dunn explains that in the Israeli culture, "righteous" was understood in relational terms, as the fulfilment of an obligation: "The

---

(*peitharcheō*), purity (*hagnotēs*), respectable (*kosmios*), righteousness (*dikaiosynē*), sincere (*anypokritos*), submissive (*eupeithēs*), truthful (*alētheia*), worthy of respect (*semnotēs*).

king was righteous when he fulfilled his obligations to his subjects. The judge was righteous when he administered justice to rich and poor impartially."[21] Righteousness was therefore seen as the general foundation of social harmony and peace, and Swartley confirms this point when he adds that the Jewish notion of shalom was closely associated with innocence from moral wrongdoing and was thus closely linked to justice and righteousness.[22] In a similar vein, Youngblood points out that righteousness is frequently linked together with peace in the Scriptures, because without a righteous life no one is able to find internal peace.[23] Therefore, the absence of this subset of virtues from the fruit of the Spirit can be explained to some extent by the fact that the nine facets of the fruit—and peace in particular—cover personal purity and righteousness. The same can be said about the attribute "submissive" (*eupeithēs*), which appears only once in Jas 3:17 in a position where it, too, is associated with interpersonal peace and harmony ("peace-loving, considerate, submissive, full of mercy").

- Three attributes are linked to specific social positions held by the believer or to the social standing of the person in the community: able to teach (*didaktikos*, associated with the overseer [1 Tim 3:2]), respectable (*kosmios*), and worthy of respect (*semnos*). As such, they are too situated for qualifying for general virtues and will thus be disregarded for the current analysis.

- Three further characteristics are related to various actions rather than personality traits, referring more to what one *does* than to what one is like, and can thus be omitted from the list: obedient (*peitharcheō*) appears four times, always in a verb form (twice obeying God and the Holy Spirit [Acts 5:29, 32]; once authorities

21. James D. G. Dunn, *New Testament Theology: An Introduction* (Nashville: Abingdon, 2009), 77.

22. Swartley, "Peace," 583.

23. Youngblood, "Peace," 732.

[Titus 3:1]; and once in the sense of taking human advice [Acts 27:21]); diligence (*spoudē*) is related to zeal and effort, as in 2 Pet 1:5: "Make every effort [*spoudēn*] to add to your faith goodness"; and forgiving (*charizomai*) concerns the fundamental interpersonal behaviour of giving up resentment against someone or releasing someone from guilt (e.g., 2 Cor 2:10).

- The above points leave only two of the fifteen virtues unaccounted for one way or another: humility (*tapeinophrosynē*) and hope (*elpis*).

Humility

Humility is usually regarded as the opposite of pride and is therefore a core Christian virtue,[24] with its central meaning well described in Phil 2:3: "In humility value others above yourselves." It therefore refers to a modest, noninflated view of one's own importance. Curiously, however, despite its high profile and seemingly straightforward content, theologians, philosophers, and psychologists have found it a real challenge to go beyond such a general characterisation and offer a more precise definition of what humility entails. This is largely due to the fact that it is easier to describe humility in terms of what it is not (e.g., pride, arrogance, selfishness, conceit, etc.) than what it is; as Nadelhoffer and Wright summarise in a review article, scholars have been divided about whether humility is a trait with its own set of features or simply the absence of other negative traits.[25] According to Gulliford and Robert, this curious characteristic manifests itself in the fact that "any time a person performs a humble action, or expresses humility by way of an emotional state (e.g., joy in another person's triumph) or lack thereof

---

24. E.g., Nadelhoffer and J. Wright argue that humility should be considered a "foundational" virtue, as it is necessary for the full development of a "virtuous character." Thomas Nadelhoffer and Jennifer Cole Wright, "The Twin Dimensions of the Virtue of Humility: Low Self-Focus and High Other-Focus," in *Virtue and Character*, vol. 5 of *Moral Psychology*, ed. Walter Sinnott-Armstrong and Christian B. Miller (Cambridge, MA: MIT Press, 2017), 328.

25. Nadelhoffer and J. Wright, "Humility," 311.

(e.g., defensiveness), the motivation comes from somewhere other than humility"[26]—that is, humility is not a source of action or a form of self-control, but rather a quality accompanying the outworking of some other virtue such as love, generosity, forgivingness, compassion, gratitude, or righteousness. It thus characterises a person "who lacks one of the vices of pride,"[27] and this "virtue by absence" character is evidenced by the fact that, as N. T. Wright explains, in traditional Christian thought "one of the highest virtues was the state where one was no longer conscious of one's own virtue."[28]

We have seen in the discussion of gentleness above that there is a definite semantic overlap between humility, gentleness, and even timidity (as in 2 Cor 10:1),[29] which creates a direct link with the fruit of the Spirit. This link has also been confirmed by Nadelhoffer and Wright, who point out that humility has often been defined in terms of interpersonal qualities such as gentleness as well as empathy and respect for others.[30] A further connection with the fruit is highlighted by Barclay, who argues that patience also forms part of the basis of humility, because being "patient in spirit" prevents someone from taking the centre place in a picture.[31] A link is also implied by Eccl 7:8: "Patience is better than pride." Indeed, humility can be seen as a potent prosocial value, because a humble person is interested in promoting or protecting others' well-being,[32] which points to a further connection with an element of the fruit: self-giving, compassionate love. In the light of these considerations, the essence of humility can be seen to be covered by the fruit of the Spirit indirectly, through a number of different channels.

---

26. Liz Gulliford and C. Robert Roberts, "Exploring the 'Unity' of the Virtues: The Case of an Allocentric Quintet," *Theory and Psychology* 28, no. 2 (2018): 213.

27. Gulliford and Roberts, "Unity of Virtues," 213.

28. N. T. Wright, *After You Believe*, 240.

29. See also Cole, *Galatians*, 221, and Fung, *Galatians*, 270, for similar views.

30. Nadelhoffer and J. Wright, "Humility," 314.

31. Barclay, *Flesh and Spirit*, 92.

32. Nadelhoffer and J. Wright, "Humility," 318, 328.

Hope

In psychology, hope can be defined as "an anticipatory state that results from perceiving the mere possibility of a desired outcome,"[33] or "a future-oriented emotion that requires a full or partial expectation of what is to come."[34] With regard to Christian hope, the possibility of a desired outcome is underpinned by one's faith, as confirmed by Heb 11:1: "Faith is confidence in what we hope for and assurance about what we do not see." Accordingly, N. T. Wright offers the following summary: "Hope is the settled, unwavering confidence that this God will not leave us or forsake us, but will always have more in store for us than we could ask or think."[35]

Hope is thus a central aspect of the Christian character, and it is closely linked to several facets of the fruit of the Spirit:

- Hope can be seen as a companion of joy and peace, as attested to by Rom 15:13: "May the God of hope fill you with all joy and peace as you trust in him, so that you may overflow with hope by the power of the Holy Spirit." In Rom 12:12 Paul also encourages believers to "be joyful in hope."
- Hope is a member of the triad of faith, hope, and love (1 Cor 13:6–7, 13; Col 1:4–5; 1 Thess 1:3; 5:8). In his commentary on the epistle to the Galatians, Jerome states in this respect, "Among the 'fruits of the Spirit' faith holds the seventh and sacred place, being elsewhere one of three—'faith, hope and love,'"[36] and then, significantly, continues, "Nor is it remarkable that hope is not included in this catalogue [i.e., the fruit of the Spirit] since the object of hope is already included as part of faith."[37]
- Hope is closely associated with self-control and perseverance, as it

---

33. Rob M. A. Nelissen, "The Motivational Properties of Hope in Goal Striving," *Cognition and Emotion* 31, no. 2 (2017): 233.

34. Daniel T. Cordaro et al., "Contentment: Perceived Completeness across Cultures and Traditions," *Review of General Psychology* 20, no. 2 (2016): 230.

35. N. T. Wright, *After You Believe*, 203.

36. Cited in Edwards, ed., *Galatians, Ephesians, Philippians*, 85.

37. Cited in Edwards, ed., 85.

creates a narrative through which suffering can be endured:[38] "your endurance inspired by hope in our Lord Jesus Christ" (1 Thess 1:3). The link between hope and resilience has also been established in psychology, because people who experience hope have been found to be less affected by setbacks in their goal progress.[39]

- Finally, as already discussed with regard to patience, Paul connects hope to patience in Rom 8:25: "If we hope for what we do not yet have, we wait for it patiently." And Hauerwas further elaborates on this link when he states, "Through patience, we learn to continue to hope, even though our hope seems to offer little chance of fulfilment."[40] He then adds, "Yet patience equally requires hope, for without hope, patience too easily accepts the world and the self for what it is, rather than what it can or should be."[41]

These links indicate that aspects of hope are closely associated with several facets of the fruit of the Spirit, but this still leaves us with the question of why Paul did not include this prominent aspect of the Christian character in Gal 5:22–23, particularly given that he did list it alongside faith and love in 1 Cor 13:13. The answer may lie in the fact that hope is different from the other facets of the ninefold fruit in that while the other facets can be recognised in the believer's actual conduct—in how loving, kind, gentle, patient they are—hope does not have any obvious manifestations; rather, it acts as a foundation and a solidifier for the other attributes. Its future-oriented sense also distinguishes hope from the other virtues in Gal 5:22–23, and in Rom 5:3–4 it is portrayed as the culmination of a chain, constituting the outcome of the overall tested character: "We know that suffering produces perseverance; perseverance,

---

38. See Pinches, "Patience," 583.

39. Nelissen, "Hope," 227. In a similar vein, Fredrickson concludes that "people feel hope, for instance, in grim situations in which they can envision at least a chance that things might change for the better. Hope creates the urge to draw on one's own capabilities and inventiveness to turn things around. The durable resources it builds include optimism and resilience to adversity." Barbara L. Fredrickson, "Positive Emotions Broaden and Build," *Advances in Experimental Social Psychology* 47 (2013): 4.

40. Hauerwas, *A Community of Character*, 12.

41. Hauerwas, 127–128.

character; and character, hope." Schreiner comments on this personal progression, that "it assures believers that the hope of future glory is not an illusion . . . [and] that the process that God has begun he will complete."[42] Indeed, Paul affirms in the next verse that "hope does not put us to shame, because God's love has been poured out into our hearts through the Holy Spirit" (v. 5).

The Internal Coherence of the Nine Facets of the Fruit of the Spirit

The first section of this chapter proposed that the list of virtues in Gal 5:22–23 was intended to present a composite picture of a unified fruit rather than nine separate attributes, and the previous analysis of the comprehensiveness of the fruit of the Spirit indicated that the content of the fruit provides an inclusive coverage of the range of virtues mentioned elsewhere in the Scriptures. There is one more aspect of the fruit of the Spirit that needs examining to verify the unified nature of the fruit—namely, how the nine virtues are connected to each other. If they indeed represent facets of an overall character, they are expected to be interrelated at least to some extent in order to form a coherent image. It will be shown below that this assumption is born out in at least two ways: first, several of the nine virtues overlap in their semantic domain or are related to each other through intertextual links; second, internal coherence is also produced by psychological interdependence between the two defining attributes, love and self-control.

Overlapping Meaning and Intertextual Links

We saw in the previous chapter that the semantic ranges of some of the nine attributes display certain overlaps with each other; Alan Cole, for example, concludes in this respect that "the difficulty is to know where to draw the line of demarcation between one virtue and another. In most cases, the 'areas of meaning' overlap considerably."[43]

---

42. Thomas R. Schreiner, *Romans*, BECNT (Grand Rapids: Baker Academic, 1998), 256.
43. R. Alan Cole, *Galatians*, 220.

Kenneson echoes this view when he states, "There is often no tidy way to distinguish between one fruit of the Spirit and another. What we call God's steadfast love cannot be neatly distinguished from God's goodness, nor can either one be easily distinguished from God's mercy and kindness."[44] In other words, while none of the nine attributes are synonyms for each other, several display some semantic link with some others. These connections will be discussed when we identify the dimensions of the fruit of the Spirit in chapter 5, so here only a few prominent examples are given:

- Kindness, goodness, gentleness, and patience all share some common meaning with loving compassion in the sense that they concern a caring social relationship with someone (e.g., we have seen earlier that kindness can be understood as "love in action"). Indeed, 1 Cor 13:4 explicitly states that "love is patient, love is kind," and Col 3:12 urges believers to clothe themselves "with compassion, kindness, humility, gentleness and patience" because they are "members of one body" (v. 15). Calvin called patience the "gentleness of mind,"[45] and deSilva confirms that one quality the Greek word for patience denotes is "gentleness in the face of others' failures or slights."[46] Finally, the intersection of goodness and kindness is well illustrated by the fact that the Greek translation of the Old Testament, the Septuagint, renders the frequent Hebrew word describing God, *tób* ("good"), sometimes into the Greek word *agathos* (good) and other times into *chrēstos* (kind).
- Bruce calls peace and joy "spiritual twins"[47]—they are mentioned together already in Isa 55:12 ("You will go out in joy and be led forth in peace"), and Paul prays in Rom 15:13 that God will fill the believers with all joy and peace as they trust in him. Elsewhere in the same letter he compares the kingdom of God to "peace and joy in the Holy Spirit" (Rom 14:17).

---

44. Kenneson, *Life on the Vine*, 136.
45. Calvin, *Commentary on Galatians*, 5:22, in Bray, *Galatians, Ephesians*, 198.
46. deSilva, *Galatians*, 467.
47. Bruce, *Galatians*, 252.

- Finally, we have seen in the previous chapter that self-control has many shades and expressions, sharing some characteristics with patience, faithfulness, and gentleness, and this steadfastness is also linked to love in 1 Cor 13:7 when we read that love "bears all things" and "endures all things" (NRSVA). Fung argues in this respect that gentleness may be described as "a humble and pliable submission to God's will which reflects itself in humility, patience and forbearance towards others. . . . It thus implies, but is not identical with, self-control."[48]

Psychological Interdependence:
Love versus Self-Control

The internal coherence of the fruit of the Spirit can be demonstrated not only by the shared similarities of the constituent virtues but also by the psychological interdependence between them. We have already seen that several of the virtues can be understood as outworkings of compassionate love, but this may be less obvious regarding the relationship between love and the other key facet of the fruit, self-control. Yet these two central elements are not unconnected but are, as will be shown below, related to each other in a perhaps unexpected manner: love is to some extent *dependent* on self-control. It was shown in the previous chapter that self-control is a foundational virtue—a kind of "spiritual muscle"—that underpins virtuous behaviour in general, and this reliance is most prominent when it comes to the relationship between self-control and love. These seemingly distant attributes have been found in psychological research to be highly correlated with each other[49] through the mediating variables of caring and compassion: because loving compassion for others always incurs some cost to the self, it requires self-control to overcome the operation of automatic

---

48. Fung, *Galatians*, 270.

49. E.g., McGrath, Greenberg, and Hall-Simmonds found a correlation between caring and self-control approaching 0.80, which is a particularly high coefficient in psychological research. Robert E. McGrath, Michael J. Greenberg, and Ashley Hall-Simmonds, "Scarecrow, Tin Woodsman, and Cowardly Lion: The Three-Factor Model of Virtue," *Journal of Positive Psychology* 13, no. 4 (2018): 388.

selfish impulses and desires, sometimes referred to as the "universal human selfishness."[50] As Underwood summarises, "It takes work to be kind, to sacrifice one's interests and desires for the good of a brother."[51] Drawing on his own practice as a psychiatrist, M. Scott Peck explains the love–self-control link as follows: "The act of love—extending one-self— . . . requires a moving out against the inertia of laziness (work) or the resistance engendered by fear (courage). . . . It follows, then . . . that any genuine lover behaves with self-discipline and any genuinely loving relationship is a disciplined relationship. If I truly love another, I will obviously order my behaviour in such a way as to contribute the utmost to his or her spiritual growth."[52] In support of this claim, Telzer and her colleagues' neuroimaging study has identified a pronounced neuropsychological correlation between compassionate behaviour and self-control: "Individuals must weigh the relative value of helping others with their own self-interests and resolve conflict between the two in order to put the needs of another before their own. Behavioural results from our study show that costly decisions . . . are related to activation of neural regions involved in self-control."[53] Thus, pursuing compassion-ate, self-giving goals is often hindered by selfish impulses that favour not helping others, and self-control has been identified by psycholo-gists to be the necessary factor to manage such motivational conflicts[54]; as Baumeister and Exline conclude, "Stifling self-interest for the sake of the greater collective good requires self-control."[55] This link might explain why the self-control of athletes is a recurring image in several

---

50. See e.g., Baumeister and Exline, "Virtue," 1165.

51. Underwood, "Interviews with Trappist Monks," 289.

52. Peck, *The Road Less Travelled*, 119, 143.

53. Eva H. Telzer et al., "Neural Regions Associated with Self Control and Mentalizing Are Recruited During Prosocial Behaviors Toward the Family," *NeuroImage* 58 (2011): 247.

54. See e.g., C. Nathan DeWall et al., "Depletion Makes the Heart Grow Less Helpful: Helping as a Function of Self-Regulatory Energy and Genetic Relatedness," *Personality and Social Psychology Bulletin* 34, no. 12 (2008): 1653. Anne Joosten et al., "Out of Control!? How Loss of Self-Control Influences Prosocial Behavior: The Role of Power and Moral Values," *PLoS One* 10, no. 5 (2015): 13; Jeffrey M. Osgood and Mark Muraven, "Self-Control Depletion Does Not Diminish Attitudes about Being Prosocial but Does Diminish Prosocial Behaviors," *Basic and Applied Social Psychology* 37 (2015): 77.

55. Baumeister and Exline, "Virtue," 1166.

New Testament books,[56] offered as a role model to follow (we shall return to this imagery in chapter 7 when we discuss the cultivation of virtues, including self-control).

The Unity of Virtues

The final argument in favour of a composite rather than fragmented conception of the fruit of the Spirit concerns a theory that was first proposed by ancient Greek philosophers (most notably, Socrates, Plato, and Aristotle), the "unity of virtue" thesis.[57] This theory claims in its strictest form that "virtue is one,"[58] but weaker versions have also been proposed depending on how one interprets the "unity" aspect. The various versions all share, however, the common principle that, in N. T. Wright's words, "If you want truly to possess one of the cardinal virtues you must possess them all—because each is, as it were, kept in place by the others."[59] That is, the different virtues are assumed to complement each other and rely on one another. This, however, does not mean that in order to lead a virtuous life one needs to possess each virtue equally: the actual proportions will vary across cultural contexts and personalities, resulting in distinctive moral styles.[60] Yet, according to the theory, they all need to be represented to some extent for completeness in a virtuous personality, because they simply do not work effectively independently.[61]

There are two specific reasons why the unity of virtues thesis might be relevant to the virtues listed in Gal 5:22–23. First, Root Luna and her colleagues point out that the essence of the unity thesis is that the individual virtues are "part of a larger overarching construct,"[62] which in

---

56. E. g., Acts 20:24; 1 Cor 9:23–27; Gal 5:7; Phil 3:14, 2 Tim 4:7; Heb 12:1.
57. For an overview, see e.g., Gulliford and Roberts, "Unity of Virtues."
58. Gulliford and Roberts, 209.
59. N. T. Wright, *After You Believe*, 195.
60. Gary Watson, "Virtues in Excess," *Philosophical Studies* 46, no. 1 (1984): 65–66.
61. Barry Schwartz and Kenneth E. Sharpe, "Practical Wisdom: Aristotle Meets Positive Psychology," *Journal of Happiness Studies* 7 (2006): 380.
62. Root Luna, Van Tongeren, and vanOyen Witvliet, "Virtue, Positive Psychology, and Religion," 299.

this case lends itself to be identified as "the fruit of the Spirit." Second, we find some concrete references in the Scriptures to this unified nature, centred around love. Colossians 3:12–13 presents a list of seven virtues/virtuous acts and then the next verse declares: "And over all these virtues put on love, which binds them all together in *perfect unity*" (v. 14; emphasis added). This is in accordance with our earlier description of love as "the supreme virtue" in chapter 3, and Paul's famous passage on love in 1 Cor 13:4–7 spells out love's binding quality in more detail: "Love is patient; love is kind; love is not envious or boastful or arrogant or rude. It does not insist on its own way; it is not irritable or resentful; it does not rejoice in wrongdoing, but rejoices in the truth. It bears all things, believes all things, hopes all things, endures all things" (NRSVA).

Summary: The Metaphor of the Fruit Salad

In reflecting on the curious ninefold nature of the fruit of the Spirit, Derek Tidball compares the image to a fruit salad: "Even so, this fruit salad is one. We are not able, as it were, to choose to be apple people as opposed to orange people, but rather should allow the Spirit to bring out the variety of his produce in our lives, each one bringing out the full flavour of the others."[63] In line with this characterisation, the thesis of this chapter has been that the facets of the fruit of the Spirit are to be understood as the representation of a complex and yet unitary character sketch. The composite nature of the fruit (salad) was supported by four extended points. First, it was shown that the list of virtues in Gal 5:22–23 was intended to present a picture of the ideal, Christlike character rather than nine separate attributes. Second, a survey of the range of virtues mentioned in the New Testament indicated that the ninefold fruit offers a comprehensive coverage, with no glaring omissions, and can therefore be seen as the "sum of all parts." Third, an examination of the internal coherence of the nine facets of the fruit showed that they are connected

---

63. Tidball, *The Message of Holiness*, 209.

together through multiple threads of overlapping meaning, intertextual links, and psychological interdependence. A case in point of the latter concerns self-control, which has been shown to undergird all the other virtues, including compassionate love, by overcoming selfish impulses and covering the inevitable costs of caring for someone else. Finally, we briefly considered the traditional philosophical maxim of the unity of virtues and argued that it fits the composite understanding of the fruit of the Spirit, bound together by love. Bearing the rounded Christlike character that the fruit outlines in mind, the next chapter will discuss how the essence of this character sketch can be captured to good effect for theoretical and practical purposes.

5

DIMENSIONS OF THE
FRUIT OF THE SPIRIT

It was argued in the previous chapters that the nine virtues in Gal 5:22–23 outline a rounded Christlike character, and the question addressed in the current chapter is how this character can be represented to good effect for theoretical and practical purposes. The two most common approaches in the past for such a representation have involved either using the singular label "fruit of the Spirit" or going to the other extreme and listing all the nine virtues in the discussion, which can be called the itemised approach. The problem with the former is that while the label does highlight the Spirit's involvement, it is not informative about the content of the fruit; on the other hand, the itemised approach is too detailed for many purposes, and it will also be argued below that it promotes a perspective that lacks sufficient theoretical coherence and may even limit the practical implication of the fruit.

There have been some attempts in the past to propose a third option by dividing the nine facets of the fruit of the Spirit into a smaller number of clusters, usually into three triplets: *love–joy–peace, patience–kindness–goodness,* and *faithfulness–gentleness–self-control.* For example, Furnish argues that there is a "threefold rhythm" discernible within the list and that "each triad manifests not only a greater or lesser degree of rhetorical balance, but also a certain similarity of content."[1] This similarity of content has been described in different ways, but following J. B. Lightfoot's classic commentary on Galatians,[2] the established argument has been that the first group is related to habits/dispositions of the mind, the second to qualities affecting human relations, and the third to principles that guide human conduct.[3] John Stott describes the three groups as being "Godward," "manward," and "selfward," respectively.[4] The problem with such classifications is threefold: first, the labels are rather vague and overlapping[5]; second, some of the virtues either do not readily fit into the categories proposed or would fit into more than one category[6]; third, because the meaning of the individual virtues is complex and overlapping, it is difficult to group some of them neatly under a single rubric. Therefore, R. Longenecker seems to be right when he concludes that "this threefold classification, however, while possibly of heuristic or homiletic value, is highly artificial and cannot be supported by anything in the text itself,"[7] and indeed, the composite categories have not been used widely in commentaries.

This chapter revisits the question of identifying broader dimensions that underlie the fruit of the Spirit. First, a rationale will be given for the potential benefits of such an exercise, arguing that an itemised approach

---

1. Furnish, *Theology and Ethics in Paul*, 87.

2. J. B. Lightfoot, *Saint Paul's Epistle to the Galatians: A Revised Text with Introduction, Notes, and Dissertations*, 10th ed. (London: Macmillan, 1890), 212; as the author explains, "The catalogue falls into three groups of three each. The first of these comprises Christian habits of mind in their more general aspect, 'love, joy, peace'; the second gives special qualities affecting a man's intercourse with his neighbour, 'long-suffering, kindness, beneficence'; while the third, again general in character like the first, exhibits the principles which guide a Christian's conduct, 'honesty, gentleness, temperance.'"

3. See e.g., R. N. Longenecker, *Galatians*, 260; Rapa, "Galatians," 628–629.

4. John R. W. Stott, *The Message of Galatians: Only One Way* (Downers Grove, IL: InterVarsity, 1968), 148.

5. E.g., what exactly is the difference between qualities affecting human relations and principles affecting human conduct?

6. E.g., one may wonder why "gentleness" belongs to the cluster labelled "principles guiding human conduct" rather than to "qualities affecting human relations," and love is surely not merely a "habit/disposition of the mind" but would also qualify for the second cluster, "qualities affecting human relations."

7. R. N. Longenecker, *Galatians*, 260.

(i.e., discussing the nine virtues relatively independently) raises both theoretical and practical problems that are less likely to emerge with fewer dimensions. This will be followed by a survey of past attempts in psychology to establish empirically validated divisions of virtues. Finally, a three-factor division of the fruit of the Spirit will be proposed, and the three dimensions described.

Rationale for Identifying Fewer Dimensions

While it is often useful to use the shorthand "fruit of the Spirit" to refer to the ideal Christlike character outlined in Gal 5:22–23—hence the popularity of the phrase in Christian circles—the fact that this label is not informative about the content of the fruit limits its value in more in-depth analyses. We have also seen above that the option of sequentially clustering the nine virtues into three triplets ("love–joy–peace," "patience–kindness–goodness," and "faithfulness–gentleness–self-control") is not sufficiently meaningful either to hold its own in theological reflection. This has left scholars who want to explore the fruit further with one option only: adopting the itemised approach and analysing the content of the fruit through examining its nine constituent attributes independently. Such an approach inevitably splits up the discourse into discrete discussion segments (well illustrated by chapter 3), and given that there are as many as nine virtues, each characterised by rich Christian and psychological content, there is a realistic danger of not seeing the forest for the trees—that is, becoming lost in the plentiful details. This potential problem was outlined in the introductory chapter, and here we may add two further challenges in this respect. The first concerns the fact that, as we shall see below, the excessive practice of a virtue without being balanced by some others might lead to nonvirtuous conduct, but the necessary balancing is rather difficult, if not unmanageable, with nine attributes. The second challenge concerns the fact that trying to cultivate nine separate virtues can easily become overbearing or even counterproductive and demotivating. Let us elaborate on these two points further.

Is More Always Better with Virtues?

If we consider a virtue in isolation, it is natural to assume that the stronger the virtue, the better—after all, a virtue is by definition a good thing to have. At a basic level this is undoubtedly true, since it is obviously preferable to be loving than unloving, patient than impatient, or kind than unkind. As Grant and Schwartz explain, this common-sense view has also characterised psychological research: "Underlying the vast majority of existing theory and research is the assumption that positive traits, experiences, and emotions have monotonic effects on well-being and performance . . . [and that] the deficiency of a strength or virtue can harm well-being and performance."[8] However, Grant and Schwartz continue by pointing out that psychologists have typically paid "little attention to understanding when, why, and how the excess of a strength or virtue can harm well-being and performance."[9] Indeed, if we look at this matter more closely, it becomes apparent that the principle of "the more the merrier" does not always hold true about virtues, because sometimes more of a virtue is definitely not better. For example, James Hughes submits that "excessive courage can lead to foolhardiness, and excessive modesty, shyness. Excessive altruism can result in self-destructiveness. Too much prudence and self-control can result in sins of inaction."[10] In fact, this very point was already made by Aristotle when he argued that a virtue taken to an extreme can become a vice, and therefore he emphasised the need to find the right balance between extremes (e.g., courage between cowardice and recklessness);[11] for example, in his *Nicomachean Ethics* he explicitly states, "Now virtue is concerned with passions and actions, in which excess is a form of failure, and so is defect, while the intermediate is praised and is a form of success; and being praised and being successful are both characteristics

---

8. Adam M. Grant and Barry Schwartz, "Too Much of a Good Thing: The Challenge and Opportunity of the Inverted U," *Perspectives on Psychological Science* 6, no. 2 (2011): 62.

9. Grant and Schwartz, 62.

10. James J. Hughes, "Moral Enhancement Requires Multiple Virtues: Toward a Posthuman Model of Character Development," *Cambridge Quarterly of Healthcare Ethics* 24 (2015): 86.

11. See e.g., Hughes, 86; Grant and Schwartz, "Too Much of a Good Thing," 62; Ng and Tay, "Lost in Translation," 311–312.

of virtue. Therefore virtue is a kind of mean, since, as we have seen, it aims at what is intermediate."[12]

In the Bible, we also find a surprisingly explicit warning to the same effect in Ecclesiastes: "Do not be over-righteous, neither be overwise—why destroy yourself? . . . Whoever fears God will avoid all extremes" (7:16, 18). This issue was then picked up and elaborated on by the famous sixth-century theologian and bishop of Rome, Gregory the Great:[13] in his highly influential work on pastoral care, *The Book of Pastoral Rule*, he adopted a dynamic perspective on virtues, declaring that "one and the same exhortation does not suit all, inasmuch as neither are all bound together by similarity of character. For the things that profit some *often hurt others*."[14] EXCURSUS 3 offers more detail about Gregory's relevant teaching, according to which even good Christian virtues can have liabilities and should therefore be "admonished" if they are not embedded in the fitting personality context.

Excursus 3: Gregory the Great's Dynamic View on Virtues in *The Book of Pastoral Rule*

The essence of Gregory the Great's teaching on virtues is that their usefulness varies according to people's personal characteristics. To illustrate this he focuses on specific combinations of personality features in his book, *The Book of Pastoral Rule*, which has been one of the most influential works on pastoral care in the Christian literature. Gregory lists thirty salient contrasts to be considered in this respect, ranging from "the joyful and the sad" to more complex distinctions such as "those who do not even begin what is good, and those who fail entirely to complete the good begun."

---

12. Aristotle, *Nicomachean Ethics*, II/6. For summaries, see Grant and Schwartz, "Too Much of a Good Thing," 61–62; Schwartz and Sharpe, "Practical Wisdom," 383.

13. I am grateful to Derek Tidball for drawing my attention to this valuable link.

14. Gregory the Great, "The Book of Pastoral Rule," in *A Select Library of the Nicene and Post-Nicene Fathers of the Christian Church*, ed. Philip Schaff and Henry Wace, trans. James Barmby (New York: Christian Literature Company, 1895), 12b:24; emphasis added.

Significantly, some of these contrasts concern values subsumed by the fruit of the Spirit; for example, "the impatient and the patient," "the kindly disposed and the envious," and "the meek and the passionate." Instead of declaring the expected maxim—namely, that all the virtues are fine and their opposites are vices—Gregory points out that a virtue might also be *deficient* if it is not combined with other complementary attributes; for example,

- "The patient are to be admonished that they grieve not inwardly for what they bear"[15] and "therefore should be told to study to love those whom they must needs bear with; lest, if love follow not patience, the virtue exhibited be turned to a worse fault of hatred."[16]
- Even the kindly-disposed should be told "that if they make no haste to imitate the good which they applaud, the holiness of virtue pleases them in like manner as the vanity of scenic exhibitions of skill pleases foolish spectators."[17]

The dynamic interaction of virtues and vices is particularly clear with regard to the "meek–passionate" contrast:

> Sometimes the meek, when they are in authority, suffer from the torpor of sloth, which is a kindred disposition, and as it were placed hard by. And for the most part from the laxity of too great gentleness they soften the force of strictness beyond need. . . . Often, then, the meek grow torpid in the laziness of inactivity; often the passionate are deceived by the zeal of uprightness. Thus to the virtue of the former a vice is unawares adjoined, but to the latter their vice appears as though it were fervent virtue.[18]

---

15. Gregory the Great, 12b:30.
16. Gregory the Great, 12b:31.
17. Gregory the Great, 12b:32.
18. Gregory the Great, 12b:39–40.

Consequently, Gregory recommends, "The meek are to be admonished that they study to have also the zeal of righteousness: the passionate are to be admonished that to the zeal which they think they have they add meekness,"[19] because "he then is in no wise full of the Holy Spirit, who either in the calm of meekness forsakes the fervour of zeal, or again in the ardour of zeal loses the virtue of meekness."[20] Thus, even good Christian virtues can have certain liabilities and should therefore be "admonished" if they are not embedded in the fitting personality context.

In sum, Gregory's teaching represents a modern conception of the dynamics of personality traits in the sense that it foregrounds the advantage of viewing the various virtues through their interactions and treating them within broader conglomerates rather than in isolation.

Modern psychological research offers support to Gregory's view. Several meta-analyses have shown that positive attributes and traits, if taken too far, can become detrimental.[21] For example, excessive concern for others might lead someone to give away too much time, energy, or possessions;[22] too high levels of empathy can cloud one's judgment and might lead to self-sacrificing behaviours at the expense of achieving one's own important goals;[23] too much volunteering may decrease psychological well-being because of role overload and insufficient time for other meaningful activities;[24] too much self-control might go at the expense of

---

19. Gregory the Great, 12b:40.
20. Gregory the Great, 12b:40.
21. See e.g., Grant and Schwartz, "Too Much of a Good Thing"; Ng and Tay, "Lost in Translation"; Schwartz and Sharpe, "Practical Wisdom"; Christopher W. Wiese et al., "Too Much of a Good Thing? Exploring the Inverted-U Relationship between Self-Control and Happiness," *Journal of Personality* 86 (2018): 380–96.
22. Watson, "Virtues in Excess," 57.
23. Grant and Schwartz, "Too Much of a Good Thing," 65.
24. Grant and Schwartz, 65.

prioritising relationships[25] or taking risks;[26] too high a degree of happiness can lead to undesirable engagement in risky behaviour.[27] Of course, the validity of such claims is always dependent on the specific circumstances and on what is meant by "taking a virtue too far"—for example, a series of studies by Wiese and his colleagues has recently found that, contrary to the well-documented results that too much self-control might inhibit life enjoyment, the more self-control people displayed in their particular samples, the happier they were.[28]

Notwithstanding any ambiguous cases, the above considerations suffice to demonstrate the need for a more nuanced view of virtue strength, and this need is further reinforced by the observation that the excess of one virtue can interfere with another virtue, resulting in *virtue conflict*; Walker, for example, reminds us of situations when exercising the virtue of truthfulness can only happen at the expense of the virtue of tact.[29] Indeed, the pursuit of a virtue will often have consequences for other aspects of one's life, including performing other virtuous acts, and without careful balancing, this consequence might turn out to be negative. Accordingly, sometimes one must observe Hamlet's well-known saying, "I must be cruel only to be kind,"[30] for example, when doctors or lawyers manoeuvre the competing calls for empathy with and detachment from their clients for best practice.[31] After all, even Jesus is recorded to have had to escape the crowds at certain times (e.g., Mark 1:45; 6:31–32; Luke 4:42–43). All these considerations justify Schwartz and Sharpe's conclusion that "there must be balance among virtues as opposed to the cultivation of signature strengths. The right balance depends on the particular context, and practical wisdom is essential to achieving that balance."[32]

---

25. McGrath, Greenberg, Hall-Simmonds, "Three-Factor Model of Virtue," 388.
26. Hughes, "Moral Enhancement," 90.
27. Cohrs et al., "Contributions of Positive Psychology to Peace," 592.
28. Wiese et al., "Too Much of a Good Thing?," 393.
29. A. D. M. Walker, "The Incompatibility of the Virtues," *Ratio* 6, no. 1 (1993): 44.
30. Shakespeare, *Hamlet*, Act 3, Scene 4.
31. Grant and Schwartz, "Too Much of a Good Thing," 65.
32. Schwartz and Sharpe, "Practical Wisdom," 386.

How can we exercise the required balance? In Phil 1:9–10 we learn that the virtue of love needs to be combined with "knowledge" and "depth of insight" to achieve righteous conduct: "And this is my prayer: that your love may abound more and more in knowledge and depth of insight, so that you may be able to discern what is best." Similarly, in 2 Pet 1:5–7 a detailed catalogue of virtues also includes "knowledge," and Richard Bauckham points out about this inclusion that although the notion of knowledge may seem out of place in the list, it represents "the wisdom and discernment which the Christian needs for a virtuous life and which is progressively acquired. It is practical rather than purely speculative wisdom."[33] This understanding parallels closely Aristotle's view that all the virtues need to be directed by what he calls "practical wisdom" (*phronesis*). There has been a great deal written in philosophy and virtue ethics about this enigmatic and somewhat controversial quality,[34] but for the current discussion it suffices to conclude that the effective pursuit of virtues requires careful and insightful balancing, consciously taking into account various priorities and conditions (we shall come back to the relationship between virtues and knowledge in chapter 7). Such a sensitive balancing act, however, cannot be carried out effectively with a long list of nine attributes—for theoretical clarity, we need a more parsimonious set that delineates critical priorities.

Can the Appeal to Cultivate Nine Virtues Be Counterproductive?

When we consider the practical aspects of cultivating virtues, we may realise that sometimes having fewer virtue dimensions can actually be more productive. In Gal 5:22–23, the apostle clearly wanted to provide rich details for his characterisation of the Christlike personality by offering an extensive list of attributes, and we shall see in chapter 7 how helpful this is, for example, when trying to put self-giving love

---

33. Richard J. Bauckham, *Jude, 2 Peter*, WBC 50 (Waco: Word, 1983), 186.

34. See e.g., Darnell et al., "Phronesis," 101–29; Daniel Lapsley, "Phronesis, Virtues and the Developmental Science of Character: Commentary on Darnell, Gulliford, Kristjánsson, and Paris," *Human Development* 62 (2019): 130–41.

into practice as we are given specific guidelines to be kind, generous, patient with others. The other side of the coin is, however, that the virtues making up the fruit of the Spirit are ideal, Christlike personality traits, and most humans can only approximate them without consistently reaching them in their lives. This being the case, having nine such not-fully-achievable targets can lead to demotivation, a scenario that has been expressively summed up by Winward:

> If we use the nine fruits of the Spirit as a standard for self-examination, we may perhaps see in our lives some of the exact opposites. Love, joy, peace? but we are cold and unconcerned, moody and gloomy, worried and quarrelsome. Patience, kindness, goodness? but we are often bad-tempered and irritable, unfriendly and unhelpful, mean and evil. Faithfulness, gentleness, self-control? but sometimes we are unreliable and disloyal, ill-mannered and harsh, slack and undisciplined. To see ourselves as we are takes the heart out of us, saps our vitality. We can become so discouraged that we lose all incentive to change. "Count me out," you may say. "Becoming like Christ may well have been the aim of those saints with a halo, but it's obviously not for me."[35]

In other words, viewing the fruit of the Spirit as nine separate attributes can be perceived as counterproductive as it foregrounds nine areas where one falls short of the mark. This is an important consideration, because a central principle of contemporary motivation science is that motivation to perform a task is dependent on the individual's *expectancy of success*; effort is unlikely to be invested in the task if people are not convinced that they can succeed no matter how hard they try.[36] Accordingly, a more concise list of targets may better serve the purpose of motivating people by making the overall goal look more achievable and by helping to concentrate their energies on key issues.

---

35. Winward, *Fruit of the Spirit*, 14.
36. See e.g., Zoltán Dörnyei and Ema Ushioda, *Teaching and Researching Motivation*, 3rd ed. (London: Routledge, 2021), 18–20.

Divisions of Virtues in Psychology

We have seen earlier that the traditional method in theology to reduce the number of the components of the fruit of the Spirit has been to divide up the nine facets sequentially into three triplets ("love–joy–peace," "patience–kindness–goodness," and "faithfulness–gentleness–self-control"). Personality psychology has followed a different approach to forming broad personality dimensions by applying the principles of a statistical procedure called "factor analysis," resulting, for example, in the currently best-known personality construct, the Big Five model.[37] Without going into technical detail about the procedure,[38] the essence of factor analysis is to identify a small number of "latent dimensions" (called "factors") that can sufficiently represent—and thus subsume—the relevant multiple personality variables that the researcher is considering. The main difference between this approach and simply dividing up the virtues into clusters is that in the latter case a virtue can belong only to one cluster (e.g., love only belongs to the "love–joy–peace" cluster), whereas a psychological variable can be meaningfully related to more than one underlying factor (e.g., love can be the dominant contributor to factor A but may also impact factor B). Given the extent to which the nine virtues in Gal 5:22–23 overlap (as discussed in the previous chapter), such a flexible and nonexclusive method may be fitting for our analysis, and indeed, factor analysis has been successfully used in positive psychology for the purpose of categorising virtues.[39] In the following we shall consider three different factor solutions that have been developed in this way.

In their study, Robert McGrath and his colleagues started out with the extensive list of human virtues summarised in Peterson and

---

37. E.g., Costa and McCrae, "The Revised Neo Personality Inventory." It is made up of five broad personality traits: openness, conscientiousness, extraversion-introversion, agreeableness, and neuroticism-emotional stability.

38. See e.g., Zoltán Dörnyei, *Research Methods in Applied Linguistics: Quantitative, Qualitative and Mixed Methodologies* (Oxford: Oxford University Press, 2007), 233–36.

39. See Gulliford and Roberts, "Unity of Virtues," 215; and McGrath, Greenberg, and Hall-Simmonds, "Three-Factor Model of Virtue," 373.

Seligman's seminal work on character strengths and virtues[40] (mentioned in chapter 1), and they proposed a three-component model to describe the main virtue dimensions: *caring, self-control,* and *inquisitiveness.* The first was associated with attributes such as kindness, love, and forgiveness, the second with perseverance, self-regulation, and prudence. The third factor, inquisitiveness, was characterised by a bit of a mixture, subsuming variables such as curiosity, bravery, creativity, and hope.[41] However, we have seen earlier that hope is a close companion to joy and peace, and interestingly, McGrath et al. also found that their inquisitiveness factor correlated positively with self-esteem and affect. In fact, as the authors summarise, "What was unanticipated was that inquisitiveness was the best single predictor of both positive affect and self-esteem. In fact, these correlations were stronger than those with variables more directly related to the traditional concept of inquisitiveness, such as enjoyment of reading or art."[42] It seems therefore that the inquisitiveness factor is closely associated with joyful well-being, while the other two emerging factors with loving care and perseverance, respectively.

The validity of McGrath's findings is supported by an earlier study of the dimensionality of Peterson and Seligman's list by Jessica Shryack and her colleagues, who analysed three-, four-, and five-factor solutions; they, too, found support for a three-component solution,[43] and the content of their factors displays a close resemblance to the McGrath et al. model: (1) interpersonal *strengths* (e.g., kindness, fairness), which is similar to "caring"; (2) *temperance strengths* (e.g., perseverance, self-regulation), which is similar to "self-control"; and (3) *intellectual strengths* (e.g., creativity, judgment), which is similar to "inquisitiveness."

Drawing on Robert Roberts's substantial past research on virtues,[44]

---

40. Peterson and Seligman, *Character Strengths and Virtues.*

41. McGrath, Greenberg, and Hall-Simmonds, "Three-Factor Model of Virtue," 374.

42. McGrath, Greenberg, and Hall-Simmonds, 381.

43. Jessica Shryack et al., "The Structure of Virtue: An Empirical Investigation of the Dimensionality of the Virtues in Action Inventory of Strengths," *Personality and Individual Differences* 48 (2010): 718.

44. E.g., Robert C. Roberts, *Spiritual Emotions: A Psychology of Christian Virtues* (Grand Rapids: Eerdmans, 2007).

Gulliford and Roberts have proposed a different threefold division of good character traits, which nevertheless has a strong resemblance to the above solutions: (1) *intelligent caring*, involving features such as justice, compassion, and generosity; (2) *willpower*, subsuming self-control, perseverance, and patience; and (3) *humility*, concerning characteristics such as being unpretentious, gentle, and properly deferential. We have seen earlier that there has been considerable ambiguity about the exact nature of humility, but it is noteworthy that Gulliford and Roberts's other two virtue components largely coincide with the caring and self-control dimensions of McGrath and colleagues' model.

Dimensions of the Fruit of the Spirit

With regard to identifying dimensions underlying the nine facets of the fruit of the Spirit, the psychological analogies reviewed above suggest a three-component model, which contains (1) an interpersonal caring dimension and (2) a self-control dimension. As we shall see below in more detail, these two factors offer a very good fit with the fruit of the Spirit, given that the key virtues at the two bookends of the list in Gal 5:22–23 are compassionate love and self-control, described earlier as "supreme" and "foundational" virtues, respectively. Regarding the third factor, the Galatians list does not contain intellectual virtues (e.g., creativity or curiosity) that were identified as a third psychological dimension, but recall that McGrath and his colleagues connected the "inquisitiveness" factor with joyful well-being, which is well represented by some of the Galatians virtues (most notably by joy and peace). These considerations, therefore, point to a three-factor division of the fruit of the Spirit, and the three dimensions can be labelled as *loving compassion*, *spiritual contentment*, and *steadfast perseverance*. Such a classification also makes intuitive sense, as it outlines a rounded character which is inherently outward-facing and loving, which has internal spiritual peace at its foundation, and which is sustained by self-discipline and endurance. Before we examine these three dimensions more closely, we should note one more important aspect of the dimensionality of the fruit of the Spirit: its twofold nature in terms of individual and communal relevance.

Individual versus Communal Implications of the Fruit

When we surveyed the components of the fruit of the Spirit in chapter 3, it was repeatedly underlined that all the facets had prominent *communal* implications. This was not a coincidence, because as Richard Hays rightly reminds us, the Pauline Epistles are messages to Christian communities, "written to strengthen and support group identity in fledgling mission churches."[45] Thus, Paul's ultimate aim was to build up the community of believers, as is profoundly expressed in Phil 2:1–4: "If then there is any encouragement in Christ, any consolation from love, any sharing in the Spirit, any compassion and sympathy, make my joy complete: be of the same mind, having the same love, being in full accord and of one mind. Do nothing from selfish ambition or conceit, but in humility regard others as better than yourselves. Let each of you look not to your own interests, but to the interests of others" (NRSVA).

A particularly revealing manifestation of this community-building agenda can be found in Eph 4:2–6, where several of the facets of the fruit of the Spirit are explicitly linked to a communal orientation: "Be completely humble and gentle; be patient, bearing with one another in love. Make every effort to keep the unity of the Spirit through the bond of peace. There is one body and one Spirit, just as you were called to one hope when you were called; one Lord, one faith, one baptism; one God and Father of all, who is over all and through all and in all."

Such a communal orientation—"unity through the bond of peace"— also underlies the whole letter to the Galatians,[46] culminating in the contrast between the self-centred egocentricity of the list of vices in Gal 5:19–21 and the subsequent list of virtues,[47] which N. T. Wright simply

---

45. Hays, "Galatians," 32.

46. As Hays explains, "Paul's concern for communal unity surfaces clearly in the concluding hortatory portion of the letter to the Galatians. Not only is his list of 'works of the flesh' (5:19–21) heavily weighted toward offenses against the unity of the community ('enmities, strife, jealousy, anger, quarrels, dissensions, factions, envy'), but the vice and virtue lists of 5:16–24 are also bracketed by clear directives against conflict in the church (5:13–15; 5:25–6:5)." Richard B. Hays, *The Moral Vision of the New Testament: A Contemporary Introduction to New Testament Ethics* (London: T&T Clark, 1996), 33.

47. Martyn (*Galatians*, 498) states, "Paul transforms lists of vices and virtues into something fundamentally different—marks of a community under the sway of the Flesh contrasted with

characterises as "a list of the qualities you would want to see in your neighbours."[48] B. Longenecker captures this collective theme clearly: "Paul's
case throughout Galatians is, then, primarily a charter and blueprint for
social relationships within the eschatological community in which the
sovereign creator is transforming people in conformity with the character
of the loving and self-giving son."[49] As we shall see below, all the three
dimensions of the fruit manifest this community-centred "blueprint for
social relationships."

Loving Compassion

The most salient dimension of the fruit of the Spirit is bound to be
centred around love. We saw in chapter 3 that love is the supreme virtue
not only amongst the facets of the fruit of the Spirit but more generally
in the whole of Scripture: it reflects God's very nature (1 John 4:8) and it
fulfils the entire law (Gal 5:14). It was shown that biblical love (*agapē*) only
concerns one segment of the semantic range of the English word "love,"
compassionate love, and given that all the other facets of the fruit of the
Spirit include a prosocial orientation, they can be seen as an elaboration of
the selfless, compassionate, loving concern for others. More specifically,
it was argued that kindness, goodness, gentleness, and patience in particular share common meaning with loving compassion in the sense that
they all concern aspects of a caring social relationship with someone[50]—
compassionate love in action—and we saw that faithfulness also contributes
to this dimension through benevolence (also labelled unconditional kindness), which has been found to be a determinant of trustworthiness in
psychology. In her research of Trappist monks, Underwood showed a

marks of a community under the leading of the Spirit." Cohick's ("Fruit of the Spirit," 333)
conclusion echoes this point: "The Holy Spirit works to transform a believer into Christ's likeness. This work has a communal dimension, for Paul calls church members to demonstrate godly
behaviour rather than biting, devouring, and envying one another (Gal. 5:15, 26). The Holy Spirit
unifies the church as the fruit of the Spirit is manifested."

48. N. T. Wright, *Galatians*, 338.

49. B. W. Longenecker, *The Triumph of Abraham's God*, 72.

50. Peterson and Seligman's (*Character Strengths and Virtues*, 326) seminal work on virtues in
positive psychology also confirms that "kindness, generosity, nurturance, care, compassion, and
altruistic love are a network of closely related terms indicating a common orientation of the self
toward the other."

link between compassionate love and inner peace, as many participants regarded inner peace as a sign that the balancing of various considerations in exercising compassionate love "was going in an appropriate direction."[51] Finally, loving compassion correlates with self-control, because the latter is required to "cover the costs" of self-giving other-centredness.

The loving compassion dimension of the fruit of the Spirit encompasses "communal responsiveness"—that is, watching out for another's well-being, needs, and desires, as well as trying to help and support the other.[52] The disposition of caring for the good of the other has often been discussed in psychology under the rubric of *altruism*,[53] but Underwood argues that compassionate love stretches beyond altruism as it "captures an investment of self deeper than 'altruism' suggests."[54] Behavioural manifestations of this loving compassion orientation are wide-ranging, including providing social support, financial aid, volunteering time, caregiving, helpfulness, and self-sacrifice.[55]

Spiritual Contentment

If loving compassion is primarily communal in nature, the second dimension of the fruit of the Spirit, *spiritual contentment*, may be seen as its internal companion, because it is centred around the personal serenity of the believer (although we shall see below that this tranquil disposition of inner spiritual peace also serves as the foundation of communal harmony). The key virtues associated with spiritual contentment are joy and peace, the "spiritual twins"[56] that are often mentioned together in the Bible as complementary companions. In the Old Testament, for example, Isa 55:12 prophesies, "You will go out in joy and be led forth in peace," and Prov 12:20 declares that "those who promote peace have joy." In the New Testament, the peace and joy couplet in Rom 14:17 is used to characterise the whole of the kingdom of God ("For the kingdom of

---

51. Underwood, "Interviews with Trappist Monks," 295.
52. Sternberg, *Psychology of Love*, 50.
53. See e.g., Stephen Stich, John M. Doris, and Erica Roedder, "Altruism," in *The Moral Psychology Handbook*, ed. John M. Doris (New York: Oxford University Press, 2010).
54. Underwood, "Interviews with Trappist Monks," 292.
55. E.g., DeWall et al., "Depletion," 1653; Fehr and Sprecher, "Compassionate Love," 113.
56. Bruce, *Galatians*, 252.

God is not a matter of eating and drinking, but of righteousness, peace and joy in the Holy Spirit"), and the Bible passage that offers one of the most expressive descriptions of internal peace, Phil 4:4–7, starts with the trumpet call to "rejoice" (v. 4) so that "the peace of God, which transcends all understanding, will guard your hearts and your minds in Christ Jesus" (v. 7). This passage also shows that the composite content of joy and peace is deeply spiritual, which is again highlighted in Paul's prayer in Rom 15:13: "May the God of hope fill you with all joy and peace as you trust in him, so that you may overflow with hope by the power of the Holy Spirit." Also, in Phil 4:11–13 the apostle models how tranquillity has been realised in his own life, leaving no doubt about its divine origin: "I have learned to be content whatever the circumstances. I know what it is to be in need, and I know what it is to have plenty. I have learned the secret of being content in any and every situation, whether well fed or hungry, whether living in plenty or in want. I can do all this *through him who gives me strength*" (emphasis added).

The discussion in chapter 3 emphasised that an important aspect of biblical peace is its relational aspect,[57] promoting communal harmony, and this communal dimension matches the collective nature of joy, which in the Bible is frequently described as a quality of community life. Consistent with this, Brueggemann argues that the biblical shalom "refers to all those resources and factors that make communal harmony joyous and effective,"[58] and Eph 4:1–3 underlines the role of two other facets of the fruit as building blocks of corporate peace: patience and gentleness. Colossians 3:15 relates corporate harmony to someone's inner peace—"Let the peace of Christ rule in your hearts, since as members of one body you were called to peace"—yet this is not a one-way but a dynamic relationship, because we saw earlier (CONCEPT 3.4 in chapter 3) that people who experience relatively more inner contentment tend to be more peaceful towards others.[59]

---

57. As deSilva (*Galatians*, 466) sums up, "The Hebrew concept of shalom, the enjoyment of solid and edifying connections with others throughout the community and beyond, cannot be far in the background for Paul."

58. Brueggemann, *Peace*, 14.

59. Nelson, "Peacefulness," 28.

Steadfast Perseverance

The believer's *steadfast perseverance* is undoubtedly a vital personality dimension. In 2 Cor 6:4–10, the apostle Paul lists a number of aspects of his own mission which make it worthwhile to commend it to the Corinthians, and his "great endurance" (v. 4) is the very first of the virtues mentioned. Even more compellingly, Mark 13:13 cites Jesus declaring that "the one who stands firm to the end will be saved" (see also Matt 10:22; Luke 21:19). The most obvious facet of the fruit of the Sprit to be linked to this crucial factor is *self-control*, and two other virtues contributing to it directly are *patience* and *faithfulness*, with the former referring to steadfast endurance and forbearance, the latter involving dependability and trustworthiness. The discussion in chapter 3 also underlined the connection between self-control and *gentleness*, as the latter involves "strength under control" by disallowing provocation to anger. Moreover, we have seen in chapter 4 that self-control correlates with compassionate love, because other-centredness incurs costs that are covered by one's self-discipline. This important link between steadfast perseverance and love is further strengthened in 1 Cor 13:4–7, where it is explicitly stated that "love is patient," love "is not irritable," and it "bears all things" and "endures all things" (NRSVA).

It was argued in chapter 3 that a central aspect of self-control concerns its *communal* nature—that is, the self-discipline required in a community to maintain harmonious relationships. This aspect has been studied in psychology under the label of "social resilience," which has been defined by John Cacioppo and his colleagues as "the capacity to foster, engage in, and sustain positive relationships and to endure and recover from life stressors and social isolation."[60] Its manifestation is, as the authors continue, "the transformation of adversity into personal, relational, and collective growth through strengthening existing social engagements, and developing new relationships, with creative collective actions."[61] In a high-profile paper in psychology, Christopher Cohrs and his colleagues further argue that resilient communities provide their

---

60. John T. Cacioppo, Harry T. Reis, and Alex J. Zautra, "Social Resilience: The Value of Social Fitness with an Application to the Military," *American Psychologist* 66, no. 1 (2011): 44.

61. Cacioppo, Reis, and Zautra, 44.

members with support and resources to cope with adversity and foster well-being, and that such communities tend to be more able to withstand internal conflict through more effective communication, mediation, and collective decision-making.[62]

Summary: "A Cord of Three Strands Is Not Quickly Broken"

This chapter set out to identify a small number of dimensions underlying the fruit of the Spirit that represent the essential features of the ninefold fruit. It was argued that such a parsimonious framework can offer a number of advantages: First, it allows us to communicate the nature of the ideal Christlike character without the danger of losing focus amidst the details of a long list of components. Second, a parsimonious framework can highlight character priorities and can thus help one to consider how to balance these against each other to best effect in order to avoid any excessive, and potentially counterproductive, practice of a virtue. Third, having a shorter list with straightforward priorities is also beneficial for practical purposes, because urging people to improve in as many as nine areas of their lives can easily become overbearing and demotivating.

Several recent psychological investigations of virtues have produced classifications with three main components, and while the labels given to the factors have differed somewhat, two emerging dimensions tended to coincide with two central aspects of the fruit of the Spirit, compassionate love and self-control, with a third correlating with joyful well-being. Following these analogies, a three-component division of the fruit of the Spirit was proposed:

- **loving compassion**, concerning a compassionate orientation centred around the well-being and needs of others;
- **spiritual contentment**, referring to a tranquil disposition of serenity and joyful spiritual peace;

---

62. Cohrs et al., "Contributions of Positive Psychology to Peace," 595.

- **steadfast perseverance**, involving self-disciplined and enduring conduct in the face of challenges and adversities.

It was shown that these three dimensions offer a good fit with the nine facets of the fruit of the Spirit, as they cover all the constituent virtues adequately. Together, the three dimensions outline a rounded Christian character, which is inherently outward facing and loving, which has internal spiritual peace at its foundation, and which is sustained by self-control and tenacity.

In his seminal work on virtues, Alasdair MacIntyre defines a virtue as an "acquired human quality the possession and exercise of which tends to enable us to achieve those goods which are internal to practices and the lack of which effectively prevents us from achieving any such goods."[63] The threefold fruit of the Spirit is fully consistent with this definition, as its loving compassion dimension enables people to fulfil the law and the greatest commandment, and it also contains the necessary support— spiritual contentment and steadfast perseverance—whose absence would likely impede the pursuit of the greater good. The social manifestation of this disposition is a loving and unified community of the saints that is sufficiently resilient to carry out the stewardship duties that humanity has been charged with at the beginning of its existence.

Ecclesiastes 4:12 declares that "a cord of three strands is not quickly broken." Although in its specific scriptural context this proverbial saying concerns the strength of human fellowship and mutual support rather than character strengths, the image confers general wisdom that can be applied to our current subject[64]: similar to a three-ply cord, the three dimensions of the fruit constitute a potent whole, with loving compassion braided together with spiritual contentment and steadfast perseverance. The latter is by definition a prerequisite for overcoming inherent self-

---

63. MacIntyre, *After Virtue*, 191.

64. Treier explains that the saying, which is traceable to an ancient Sumerian proverb, makes no reference to the three theological virtues of faith, hope, and love, because "virtues are only indirectly personal; they are dispositions or character traits, not agents themselves." However, he does not exclude the hearing of different echoes in the language of the proverb in general. Daniel J. Treier, *Proverbs and Ecclesiastes*, Brazos Theological Commentary on the Bible (Grand Rapids: Brazos, 2011), 164.

centredness and emerging obstacles, while Nelson provides evidence from psychology that inner peace will "allow a person to give relatively more attention to the concerns of others and to relationship issues."[65] In Rom 12:10–12, Paul presents, in slightly different words, the same threefold combination of what "genuine love" should involve: "love one another with mutual affection [loving compassion] . . . rejoice in hope [internal contentment], be patient in suffering, persevere in prayer [steadfast perseverance]" (NRSVA).

---

65. Nelson, "Peaceful Personality," 72.

6

THE FRUIT OF THE SPIRIT AND SPIRITUAL TRANSFORMATION IN THE BIBLE

The fruit of the Spirit was defined in chapter 2 as the ideal outcome of a divinely orchestrated transformation process to produce a Christlike character in the believer. The previous chapters have examined the nature of this character from a number of different angles, but have not addressed the spiritual development whereby this character develops. From a theological perspective, understanding this transformation is of special significance, because without seeing how the fruit fits into the core Christian story, we cannot establish its true biblical role or value. Therefore, the main objective of the current chapter is to specify the place of the fruit of the Spirit within the believer's spiritual formation.

A prerequisite to the task of relating the ninefold fruit to Christian development is to have a specific framework of spiritual growth within which the fruit can be evaluated. However, identifying such a framework is somewhat of a challenge, because there does not appear to exist a single robust outline of spiritual transformation that is universally accepted in the theological mainstream. As we shall see in this chapter, the Bible portrays spiritual formation through a rich variety of concepts, metaphors, and images that describe expressively the process of human development and transformation, without, however, providing a single unified and explicitly articulated template in this respect. Although Christian thinkers over the centuries have offered several summations and interpretations of the economy of salvation from different theological vantage points, there has been no authoritative definition provided by an ecumenical council,[1] and the contemporary theological landscape is rather fragmented.

In the absence of such a consensus of thought, the current discussion will apply the following investigative strategy: To start with, spiritual growth will be considered in the most general sense as the process leading to *spiritual maturity*, and it will be examined how the ninefold fruit relates to this developmental process. Following this, in order to obtain a representative range of the most salient theological construals of spiritual transformation, three clusters of relevant concepts will be selected for an analysis of how they accommodate the fruit of the Spirit: (1) sanctification, justification, and related concepts; (2) deification/theosis and related concepts; and (3) variations on being conformed to the divine image.

Ultimately, the central question addressed in this chapter is how important it is for believers to develop the fruit of the Spirit as part of their spiritual development. It will be argued that the fruit represents more than merely a selection of commendable personal qualities that Christians are encouraged to emulate. To be sure, the virtues in Gal 5:22–23 are laudable, and elsewhere in the Bible they are repeatedly presented as attributes to be cultivated; but in the current chapter the focus will be on the fruit also being presented as a central component in new creation as well as in the transformation of believers into citizens of the kingdom of God. It will be proposed that the fruit of the Spirit can be viewed as the most concrete and specific portrayal of the outcome of the spiritual transformation process described in the biblical corpus.

---

1. See Paul M. Collins, *Partaking in Divine Nature: Deification and Communion* (London: Bloomsbury T&T Clark, 2010), 47.

Spiritual Maturity and the Fruit of the Spirit

The process of the believer's spiritual development is a central theme in the biblical canon; it is widely recognised as common ground in mainstream Christianity that, in William Alston's words, "God is at work within the believer to transform her into the kind of person God wants her to be, the kind of person capable of entering into an eternal loving communion with God."[2] Let us begin the survey of the biblical portrayal of Christian spiritual development with arguably the most generic term in this respect, *spiritual maturation*. The Greek word for "mature" is *teleios*, and N. T. Wright explains that it conveys two related senses: a sense of something having reached its goal and a sense of maturity or completeness.[3] Indeed, in Jas 1:4 *teleios* is paired up with *holoklēros* (wholeness): "Let perseverance finish its work so that you may be mature and complete, not lacking anything." *Teleios* occurs in the Scriptures almost twenty times, but in a monograph on maturation in the Pauline Epistles, James Samra emphasises that the representation of spiritual growth is not restricted to this word only[4]—indeed, as we shall see below, the notion of "growing in the knowledge of God" (Col 1:10) permeates the whole of the New Testament under different labels.

For the apostle Paul, building up mature believers was a paramount goal, comparable only to his evangelistic mission, and a central purpose of his letters was to promote the spiritual maturity of their recipients.[5] Indeed, Col 1:28 characterises Paul as "admonishing and teaching everyone with all wisdom, so that we may present everyone fully mature in Christ," and in Phil 3:12–15, Paul presents himself as a role model in this respect, as someone whose own maturation is still a work in progress—"Not that I have already obtained all this, or have already arrived at my goal" (v. 12)—but who is "pressing on," and

---

2. William P. Alston, *Divine Nature and Human Language: Essays in Philosophical Theology* (Ithaca, NY: Cornell University Press, 1989), 231.

3. N. T. Wright, *After You Believe*, 185.

4. Samra, *Being Conformed to Christ*, 7.

5. Samra, *Being Conformed to Christ*, 43; as he later reiterates, "One could even argue, given the purpose of his epistles, that every statement we have from the Apostle is in some way oriented toward the maturation of his readers" (170).

then he concludes, "All of us, then, who are mature should take such a view of things" (v. 15). The importance of aiming for spiritual maturity is also highlighted at the beginning of the same epistle, when Paul declares that although it is his "desire to depart and be with Christ" (Phil 1:23), "it is more necessary for you that I remain in the body . . . for your *progress* and joy in the faith" (vv. 24–25; emphasis added). Note that the same word is used here for progress (*prokopē*) as in Gal 1:14 regarding Paul's theological studies—"I was advancing [*proekopton*] in Judaism beyond many of my own age among my people and was extremely zealous for the traditions of my fathers"—and in Luke 2:52 for Jesus's maturation: "And Jesus grew [*proekopten*] in wisdom and stature, and in favour with God and man."

The Image of the Growing Child and the Flesh–Spirit Contrast in Spiritual Maturity

The emphasis on promoting Christian maturity is also explicit in Paul's letter to the Galatians, and in 4:19 he uses the vivid picture of the anguish of a mother to raise her child in this respect: "My dear children, for whom I am again in the pains of childbirth until Christ is formed in you . . ." Such expressive parent–child language recurs several times in the Scriptures carrying the same connotation of spiritual growth. For example, in 1 Cor 3:1–3 Paul compares the immature Corinthian believers to infants who are not ready for solid food yet, and the same image is expressed in Heb 5:12–14, where baby food is equated with elementary teachings, and "solid food is for the mature" (v. 14). The latter passage also states that "infants," who are still on "milk, not solid food" and who are "not acquainted with the teaching about righteousness," need to become "mature" disciples who "have trained themselves to distinguish good from evil," leading to the concluding exhortation, "Therefore let us move beyond the elementary teachings about Christ and be taken forward to maturity" (6:1).[6] The parent–child image reappears in 1 Pet 2:2,

---

6. See Brian D. Majerus and Steven J. Sandage, "Differentiation of Self and Christian Spiritual Maturity: Social Science and Theological Integration," *Journal of Psychology and Theology* 38, no. 1 (2010): 45.

this time specifically linked to salvation—"Like newborn babies, crave pure spiritual milk, so that by it you may grow up in your salvation"—and in 1 Cor 14:20 Paul urges the believers to "stop thinking like children. In regard to evil be infants, but in your thinking be adults."

As mentioned above, in 1 Cor 3:1–3 the believer's lack of maturation is expressed through the metaphor of spiritual infancy, and this passage holds particular significance for the current discussion because it explicitly links the process of spiritual formation to the transformation from being "worldly" (*sarkinos*, literally "fleshly") to becoming "people who live by the Spirit": "Brothers and sisters, I could not address you as people who live by the Spirit but as people who are still worldly ['fleshly']—mere infants in Christ. I gave you milk, not solid food, for you were not yet ready for it. Indeed, you are still not ready. You are still worldly ['fleshly']." What Paul is declaring here is nothing less than a central tenet of developing Christian maturity: believers need to grow up spiritually from being infants dominated by the flesh to mature people who live by the Spirit.[7] In other words, this passage portrays spiritual maturation as a journey from a primarily flesh-bound towards a more Spirit-bound existence. Let us have a look at the implication of this tenet for the reading of Gal 5.

Reading Together 1 Cor 3:1–3 and Gal 5:16–25

The flesh–Spirit contrast is a central theme in Paul's theology (see CONCEPT 6.1 for a brief summary), and its inclusion in 1 Cor 3:1–3 creates an obvious link with Gal 5:16–25, the locus of the description of the fruit of the Spirit, because the latter passage is also one of the key biblical texts regarding Paul's teaching about the antithesis between the flesh and the Spirit. The Galatians passage is framed by two exhortations that set the tone—"walk by the Spirit, and you will not gratify the desires of the flesh" (v. 16 ESV) at the beginning and "since we live by the Spirit, let us keep in step with the Spirit" (v. 25) at the end. The flesh–Spirit distinction is reiterated in v. 17 explicitly: "For the flesh desires what is contrary

---

7. For an analysis of this passage that similarly highlights a developmental angle while focusing on the flesh's impeding role, see Steven L. Porter, "The Gradual Nature of Sanctification: Σάρξ as Habituated, Relational Resistance to the Spirit," *Themelios* 39, no. 3 (2014): 479.

to the Spirit, and the Spirit what is contrary to the flesh. They are *in conflict with each other*" (emphasis added). This unequivocal contrasting is then fully matched by the central part of the passage (vv. 19–23), which offers expository support by means of the juxtaposition of two extensive lists, the first made up of sins related to the flesh, the second of virtues related to the Spirit.[8]

Concept 6.1: The Flesh–Spirit Conflict in Pauline Theology

Paul's epistle to the Romans (especially 7:14–23 and 8:5–8) contains several expressions of the antithesis between two mindsets, one centred around the flesh, the other around the Spirit. The essence of this conflict is summarised in 8:5–6 as follows: "Those who live according to the flesh have their minds set on what the flesh desires; but those who live in accordance with the Spirit have their minds set on what the Spirit desires. The mind governed by the flesh is death, but the mind governed by the Spirit is life and peace." Galatians 3:3 and 5:16–17 reiterate the contrast between the two diametrically opposed directions associated with the flesh and the Spirit, and Barclay submits that the two notions are in fact the "dominant categories in Paul's ethics in Galatians."[9] This affirms the more general existence of what Moo calls a "'two regime' framework that is fundamental to all of Paul's teaching (and, indeed, to all of the New Testament)."[10]

---

8. Runge captures the essence of this passage as follows: "This section opens and closes with exhortations, with verses 17–24 offering expository support for both sets. The opening positive/negative pair are about as direct and emphatic as one can get. The closing ones, though also offering positive/negative statements reiterating much the same sentiment, adopt a less-direct tone by shifting to 'Let us' statements. The two sets of exhortations bookend one of the New Testament's most powerful and beloved rhetorical appeals for the Spirit-filled life." Steven E. Runge, *Galatians: A Textual Guide*, High Definition Commentary (Bellingham, WA: Logos Bible Software, 2019).

9. Barclay, *Obeying the Truth*, 29.

10. Moo, *Romans*, 240.

As stated in Rom 8:6, the two opposing mindsets are associated with two distinct life trajectories: one leading to death, the other to life. For emphasis, Paul reiterates this point a few verses later: "If you live according to the flesh, you will die; but if by the Spirit you put to death the misdeeds of the body, you will live" (8:13). This duality echoes Paul's earlier teaching in Rom 5:12–21 concerning the two opposing trajectories associated with the first and the last Adam, one leading to sin and death, the other to righteousness and life; indeed, in his commentary on Romans, N. T. Wright suggests that the whole of Rom 8:1–11 is best seen as the unfolding of the Adam–Christ contrast.[11]

Given that the two conflicting mindsets coexist in parallel, they present an ongoing battleground for the Christian believer,[12] and in Gal 6:8 Paul demarcates two courses to choose from in the Christian fight: "Whoever sows to please their flesh, from the flesh will reap destruction; whoever sows to please the Spirit, from the Spirit will reap eternal life." Referring to the two alternatives represented by the first and the last Adam, but also relevant to the fatal tension between the flesh and the Spirit, Dunn describes this ultimate conflict as Paul's version of the "epochal choice between death and life laid before Israel in the climax to the Deuteronomic covenant."[13]

Commentators have traditionally interpreted the flesh–Spirit contrast in the Galatians passage as two *alternatives* to choose from (as illustrated in CONCEPT 6.1) rather than in terms of *development* from one

---

11. E.g., N. T. Wright suggests that the clue to understanding the whole passage of Romans 8:1–11 is to see it as "the unfolding of the Adam/Christ contrast of 5:12–21." N. T. Wright, "The Letter to the Romans: Introduction, Commentary, and Reflections," in *The New Interpreter's Bible: A Commentary in Twelve Volumes*, ed. Leander E. Keck (Nashville: Abingdon, 2002), 574.

12. As Runge (*Galatians*) expressively puts it, "Believers are inescapably trapped in the middle of this battlefield (v. 17a). There is no possibility of appeasing both sides, no middle ground."

13. James D. G. Dunn, *The Theology of Paul the Apostle* (Grand Rapids: Eerdmans, 1998), 94; for a similar view, see Brendan Byrne, *Romans*, SP 6 (Collegeville, MN: Liturgical Press, 1996), 241.

to the other. While understanding the contrast as the believer's struggle between two opposite tendencies is in harmony with Paul's message both in Gal 5 and Rom 7–8,[14] 1 Cor 3:1–3 adds to this picture a further, *developmental dimension*: growing spiritual maturity involves increasingly choosing the Spirit over the flesh—that is, the process is aimed at developing an increased proclivity to attune to the Spirit in one's daily conduct rather than succumb to the temptations and influences of the flesh. Within this paradigm, therefore, the Galatians passage can be seen as an elaborate description of the two poles of the human transformation process outlined in 1 Cor 3:1–3, spelling out in rich detail the starting point of spiritual growth and its final destination. The fruit of the Spirit represents the latter, the ultimate aspired-to target for Christian development.

In summary, reading together 1 Cor 3:1–3 and Gal 5:16–25, Paul's message about believers' required development presents a clear conception of moral/spiritual formation as a move from a flesh-centred state that is riddled with sins to a Spirit-centred state of Christlike character as illustrated by the fruit of the Spirit. In conveying this message, Paul's strategy is not so much to explain the economy of spiritual formation (i.e., the mechanisms whereby the transformation takes place) as to describe the two poles of the maturation process (i.e., the start and the desired finish) in unambiguous terms, offering a detailed list of descriptors for each. All this points to the more general conclusion that spiritual growth is operationalised in Scripture as a process of character formation from a lack of righteousness to achieving moral integrity, approximating as closely as possible the ideal Christlike character outlined in Gal 5:22–23.

Undoubtedly, drawing a direct parallel between the fruit of the Spirit and the target of biblical moral/spiritual formation is a substantial claim. In order to verify it, we shall examine below whether the same link can be

---

14. See e.g., David Wenham, "The Christian Life: A Life of Tension? A Consideration of the Nature of Christian Experience in Paul," in *Pauline Studies: Essays Presented to Professor F. F. Bruce on His 70th Birthday*, ed. Donald A. Hagner and Murray J. Harris (Exeter: Paternoster, 1980), 89.

established between the fruit and other key biblical metaphors of spiritual growth—most notably, sanctification, deification, and becoming conformed to the divine image.

Biblical Metaphors and Images of Spiritual Formation

In his summary of New Testament theology, Dunn argues that insufficient recognition has been given in the past to the wide variety of the New Testament's soteriological language and metaphorical imagery that describes the process of salvation.[15] He contends that, in stark contrast to the unifying efforts of contemporary theologians to synthesise the relevant biblical terms, "Paul and the other NT writers do not seem to have been concerned about the diversity of the imagery they used and whether the metaphors could be neatly integrated with one another. On the contrary, their concern seems to have been rather to bring to as vivid expression as possible the existential reality of their varied experience of saving power, even when it meant ransacking the range of imagery available."[16] Indeed, even a cursory look at the relevant theological terminology reveals two salient features: First, there is a profusion of terms related to spiritual transformation such as "conversion," "regeneration," "justification," "sanctification," "glorification," "deification" (and its synonyms, "divinization" and "theosis"), "adoption," "participation," being "conformed to the divine image," and "union with God."[17] Second, the various terms tend to be used in the literature in a nonuniform manner, sometimes as synonyms, sometimes as overlapping categories, and sometimes as constituent components of more complex models. Excursus 4 explores the main reasons for the existence of this bewildering terminological tapestry.

---

15. Dunn, *New Testament Theology*, 91.
16. Dunn, 91.
17. Some of these terms have been further divided: e.g., "definitive," "progressive," and "entire" sanctification; "ethical" and "realistic/ontological" deification.

Excursus 4: Ambiguities Surrounding Metaphors and Images Related to Spiritual Transformation

The Bible does not contain a uniform, in-depth description of the process of spiritual transformation within a convert, and some scholars maintain that the exact economy of salvation is unfathomable.[18] While comprehending the specific mechanisms of salvation may well be beyond human understanding, the Scriptures do express the profound sense of being saved by using a variety of metaphors. Kevin Vanhoozer argues that the Bible is replete with metaphors exactly because such creative language use is necessary to relate the essentially indescribable to the realities of the readers' own world.[19] This appears to be particularly true of aspects of the processes related to salvation, and in fact, Dunn points out that even the concept of "salvation" (sōtēria) itself, which is often used in theology as a higher-order technical term to subsume several related subprocesses, is only one of many relevant biblical metaphors, denoting the wholeness of a healthy person, and thus being familiar to contemporary readers in the everyday sense of "bodily health, preservation."[20] To take another example, the word "justification" (dikaiōma) was a legal term meaning acquittal—that is, declaring innocent in a court case—and Dunn concludes that by drawing on such known images, Paul attempted to express as fully as possible a reality "which defied a simple or uniform or unifaceted description. . . . The vitality of the experience made

---

18. E.g., Alston (*Divine Nature and Human Language*, 227) simply concludes about the divine mechanisms involved in salvation that "we could not expect to grasp them," and adds that "we should be alive to the possibility that God works differently with different people in different situations."

19. Kevin J. Vanhoozer, *Pictures at a Theological Exhibition: Scenes of the Church's Worship, Witness and Wisdom* (Downers Grove, IL: IVP Academic, 2016), 28.

20. Dunn, *The Theology of Paul*, 332.

new metaphors necessary if the experience was to be expressed in words."[21]

While metaphors can create a rich and expressive texture of a semantic domain, they are not technical terms with well-defined, specific referents. This means that they are used in the Scriptures in multiple senses that are sometimes only loosely related to each other. This, however, creates a tension between how metaphors are used in the biblical corpus and how they are integrated into the conceptual language of academic theological discourse. The concept of "sanctification" might illustrate this tension well. The verb "to sanctify" (*hagiazō*) literally means "to make somebody/something holy," and because the adjective "holy" is very broadly used in the Bible, the related verb form also occurs in many different semantic contexts. As Graham Cole explains about technical terms in the theological register, "The word 'sanctification' in the latter [i.e., as a technical term] refers to a master concept that the history of theological discussion has made both more complex (with its subcategories) and nuanced (with its distinctions) than the biblical concepts themselves."[22]

A further terminological challenge concerning the process of spiritual transformation and salvation is that it holds together two different perspectives, one concerning a single event (i.e., an initial turning point), the other an ongoing, gradual process of spiritual growth: while most biblical scholars would agree that a believer's salvific transformation has a definite and clear-cut beginning, the Scriptures also offer multiple indications that there is some additional progressive outworking of salvation following this initial event in the form of the convert's spiritual maturation

---

21. Dunn, 332.

22. Graham A. Cole, "Sanctification," in *Dictionary for Theological Interpretation of the Bible*, ed. Kevin J. Vanhoozer (London: SPCK, 2005), 721–722.

towards being conformed to the divine image.[23] Not only does this twofold process raise profound theological questions about the two phases' relationship with each other and about their relative impact on the believer, but a further complication is posed by the fact that several biblical passages fail to differentiate the two temporal phases explicitly. For example, while in theological discourse we often find a clear distinction between "justification" and "sanctification," with the former typically referring to the first phase of salvation (i.e., the turning point) and the latter to the second (i.e., to the progression towards maturity), in the Scriptures this difference is sometimes blurred, as for example in 1 Cor 6:11, which offers a sequence in which sanctification *precedes* justification: "You were washed, you were sanctified, you were justified in the name of the Lord Jesus Christ and by the Spirit of our God." It is therefore not always straightforward how exactly to map the various related terms used in the Bible onto the overall timeline of spiritual transformation. In this respect, Henri Blocher offers an insightful warning about any theological discussion of spiritual progress in general: "We are to handle the theme of progress carefully. Metaphors are not to be pressed, and the analogy of biological growth cannot be applied in a rigid manner: regression and pathological stagnation are (alas!) spiritually common! . . . Like life in general, sanctification knows a combination of special moments, seasons of intense transformation, critical transitions as well as more linear continuity."[24]

A further source of difficulty in aligning biblical metaphors and theological technical terms is that the development of the latter has also been shaped by denominational priorities. An obvious example is the term "justification," which was at the heart of the

---

23. For balanced overviews, see e.g., Dunn, *The Theology of Paul*, 328–333; Dunn, *New Testament Theology*, 92; 147–148.

24. Henri Blocher, "Sanctification by Faith?," in *Sanctification: Explorations in Theology and Practice*, ed. Kelly M. Kapic (Downers Grove, IL: IVP Academic, 2014), 74.

theological disputes during the Protestant Reformation and which was, accordingly, assigned unique significance in some denominations. Dunn cites the treatment of this term as an example of how one of Paul's several metaphors has been exalted into "some primary or normative status so that all the others must be fitted into its mould."[25] Such a privileged treatment, he argues, carries the danger of reducing the diversity and richness of the relevant experiences that the various metaphors cover. Other prominent examples of denominational prioritisation include the Wesleyan emphasis on "entire sanctification" as well as the different understandings of the notion of deification/theosis by the Western and the Orthodox churches (to be discussed later). Moreover, not only have different theological traditions prioritised certain terms and concepts at the expense of others, they have also used some of the terms in different senses. Kelly Kapic explains, for example, that although Luther did use the term "sanctification" in his writings, he did not distinguish it from justification as a separate act,[26] which is in contrast with the Calvinist practice, whereby justification and sanctification are viewed as two distinct (though complementary) concepts.[27]

To summarise, even this brief overview is enough to illustrate that a number of different factors can profoundly shape the interpretation of the biblical metaphors related to spiritual transformation and growth, leading to theoretical positions that are not always fully compatible with each other. It is noteworthy, however, that these positions have not been static over the centuries but

---

25. Dunn, *The Theology of Paul*, 332.

26. That is, Luther used the term in the sense of definitive rather than progressive sanctification; Kelly M. Kapic, "Faith, Hope and Love: A Theological Meditation on Suffering and Sanctification," in *Sanctification: Explorations in Theology and Practice*, ed. Kelly M. Kapic (Downers Grove, IL: IVP Academic, 2014), 217.

27. See e.g., Kevin J. Vanhoozer, "In Bright Shadow: C. S. Lewis on the Imagination for Theology and Discipleship," in *The Romantic Rationalist: God, Life, and Imagination in the Work of C. S. Lewis*, ed. John Piper and David Mathis (Wheaton: Crossway, 2014), 9.

have evolved parallel to the transformation of Christendom in the world. A remarkable example of the changing theological landscape was the production of the *Joint Declaration on the Doctrine of Justification*[28] by the Catholic Church and the Lutheran World Federation in 1999, expressing a common understanding of the traditionally divisive notion of justification, thereby resolving a 500-year-old conflict. There have also been several attempts over the past two decades to develop a more ecumenical interpretation of the concept of deification/theosis by reconciling Eastern Orthodox and Western perceptions (see below).

As mentioned in the introduction of this chapter, in order to obtain a representative range of salient theological construals of spiritual transformation, three clusters of terms have been selected: (1) sanctification, justification, and related concepts; (2) deification/theosis and related concepts; and (3) variations on being conformed to the divine image. For the purpose of providing some initial orientation—and admittedly at the risk of oversimplification—the metaphors in the first cluster are most often used in paradigms that interpret spiritual formation largely *figuratively*, emphasising the believer's moral transformation. Deification/theosis takes a more *ontological* approach by also suggesting the involvement of a level of experiential reality in the process. The metaphor at the centre of the third cluster, being conformed to the divine image, has been associated equally with the figurative and the ontological senses, and several scholars would consider it the principal expression to subsume all the different forms of spiritual development in the New Testament; it is this reason that warrants a separate discussion of this metaphor, even though it is often used alongside both justification/sanctification and theosis in the literature.

---

28. "Joint Declaration on the Doctrine of Justification," The Lutheran World Federation, https://www.lutheranworld.org/jddj.

In the following discussion, these three groups of concepts will be taken as representative of the variety of expressions of spiritual maturation, and it will be examined to what extent the fruit of the Spirit represents the end-product for each of them. We shall start the exploration by offering a brief description of the relevant concepts, but it needs to be emphasised that this overview is merely to provide a broad characterisation of the issues rather than to evaluate or contrast the various notions—the latter task would require a more extensive and nuanced treatment of the various concepts and categories, one that goes beyond the scope of the current book.

Sanctification, Justification, and Related Concepts

There is a cluster of terms in the theological literature—"conversion," "regeneration," "justification," "sanctification," as well as subcategories of sanctification such as definitive, progressive, and entire sanctification—that are often used in the same broad thematic domain, often with overlapping or even exchangeable semantic meaning. Excursus 4 showed that this complicated terminological situation is partly rooted in the lack of an exact correspondence between biblical metaphors and theological technical terms. To illustrate this issue further, let us consider the relationship between the two key terms within this cluster, "justification" and "sanctification." While the most common theological understanding would suggest that justification refers to the dramatic starting point of the salvation process and sanctification concerns some kind of subsequent progressive spiritual "fine-tuning" as believers are discipled into becoming citizens of the kingdom of God, some verses of Scripture are not fully consistent with such a clear-cut sequential understanding; here are two oft-cited examples:

And that is what some of you were. But you were washed, you were sanctified, you were justified in the name of the Lord Jesus Christ and by the Spirit of our God. (1 Cor 6:11)

> And those he predestined, he also called; those he called, he also jus-
> tified; those he justified, he also glorified. (Rom 8:30)

In the first passage, the usual order of the terms "justified" and "sanctified" is reversed, while in the second example, sanctification is simply
omitted from the order of salvation, thereby causing understandable
theological headaches.[29] The picture is further complicated by the fact
that the term "justification" assumed special significance during the
Reformation; as the preamble of the *Joint Declaration on the Doctrine of
Justification* by the Lutheran World Federation and the Roman Catholic
Church states, "The doctrine of justification was of central importance
for the Lutheran Reformation of the sixteenth century. . . . The doctrine
of justification was particularly asserted and defended in its Reformation
shape and special valuation over against the Roman Catholic Church and
theology of that time . . . From the Reformation perspective, justification
was the crux of all the disputes."[30]

As is well known, the dispute was to a great extent related to the
agency involved in salvation, contrasting the role of divine agency/grace
and human efforts/works. Luther famously held the principle that we are
justified—or made righteous in God's eyes—by faith and not by works,[31]
and accordingly, as Dunn underlines, "In Lutheranism the metaphor of
'justification' became the article by which the church stands or falls, and
all the other metaphors were subordinated to it."[32] Although Luther did
sometimes use the term "sanctification," he did it in a secondary manner and not entirely consistently,[33] and as a result, in Lutheran theology
sanctification has often been sidelined. For example, the three-volume
summary of systematic theology by renowned Lutheran theologian

---

29. See e.g., Haley Goranson Jacob, *Conformed to the Image of His Son: Reconsidering Paul's Theology of Glory in Romans* (Downers Grove, IL: IVP Academic, 2018), 5–6.

30. https://www.lutheranworld.org/jddj.

31. For an accessible summary, see Tomlin, *Spiritual Fitness*, 92–97.

32. James D. G. Dunn, "If Paul Could Believe Both in Justification by Faith and Judgment according to Works, Why Should That Be a Problem for Us?," in *Four Views on the Role of Works at the Final Judgment*, ed. Robert N. Wilkin et al. (Grand Rapids: Zondervan, 2013), 121.

33. See e.g., Kapic, "Faith, Hope and Love," 217; A. Sheir-Jones, "Sanctification," in *New Dictionary of Theology: Historical and Systematic*, ed. Martin Davie et al. (Downers Grove, IL: IVP Academic, 2016), 805–806.

Wolfhart Pannenberg[34] does not include a focused discussion of sanctification at all, and the term "sanctification" does not appear in the main body of the entire *Joint Declaration* mentioned above (and indeed, in Lutheran circles sanctification has sometimes been explicitly considered a problem issue that is best avoided[35]).

This prioritisation of justification, however, reduced the theological space to address ongoing spiritual growth or the believer's own efforts to lead a more righteous life—efforts that the Bible recurringly calls for. As a result of this narrowing, Calvinist views have deviated from the Lutheran tradition in that they also highlight the importance of sanctification. In the current discussion we shall follow the arguably most common theological interpretation of the two notions, namely that sanctification involves ongoing spiritual formation following the initial "turning point" usually referred to as justification, conversion, or regeneration. Accordingly, for the purpose of exploring spiritual formation it is sanctification that is of specific relevance, but Concept 6.2 offers a brief overview of the other terms within the cluster.

Concept 6.2: Brief Summaries of Justification, Conversion, and Regeneration

The term "justification" is derived from the verb "to justify" (*dikaioō*), which has the legal meaning of "declaring righteous," and Richard Hays describes its theological essence as "God's covenant-faithfulness which declares persons full participants in

---

34. Wolfhart Pannenberg, *Systematic Theology*, trans. Geoffrey W. Bromiley, vols. 1–3 (Edinburgh: T&T Clark, 1991–1998).

35. E.g., in a summary of the Lutheran view of sanctification, Forde goes on record to state that "talk about sanctification is dangerous. It is too seductive for the old being. What seems to have happened in the tradition is that sanctification has been sharply distinguished from justification, and thus separated out as the part of the 'salvationing' we are to do. God alone does the justifying simply by declaring the ungodly to be so, for Jesus' sake." Garhard O. Forde, "The Lutheran View," in *Christian Spirituality: Five Views of Sanctification*, ed. L. Donald Alexander (Downers Grove, IL: IVP Academic, 1988), 15.

the community of God's people."[36] He also emphasises that God's sovereign act of incorporating a person into the believers' community is not conditioned on moral uprightness on the part of the person (Rom 5:6–11), nor does it offer "a magical transformation of moral character."[37] As John Frame succinctly puts it, "Justification is God's declaring us righteous, not making us righteous."[38]

Because justification is typically understood as God's initial gift based on the believer's faith, it is closely linked to two other terms, "conversion" and "regeneration." Regarding the former, the biblical verb expressing the act of a person turning or returning to God is *strephō* and its cognate *epistrephō*. However, this verb is most often used in Scripture in its literal sense of "to turn," while its spiritual application is rare (e.g., Matt 18:3; Acts 15:3).[39] Similarly, the noun used for "converts" (*prosēlytos*) only appears four times,[40] and the New Testament contains a number of high-profile conversion stories (e.g., the conversion of Paul, the Ethiopian eunuch, or Cornelius) without using a specific term to denote the event.[41] For example, during Pentecost, which describes the dramatic conversion of the first group of people in Jerusalem, the converts are simply referred to as "those who accepted his message" (Acts 2:41).

The term "regeneration" or "rebirth" (*palingenesia*) is often used by Calvinist theologians to denote the beginning of salvation.[42] It appears in the Bible only twice (Matt 19:28; Titus 3:5), but

---

36. Richard B. Hays, "Justification," in *ABD*, ed. David Noel Freedman (New York: Doubleday, 1992), 1131.

37. Hays, "Justification," 1132.

38. John M. Frame, *Salvation Belongs to the Lord: An Introduction to Systematic Theology* (Phillipsburg, NJ: P&R, 2006), 211–212.

39. See e.g., Daniel L. Akin, "Conversion," in *Holman Illustrated Bible Dictionary*, ed. Chad Brand et al. (Nashville: Holman, 2003), 335; James I. Packer, "Conversion," in *New Bible Dictionary*, ed. I. Howard Marshall et al. (Downers Grove, IL: InterVarsity, 1996), 222.

40. Matt 23:15; Acts 2:11; 6:5; 13:43.

41. Beverly Roberts Gaventa, "Conversion," in *ABD*, ed. David Noel Freedman (New York: Doubleday, 1992), 1132; as she explains, Paul refers to the conversions of others as calling (1 Cor 1:2), purchasing (1 Cor 6:20), liberating (Rom 6:17–18), or giving grace (Rom 3:21–26) to human beings.

42. See e.g., Blocher, "Sanctification by Faith?," 59.

the concept of being "born again" is a featured theme in John 3:1–8 when Jesus explains to Nicodemus that "no one can see the kingdom of God unless they are born again" (v. 3; see also 1 Pet 1:3). As a singular and instantaneous event of spiritual renewal, "regeneration" is a companion term of conversion,[43] but Wayne Grudem submits that it can also be seen as the first phase of sanctification in the sense that it involves a spiritual and moral change.[44] Interestingly, the image of new birth has become one of the dominant metaphors of salvation in contemporary popular Christianity.[45]

Sanctification and Its Subcategories

In his systematic theology, Grudem explains that the most common understanding of sanctification concerns ongoing spiritual development towards maturity as a Christian believer: "The ordinary course of a Christian's life will involve continual growth in sanctification, and it is something that the New Testament encourages us to give effort and attention to."[46] Indeed, the NT message about the believer's spiritual formation is that it is not finished with their initial turning to God, but continues throughout their lifetime.[47] This spiritual progression is primarily discussed in contemporary theology under the rubric of "progressive sanctification" (with the "progressive" modifier sometimes omitted though implied), and in this sense the notion is a close companion of the process of developing spiritual maturity discussed earlier. Scriptural examples of the process of sanctification also include biblical passages that do not contain the word "holy" or its derivatives; for example, 2 Pet 3:18 is often seen as a

---

43. A. J. Stobart, "Regeneration," in *New Dictionary of Theology: Historical and Systematic*, ed. Martin Davie et al. (Downers Grove, IL: IVP Academic, 2016), 753.

44. Wayne Grudem, *Systematic Theology: An Introduction to Biblical Doctrine*, 2nd ed (Grand Rapids: Zondervan Academic, 2020), 925.

45. Dunn, *The Theology of Paul*, 332.

46. Grudem, *Systematic Theology*, 925.

47. A good illustration is the unmistakable ongoing element in Paul's call in 2 Cor 7:1 to "purify ourselves from everything that contaminates body and spirit, perfecting holiness out of reverence for God."

prime example of the biblical emphasis on the need for ongoing progress in the Christian life without containing sanctification language: "But grow in the grace and knowledge of our Lord and Saviour Jesus Christ."[48]

It should be noted, however, that because the verb "to sanctify" (*hagiazō*) simply means "to make holy," it has a fairly wide sphere of reference, applicable to any person, place, occasion, or object that has been "set apart" for nonsecular use.[49] For example, in psychology there is even a nontheistic, psychospiritual sense of the verb, referring to "a process through which aspects of life are perceived as having divine character and significance."[50] Moreover and consistent with the multiple senses of biblical metaphors discussed earlier, scriptural occurrences of the Greek term for "sanctification" do not always refer to an ongoing process but rather to an accomplished act (e.g., Heb 10:10: "And it is by God's will that we have been sanctified through the offering of the body of Jesus Christ once for all" [NRSV]).[51] Sometimes this realised aspect of sanctification is distinguished from the more common progressive meaning by referring to it as "definitive sanctification";[52] therefore, although the

---

48. E.g., G. A. Cole, "Sanctification," 721; Walter A. Elwell and Philip Wesley Comfort, *Tyndale Bible Dictionary* (Wheaton: Tyndale House, 2001), 1164.

49. Reginald E. O. White, "Sanctification," in *Evangelical Dictionary of Theology*, ed. Daniel J. Treier and Walter A. Elwell (Grand Rapids: Baker Academic, 2017), 770; A. Sheir-Jones, "Sanctification," 804–805. Moreover, in accordance with the broad nature of the adjective "holy," Christian believers in the New Testament are frequently (over sixty times) referred to by the noun form of the word (*hagios*), as "holy people" (NIVUK) or "saints" (NRSVA, ESV, NKJV).

50. Kenneth I. Pargament and Annette Mahoney, "Sacred Matters: Sanctification as a Vital Topic for the Psychology of Religion," *International Journal for the Psychology of Religion* 15, no. 3 (2005): 183. As Deal and Magyar-Russell summarise, psychological research on sanctification has been applied to marriage and relationships, strivings and goals, parenting, work, loss, sexuality, pregnancy, nature, forgiveness, community life, and social justice. Paul J. Deal and Gina Magyar-Russell, "Sanctification Theory: Is Nontheistic Sanctification Nontheistic Enough?," *Psychology of Religion and Spirituality* 10, no. 3 (2018): 244.

51. Murray even submits that "in the New Testament the most characteristic terms that refer to sanctification are used, not of a process, but of *a once-for-all definitive act*." John Murray, *Systematic Theology*, vol. 2 of *The Collected Writings of John Murray* (Edinburgh: Banner of Truth, 1997), 277. In contrast, Chung maintains that "the predominant occurrence of New Testament sanctification language occurs in the context of a lifelong process of ethical transformation effected by the Holy Spirit." Miyon Chung, "Conversion and Sanctification," in *The Cambridge Companion to Evangelical Theology*, ed. Timothy Larsen and Daniel J. Treier (Cambridge: Cambridge University Press, 2007), 119.

52. E.g., Blocher, "Sanctification by Faith?," 59; Frame, *Salvation Belongs to the Lord*, 213, 325; Anthony A. Hoekema, "The Reformed Perspective," in *Five Views on Sanctification*, ed. Stanley N. Gundry (Grand Rapids: Zondervan, 1987), 75–77.

applied imagery is different, definitive sanctification is simultaneous with justification[53] and with regeneration.[54] The Wesleyan tradition within Protestantism has introduced a further interpretation of sanctification, termed "entire sanctification." This was seen as building on justification by constituting a subsequent single event in which a believer attains a higher level of holiness, a distinct experience or receiving "second grace."[55]

Finally, a unique feature of progressive sanctification is that it involves an inherent theological paradox: although it is divinely fuelled by the grace of God, its successful flow also requires some sort of a collaboration of the believer,[56] as evidenced by the numerous ethical exhortations and calls for holiness throughout the biblical corpus. In other words, the success of the process of sanctification is dependent to some extent on the participant's efforts and can thus be consciously cultivated. This aspect will be discussed in detail in chapter 7, exploring possible models for harmonising the cooperation between divine and human agency.

Deification and Related Themes

Let us continue the brief overview of the theological landscape of spiritual formation by turning to a second cluster of terms and metaphors centred around the notion of "deification." In his overview of Christian theology, Anglican scholar Anthony Thiselton rightly points out that both deification and sanctification are "processes of becoming Christlike by the power of the Holy Spirit,"[57] which raises the question of how the two concepts differ from each other. To start with, "deification"—also called "theosis"[58] or "divinisation"—is not a biblical term but was developed

---

53. See e.g., Hoekema, "The Reformed Perspective," 75.
54. See e.g., Frame, *Salvation Belongs to the Lord*, 213.
55. Sheir-Jones, "Sanctification," 806; see also Grudem, *Systematic Theology*, 926.
56. See e.g., Blocher, "Sanctification by Faith?," 61; Hoekema, "The Reformed Perspective," 77.
57. Anthony C. Thiselton, *The Thiselton Companion to Christian Theology* (Grand Rapids: Eerdmans, 2015), 279.
58. According to Stamoolis, some scholars prefer to retain the Greek form of the term, *theōsis*, rather than use the Latin-based version ("deification") to avoid the latter's pantheistic overtones. James J. Stamoolis, "Theosis," in *Evangelical Dictionary of Theology*, ed. Daniel J. Treier and Walter A. Elwell (Grand Rapids: Baker Academic, 2017), 875.

after several centuries of theological reflection about biblical references to a more organic/ontological transformational communion with God than what sanctification usually represents (see CONCEPT 6.3). Although the concept frequently occurs in the writings of the church fathers—from Clement and Irenaeus to Athanasius and Augustine—it was not developed into a firm doctrine by them but was used in a rather nontechnical and nonuniform manner, simply taking it for granted that the readers knew what the notion meant.[59] Indeed, even what is usually considered the first definition of the term (by Pseudo-Dionysius around the turn of the sixth century AD) is rather general: "Deification is the attaining of likeness to God and union with him so far as is possible."[60] Yet, despite the somewhat underspecified nature of the concept, it was the dominant model of salvation in the early Christian tradition,[61] and later it became a core component of Eastern Orthodox theology. The notion has also generated a great deal of traction in Western theological reflection, both in Protestant and Catholic circles,[62] and Olson, for example, states, "When

---

59. Daniel A. Keating, "Typologies of Deification," *International Journal of Systematic Theology* 17, no. 3 (2015): 277. Likewise, in the introduction to an edited volume on deification in Christian theology, Finlan and Kharlamov conclude, "The popularity of the idea is matched by a lack of precise definition. The church fathers argue for, rather than spell out, deification." Stephen Finlan and Vladimir Kharlamov, "Introduction," in *Theosis: Deification in Christian Theology*, ed. Stephen Finlan and Vladimir Kharlamov (Eugene, OR: Pickwick, 2006), 4. For similar conclusions, see e.g., Athanasios Despotis, "From Conversion according to Paul and 'John' to Theosis in the Greek Patristic Tradition," *Horizons in Biblical Theology* 38 (2016): 94–95; Paul L. Gavrilyuk, "The Retrieval of Deification: How a Once-Despised Archaism Became an Ecumenical Desideratum," *Modern Theology* 25, no. 4 (2009): 651; Norman Russell, *The Doctrine of Deification in the Greek Patristic Tradition* (Oxford: Oxford University Press, 2006), 1.

60. Cited by Russell, *The Doctrine of Deification*, 1. Moreover, as Williams concludes in her authoritative monograph on the subject, even the Byzantine theologian who is most closely associated with the development of a deification theology, Gregory Palamas (1296—1359), tends to offer a cluster of related terms by means of explanation instead of a definition proper, including "virtue, knowledge, vision, contemplation, light, glory, grace, adoption, participation and union." The closest Palamas ever got to offering a definition involved citing Maximus the Confessor, stating that theosis is a "mystical union with God beyond intellect and reason." Anna N. Williams, *The Ground of Union: Deification in Aquinas and Palamas* (New York: Oxford University Press, 1999), 105–106.

61. Williams, *The Ground of Union*, 27.

62. E.g., Michael J. Christensen and Jeffery A. Wittung, eds., *Partakers of the Divine Nature: The History and Development of Deification in the Christian Traditions* (Grand Rapids: Baker Academic, 2007); Collins, *Partaking in Divine Nature*; M. David Litwa, *We Are Being Transformed: Deification in Paul's Soteriology* (Berlin: De Gruyter, 2012); David Vincent Meconi and Carl E.

asked to identify who is talking about deification in Western theological circles, my initial response is 'Who isn't?'"[63]

Concept 6.3: On the Meaning of Deification

The best place in the Bible to start getting a sense of the notion of deification is 2 Pet 1:4, which most scholars would regard as the proof text for the concept:[64] "[Jesus] has granted to us his precious and very great promises, so that through them you may become partakers [literally: sharers] of the divine nature, having escaped from the corruption that is in the world because of sinful desire" (ESV).

Emil Bartos explains that the expression "partakers of the divine nature" has become a sort of motto of Orthodox theology's view of deification: for many, "to be deified means to become 'partakers of the divine nature.'"[65] Orthodox theologians have taken it for granted that partaking involves a realistic and organic (i.e., ontological) change in the believer, one that Roger Olson describes as "a real, substance-transforming participation in God's own nature that elevates one above mere humanity."[66] However, the "partaking of the divine nature" expression is unique and highly unusual in the

Olson, eds., *Called to Be the Children of God: The Catholic Theology of Human Deification* (San Francisco: Ignatius, 2016).

63. Roger E. Olson, "Deification in Contemporary Theology," *Theology Today* 64 (2007): 188. As he continues, "It seems that almost every Protestant and Catholic theologian writing creatively and constructively in the last two to three decades has found it necessary to address the subject, and many are trying to incorporate it into their emerging theological visions." In fact, the main contribution to the doctrine of deification over the past decade has primarily come from the Western theological tradition; for an overview, see Keating, "Typologies of Deification," 267.

64. See e.g., David Vincent Meconi and Carl E. Olson, "The Scriptural Roots of Christian Deification," in *Called to Be the Children of God: The Catholic Theology of Human Deification*, ed. David Vincent Meconi and Carl E. Olson (San Francisco: Ignatius, 2016), 36; Williams, *The Ground of Union*, 27.

65. Emil Bartos, "Deification," in *New Dictionary of Theology: Historical and Systematic*, ed. Martin Davie et al. (Downers Grove, IL: IVP Academic, 2016), 246.

66. Olson, "Deification," 193.

Scriptures, and therefore its exegesis has been rather fluid—a point well illustrated by the fact that, in contrast to the Orthodox views, Karl Barth insisted that the phrase merely denotes "practical fellowship of Christians with God,"[67] and in Roman Catholic theology the concept is seen as a central component of "sanctifying grace."[68]

While the Bible contains no explicit mention of the word "deification," there is a general agreement amongst scholars that many aspects of the notion can be found throughout the writings of the Old and New Testament;[69] that is, certain Bible passages appear to point to some form of human–divine communion that goes beyond the kind of moral/spiritual maturation with which the notion of sanctification is usually associated. Three primary examples of such "circumstantial evidence" are the Genesis account of humans being created in the image and likeness of God, the incarnation, and the transfiguration (CONCEPT 6.4 summarises their relevance to deification).

Concept 6.4: Three Biblical Themes Related to Deification

Created in the image and likeness of God: In an anthology exploring the Catholic theology of human deification, Meconi and Olson submit that the "anthropological bedrock of deification is found in Scripture's opening: we are made in the image and likeness of a God."[70] While this theme is most clearly expressed in Gen

---

67. Karl Barth, *The Christian Life: Church Dogmatics IV/4; Lecture Fragments* (Grand Rapids: Eerdmans, 1981), 28.

68. See Alston, *Divine Nature and Human Language*, 243; as he adds, in *Summa Theologiae* (Iae 2a, Q.100, art. 4) Thomas Aquinas also speaks of "the light of grace" as "a participation in the divine nature."

69. See e.g., Collins, *Partaking in Divine Nature*, 38.

70. Meconi and Olson, "Christian Deification," 18.

1:26–27, these scholars also highlight Gen 3:5: "For God knows that when you eat from it your eyes will be opened, and *you will be like God*" (emphasis added), offering an intriguing argument: "The enemy of our human nature realized that he could not tempt paradisiacal creatures like Adam and Eve with anything they already possessed perfectly. The one thing for which they were created that they still lacked was that deifying union which would transform their mere human nature into something even more glorious."[71]

The incarnation: The significance of the incarnation for deification lies in the fact that it provides a biblical example for divine–human communion. As Norman Russell explains in his historical overview of the emergence of the notion of deification, many church fathers, particularly of the Alexandrian tradition, considered the concepts of the Incarnation of God and the deification of man "to be correlative to one another."[72] In this understanding—shared by patristic theologians such as Justin, Irenaeus, Origen, and Athanasius—deification is seen to represent a realistic approach to the transformation of humanity as a consequence of the incarnation.[73] After all, given that Jesus, born from the communion of Mary and the Holy Spirit, is portrayed in the Bible (e.g., at the transfiguration—see below) as a deified human being, it is not unreasonable to assume that the born-again Christian, who has the indwelling Spirit, can also share some degree of this deified nature.

The transfiguration: The biblical narrative of the transfiguration of Jesus (Matt 17:1–13; Mark 9:2–13; Luke 9:28–36) describes the supernatural, mystical experience of three disciples (Peter, James, and John), who witnessed a bright, unearthly light radiating from Jesus on the Mount of Transfiguration. This was perceived

---

71. Meconi and Olson, 19.

72. Russell, *The Doctrine of Deification*, 7.

73. According to Olsen ("Deification," 190), "[Deification] is possible only because of the Incarnation, which made divinity available to humanity, and through the Holy Spirit, who communicates it to people."

to be the mark of the metamorphosis of the Son of Man and, more generally, as the biblical model for the transformation of humanity. As such, it had a critical role in the development of the theology of deification in the Eastern Orthodox church.[74]

Two further Scripture-based theological notions, "adoption" and "union with God," are also often associated with the deification paradigm, even though not all the literature on these themes is written in this vein, and not every deification scholar would draw on these notions in support of their arguments. CONCEPT 6.5 offers a brief overview of the two concepts.

Concept 6.5: "Adoption" and "Union with God" and Their Connection with Deification

Adoption: The Bible testifies in many places that believers are the *sons* of God the Father,[75] and Paul specifically uses the term "adoption for sonship" (*huiothesia*) several times (Rom 8:15, 23; 9:4; Gal 4:5; see also Eph 1:5). This is a legal term referring to the full legal standing of an adopted male heir in Roman culture,[76] but in Paul's usage, entering into God's family is not merely a legal or theoretical abstraction but also a realistic act of sharing the Holy Spirit, as declared in Rom 8:15: "The Spirit you received

74. Vladimir Lossky, *In the Image and Likeness of God* (New York: St Vladimir's Seminary Press, 1974), 60.

75. According to Meconi and Olson ("Christian Deification," 20–21), the precursor of the notion of adoption is the OT concept of filiation (e.g., Israel is God's son: Exod 4:22; Hos 11:1), which has continuation in the NT reference to "children of God" (e.g., John 1:12; Rom 8:14, 16; 1 John 3:1), and which culminates in calling God the "Father" or "Abba" (e.g., Matt 8:6; Rom 8:15; Gal 4:6).

76. See e.g., Peter H. Davids, "Adoption," in *Evangelical Dictionary of Theology*, ed. Daniel J. Treier and Walter A. Elwell (Grand Rapids: Baker Academic, 2017), 30–31.

brought about your adoption to sonship. And by him we cry, 'Abba, Father'" (see also Gal 4:4–7). This process of adoption may be understood to result in a more organic intimacy with the divine than what the notion of sanctification usually represents; as David Litwa points out, such a kinship metaphor expresses a form of relatedness that can be called "genetic,"[77] and according to Grant Macaskil, the "intimate communion of sons with their heavenly father in the new covenant" is indeed a form of deification proper.[78] Athanasios Despot makes the organic nature of the resulting connection even more prominent when he submits that "the converts share one and the same Spirit, which is the Spirit of God the Father, the Creator, and this practically means that the Spirit re-creates, i.e., transforms the believers and makes them partakers of a transcendent and divine reality."[79]

Union with God: The notion of the "union with God" has multiple biblical sources, and it subsumes a number of different metaphors.[80] The Pauline Epistles contain no fewer than eighty-three occurrences of the term "in Christ" and a further forty-seven instances of "in the Lord (Jesus)," indicating that Paul used the phrase as shorthand for some meaning that was highly important for him. This significance is further evidenced by the fact that the notion of a union with Christ also appears in other expressions; for example, in Gal 2:20 the apostle declares that "Christ lives in me," and later that his desire about the Galatian believers is that "Christ is formed in you" (4:19). The "in Christ" image also occurs in the Johannine writings; in John 15:4 we read, "Abide in me as I abide in you" (NRSVA; the NIVUK translates the verb as "remain"), and in 1 John 2:5–6 the image is expanded: "By this we may be sure

---

77. Litwa, *We Are Being Transformed*, 12.

78. Grant Macaskill, *Union with Christ in the New Testament* (New York: Oxford University Press, 2013), 73–74.

79. Despotis, "From Conversion to Theosis," 98.

80. For a good summary, see Michael Allen, *Sanctification*, New Studies in Dogmatics (Grand Rapids: Zondervan, 2017), 143–144.

that we are in him: whoever says, 'I abide in him,' ought to walk just as he walked" (NRSVA). We also find expressions of some sort of union with God without the "in Christ" marker in the New Testament, for example the marriage between Jesus and the church.[81]

There is no consensus in the literature about the extent to which "union with God/Christ" falls under the broader category of deification, because the various expressions for participatory union can be also seen as aspects of psychological identification rather than ontological transformation.[82] On the other hand, while Dunn concludes that the locational meaning of the "in Christ" image is not entirely clear, he also points out that it unmistakably involves language of indwelling and participation,[83] and, as seen earlier, the original definitions of deification by Pseudo-Dionysius specifically include a reference to union with God. Indeed, Despotis argues that the various images of union with Christ clearly reflect an "existential transformation," which causes an "unusually serious change in the convert's biography . . . and goes beyond the limits of the human language."[84]

---

81. Campbell argues that four metaphors are particularly relevant in this respect: (1) The church as the *body of Christ* (e.g., Rom 12:4–5; 1 Cor 6:15–16; 12:12–27; Eph 1:22–23; Col 1:18), which may also be related in some ways to the *Eucharist*. (2) The believer's body is *God's temple* in which the Holy Spirit dwells (e.g., 1 Cor 3:16–17; 6:19; 2 Cor 6:16; Eph 2:22). (3) The *marriage* between Jesus and the church (e.g., Luke 5:34–35; 1 Cor 6:15–17; 2 Cor 11:2; Rev 19:7). (4) Clothing *oneself* with Christ (e.g., Rom 13:14; Gal 3:27). Constantine R. Campbell, "Metaphor, Reality, and Union with Christ," in *"In Christ" in Paul: Explorations in Paul's Theology of Union and Participation*, ed. Michael J. Thate, Kevin J. Vanhoozer, and Constantine R. Campbell (Tübingen: Mohr Siebeck, 2014), 61.

82. E.g., Vanhoozer ("In Bright Shadow," 5) states, "Union is a matter of subjective perception rather than of an objective condition." In fact, Olson ("Deification," 189) explains that for several scholars who are "wary of deification, traditional Protestant ideas such as union with Christ do all that deification is supposed to do without the latter's pitfalls."

83. Dunn, *New Testament Theology*, 91.

84. Despotis, "From Conversion to Theosis," 96. Collins (*Partaking in Divine Nature*, 48) offers a similar view: "The metaphorical status of deification is particularly important to hold on to, as the language of imitation and participation may suggest a level of experiential reality which goes beyond the metaphorical. This is in no way to deny the reality of the experience of 'mystical union' with God. But it is a warning against reducing the mystery of Christ to the mechanism of human words. This is why the notion of 'unknowing' remains so crucial in the discussion of the metaphor of deification."

Being Conformed to the Divine Image

"Being conformed to the divine image" has been understood by several scholars as the central expression of spiritual transformation in the New Testament[85]; N. T. Wright, for example, submits that "the whole New Testament insists that the point of Christian living is the remaking of humans in God's image."[86] One of the key passages containing the expression, Rom 8:29, states that Christian believers are "to be conformed to the image of his Son, in order that he might be the firstborn within a large family" (NRSVA). The Greek term for "conformed to" (*symmorphos*) literally means "jointly formed" and it can be used to express "similar" or "fashioned like/onto." How can one become "jointly formed with" or "fashioned like/onto" Jesus's image? As Haley Jacob summarises, the most common interpretation of *symmorphos*, particularly within popular Christian theology and writing, has been that of spiritual or moral conformity, not unlike sanctification.[87] Grudem further elucidates the ethical link with sanctification by emphasizing, "As we grow in holiness we grow in conformity to the image of Christ, and more and more of the beauty of his character is seen in our own lives. This is the goal of perfect sanctification, which we hope and long for."[88] Tidball captures the essence succinctly: "The heart of holiness lies in the restoration of God's image in us."[89]

---

85. E.g., Dunn (*New Testament Theology*, 94) states that in the Pauline corpus "the transformation is explicitly understood as a being conformed to the image of God in Christ," and elsewhere Dunn (*The Theology of Paul*, 468) explains that it can be regarded as "Paul's most basic conception of the salvation process . . . in particular, as transformation to become like Christ." He employs this image in several variations, using permutations of "being/becoming," "conformed to/transformed into/conformity to," and "Christ/the image of Christ." Likewise, Samra (*Being Conformed to Christ*, 110) concludes: "Our analysis of conformity to the image of Christ also supports our assertion that this motif is the central motif for Paul's concept of maturity. The motif is found in passages widely recognized as being foundational to Paul's thought (Rom 8, 12; 1 Cor 15; 2 Cor 2–4; Gal 3–4; Phil 3) and appears in connection with central themes of Pauline theology."

86. N. T. Wright, *After You Believe*, 251.

87. Jacob, *Conformed to the Image of His Son*, 5. A popular example is Boa's work on spiritual formation: Kenneth Boa, *Conformed to His Image: Biblical, Practical Approaches to Spiritual Formation*, rev. ed. (Grand Rapids: Zondervan Academic, 2020).

88. Grudem, *Systematic Theology*, 937. Hoekema ("The Reformed Perspective," 66) argues in a similar way: "Sanctification means that we are being renewed in accordance with the image of God—that, in other words, we are becoming more like God, or like Christ, who is the perfect image of God."

89. Tidball, "Holiness," 26.

The process of being "conformed to the image of his Son" (Rom 8:29) can also be understood in a less figurative and more realistic or ontological manner. In 2 Cor 3:18 Paul states that "all of us . . . are being transformed into the same image from one degree of glory to another" (NRSVA), using the same Greek word for "being transformed" (*metamorphoō*) as it appears in Mark 9:2 and Matthew 17:2 to describe the transfiguration of Jesus. This is unlikely to be a coincidence since this verb is very rare in the Scriptures,[90] and accordingly, Litwa expresses the widely held belief that "becoming the image, therefore, carries implications for deification."[91] In an analysis of Rom 8:29 and 2 Cor 3:18, Volker Rabens comes to a similar conclusion—namely, that Paul uses the expression of "being conformed to the likeness/image" with the same meaning as the "participation" element of deification, since "it is hard to imagine how in 2 Corinthians 3:18, becoming like Christ would not involve ontological change."[92]

Metaphors of Spiritual Formation and the Fruit of the Spirit

After the brief overview of the various biblical and theological terminology of spiritual transformation and growth, we are in a position to examine the claim made in the first part of this chapter that spiritual growth is operationalised in Scripture as a process of character formation aimed at approximating as closely as possible the ideal Christlike character outlined in Gal 5:22–23. This claim was shown to be valid with regard to reaching spiritual *maturity*, so let us now consider whether we can also associate the fruit of the Spirit directly with the end-products of sanctification, deification, and being conformed to the divine image.

---

90. Besides these three examples there is only one other occurrence of it in the whole of the NT canon, in Rom 12:2.

91. Litwa, *We Are Being Transformed*, 26.

92. Volker Rabens, "The Holy Spirit and Deification in Paul: A 'Western' Perspective," in *The Holy Spirit and the Church According to the New Testament*, ed. Predrag Dragutinovic et al. (Tübingen: Mohr Siebeck, 2016), 211.

Sanctification and the Fruit of the Spirit

As we have seen, at the most fundamental level sanctification means "making holy," and therefore an important question in understanding the nature of the human sanctification process is what this desired "holiness" entails. In an overview of holiness when applied to humans, Tidball argues that "holiness does not consist of stopping bad behaviour and eschewing sinful attitudes alone but of replacing them with good behaviour and pursuing Christlike attitudes. . . . Holiness is more than avoiding sin. It is cultivating the character of Christ in us."[93] Given that, as we have seen in chapter 2, the fruit of the Spirit reflects a Christlike character, we may view the process of sanctification as a process to grow the fruit in the believer, and indeed, as CONCEPT 6.6 illustrates, several theologians in the past have come to a similar conclusion.

Concept 6.6: A Selection of Scholarly Views Linking Sanctification and the Fruit of the Spirit

- "The marks of sanctification are the fruit of the Spirit (Gal 5:22-23)."[94]
- "Love . . . encompasses the fruit of the Spirit and is therefore one of the chief results of the sanctifying work of the Spirit."[95]
- "Sanctification is . . . chiefly the outflow of overflowing life within the soul, the 'fruit' of the Spirit in all manner of Christian graces (Gal. 5:22–23)."[96]
- "Because of the indwelling presence of the Holy Spirit and His power and direction, a Christian can progressively grow in sanctification. Although the old nature is present, by the power of

---

93. Tidball, "Holiness," 28.
94. Blocher, "Sanctification by Faith?," 64.
95. Stanley M. Horton, "The Pentecostal Perspective," in *Five Views on Sanctification*, ed. Stanley N. Gundry (Grand Rapids: Zondervan, 1987), 133.
96. White, "Sanctification," 771.

the Spirit the new nature can be enabled to manifest the fruit of the Spirit."[97]

- "The picture of the 'fruit' of the Spirit is the picture of a slow process that is always going on. The Spirit not only grabs us at various moments but also works inside us moment by moment, changing us to conform to the image of Christ. This is the doctrine of sanctification."[98]

- "It is the Holy Spirit who produces in us the 'fruit of the Spirit' (Gal 5:22–23), those character traits that are part of greater and greater sanctification. If we grow in sanctification we 'walk by the Spirit' and are 'led by the Spirit' (Gal 5:16–18; cf. Rom 8:14), that is, we are more and more responsive to the desires and promptings of the Holy Spirit in our life and character. The Holy Spirit is the spirit of holiness, and he produces holiness within us."[99]

Wesley also preached that entire sanctification is associated with, among other things, an increased ability to love God and one's neighbour and, what is particularly relevant from our point of view, "to bear the fruit of the Spirit."[100] Finally, it is noteworthy that when it comes to practical application in Christian counselling and therapy, sanctification is again closely associated with the fruit of the Spirit. Eric Johnson argues that Christian personal well-being is best realised through personal sanctification and that Christian mental health can be seen as synonymous

---

97. Walvoord, "The Augustinian Dispensational Perspective," 220.

98. Frame, *Salvation Belongs to the Lord*, 165.

99. Grudem, *Systematic Theology*, 932–933. Elsewhere Grudem reiterates the argument as follows: "After the initial break with sin that the Holy Spirit brings about in our lives at conversion, he also produces in us growth in holiness of life. He brings forth the '*fruit of the Spirit*' within us ('love, joy, peace, patience, kindness, goodness, faithfulness, gentleness, self-control,' Gal. 5:22–23), those qualities that reflect the character of God" (780).

100. Melvin E. Dieter, "The Wesleyan Perspective," in *Five Views on Sanctification*, ed. Stanley N. Gundry (Grand Rapids: Zondervan, 1987), 18.

with the fruit of the Spirit. Therefore he concludes, "A life characterized by love, joy, peace, patience, and so on, is what most Christian clients seek,"[101] which implies that "counsellors and therapists who work with Christians will want to work at enhancing the sanctification process in their clients as they assist them in tackling psychological issues."[102]

Deification and the Fruit of the Spirit

Russell explains in his historical overview of deification that one main line along which the concept originally developed—represented by Clement and the Cappadocian Fathers in the patristic era—construed the "ascent of the soul" through the "practice of virtue."[103] In an article considering "virtue as embodied deification," Hamalis and Papanikolaou confirm that the strong link between theosis and the Christian virtues prevailed from the apostolic age to the contemporary Eastern Orthodox Church, because the process of theosis was seen to entail the acquisition of virtues.[104] In a book-length treatise devoted entirely to the foundational passage of the theosis paradigm, 2 Pet 1:4, James Starr also concludes that partaking in the divine nature of Christ is synonymous with taking on the righteousness and moral excellence of Christ's character.[105] This ethical understanding of acquiring virtues and sharing the characteristics modelled by Jesus creates a direct connection between deification and the fruit of the Spirit, because, as Tomlin summarises, "We become God-like when we learn the virtues of love, joy, peace, patience, kindness, goodness, faithfulness, gentleness and self-control."[106] In fact, the opposite—that is, partaking in the divine nature *without* sharing the fruit of the Spirit—would be inconceivable.

---

101. Eric L. Johnson, "Sanctification," in *Baker Encyclopedia of Psychology and Counseling*, ed. David G. Benner and Peter C. Hill (Grand Rapids: Baker Academic, 1999), 1051.

102. E. L. Johnson, 1051.

103. Russell, *The Doctrine of Deification*, 14.

104. Perry T. Hamalis and Aristotle Papanikolaou, "Toward a Godly Mode of Being: Virtue as Embodied Deification," *Studies in Christian Ethics* 26, no. 3 (2013): 277–278.

105. James M. Starr, *Sharers in Divine Nature: 2 Peter 1:4 in Its Hellenistic Context* (Stockholm: Almqvist & Wiksell International, 2000), 232.

106. Tomlin, *Spiritual Fitness*, 84.

Being Conformed to the Divine Image and the Fruit of the Spirit

Given that humans were made in the image of God and that Jesus Christ is the perfect image of God (Col 1:15), commentators agree that "being conformed to the divine image" is inextricably linked to becoming aligned with the character of Christ; as Samra so clearly summarises, "To be conformed to the image of Christ is to become like Christ so that the character of Christ is manifested in the life of the believer."[107] In other words, to be conformed to the divine image is to develop a Christlike character, which has been directly linked to the fruit of the Spirit in earlier chapters. Colossians 3:9–12 makes this link with human virtues explicit: "Put on the new self, which is being renewed in knowledge in the image of its Creator. . . . As God's chosen people, holy and dearly loved, clothe yourselves with compassion, kindness, humility, gentleness and patience." Consequently, N. T. Wright submits that the essence of "Paul's whole vision of what Christian virtue is all about . . . is about being remade in God's image."[108] Complementing these points, George adds that the fruit of the Spirit may not only be the outcome but also the source of human transformation: "Each of the nine qualities flows into one another, mutually enriching and reinforcing the process of sanctification in the life of the believer."[109] Grudem expands on this dynamic, two-way relationship as follows: "The more we grow in likeness to Christ, the more we will personally experience the 'joy' and 'peace' that are part of the fruit of the Holy Spirit (Gal. 5:22), and the more we will draw near to the kind of life that we will have in heaven. Paul says that as we become more and more obedient to God, 'the fruit you get leads to sanctification and its end, eternal life' (Rom. 6:22)."[110]

---

107. Samra, *Being Conformed to Christ*, 108; see also Wood, "Christian Theories of Virtue," 295.
108. N. T. Wright, *After You Believe*, 168.
109. George, *Galatians*, 399.
110. Grudem, *Systematic Theology*, 937.

The Fruit of the Spirit and New Creation

The previous sections have established a consistent link between spiritual progression towards Christian maturity and the development of the fruit of the Spirit in the believer's personality, with the fruit offering a graphic description of the desired end-state of the developmental process. This understanding also stands to reason at a broader, creational level. We saw in chapter 5 that the composite fruit can be understood as a rounded Christlike character which is inherently outward facing, compassionate, and loving, which has internal spiritual contentment at its foundation, and which is sustained by self-discipline and steadfast perseverance. The social manifestation of this disposition is a loving and harmonious community of the saints that is sufficiently resilient to carry out the stewardship duties with which humanity has been charged. It is indicated by the Genesis accounts that the fruit of the Spirit had not been materialised in the first nuclear family, and neither were the divine principles of social living—represented by the communal aspects of fruit of the Spirit—adopted by the initial society of human stewards, leading eventually to the flood.[111] Since the "reboot" of life after the great deluge, humanity has been in the process of being transformed into citizens of the kingdom of God, and as Cole summarises, the "canonical plotline reveals the story of God's reclaiming a fallen world and establishing a new heavens and earth in which righteousness is at home."[112]

The flesh–Spirit contrast is directly relevant to this overarching transformation process, because humanity's "fleshly" inclinations were at the root of their initial antisocial and destructive behaviour, as evidenced by the "acts of the flesh" in Gal 5:19–21 or by 1 Cor 3:3: "For

---

111. It is beyond the remit of this book to examine the reasons for the absence of the fruit of the Spirit in the initial created order. Elsewhere, I have proposed a progressive creational paradigm, which can accommodate the fact that the fruit is a post-creational gift of the Holy Spirit, aimed at counterbalancing the corporeal, fleshly proclivities of humanity. Zoltán Dörnyei, *Progressive Creation and the Struggles of Humanity in the Bible: A Canonical Narrative Interpretation* (Eugene, OR: Pickwick, 2018).

112. Cole, "Sanctification," 721.

as long as there is jealousy and quarreling among you, are you not of the flesh, and behaving according to human inclinations?" (NRSVA). In contrast, the fruit of the Spirit is aimed at producing communal harmony, and indeed, Hays underlines Paul's "strong thematic emphasis on community," arguing that "Paul develops his account of the new community in Christ as a fundamental theological theme in his proclamation of the gospel."[113] Consistent with the tenor of the current discussion, Hays also associates this emphasis with the broader creational purpose of God: "What is God doing in the world in the interval between resurrection and parousia? According to Paul, God is at work through the Spirit to create communities that prefigure and embody the reconciliation and healing of the world."[114] In agreement with this understanding, Moo specifically connects the emergence of the Spirit-inspired new values to the progression from flesh-centredness to adopting the fruit of the Spirit: "'To walk according to the flesh,' then, is to have one's life determined and directed by the values of 'this world,' of the world in rebellion against God. It is a lifestyle that is purely 'human' in its orientation. To 'walk according to the Spirit,' on the other hand, is to live under the control, and according to the values, of the 'new age,' created and dominated by God's Spirit as his eschatological gift."[115]

The socialisation of humans into what Moo calls here the "new age" is often discussed in theology under the rubric of "new creation," following 2 Cor 5:17: "So if anyone is in Christ, there is a new creation: everything old has passed away; see, everything has become new!" (NRSVA). (For a brief overview of "newness" and "new creation" in the Bible, see CONCEPT 6.7.) In the light of this transformational quality of new creation, it is no accident—in fact, it was to be expected—that the theme also surfaces in Galatians, where reading together 5:6 and 6:15, "new creation" can be

---

113. Hays, *Moral Vision*, 32.
114. Hays, 32.
115. Douglas J. Moo, *The Epistle to the Romans*, NICNT (Grand Rapids: Eerdmans, 1996), 485. Likewise, N. T. Wright (*After You Believe*, 236) asserts that "the point was made, graphically and unmistakably: this was a different way to be human. Nobody had ever thought of living like that before."

equated with "faith expressing itself through love"[116]—that is, the manifestation of the fruit of the Spirit.[117]

Concept 6.7: "Newness" and "New Creation" in the Bible

In his seminal paper, "The Concept of Newness in the New Testament," Roy Harrisville asserts that the "NT kerygma includes the idea that in Jesus something entirely new has occurred, that in him a new time phase, a 'new aeon' has begun by which the redemptive activity of God comes to its conclusion."[118] The books of the New Testament refer to this emerging "newness" in a variety of terms such as "new wine" (Mark 2:22; Luke 5:37–38), "new teaching" (Mark 1:27), "new command" of love (John 13:34; 1 John 2:8), "new covenant" (Luke 22:20; 1 Cor 11:25; 2 Cor 3:6; Heb 8:8, 13; 9:15; 12:24), "new creation" (2 Cor 5:17; Gal 6:15), "new man/ humanity" (Eph 2:15; 4:24; Col 3:9–10), "new song" (Rev. 5:9; 14:3), and "new name" for believers (Rev. 2:17; 3:12). Revelation also describes that in eschatological times—"at the renewal of all things" (Matt 19:28)—there will be "a new heaven and a new earth" (Rev 21:1; cf. 2 Pet 3:13) and a "new Jerusalem" (Rev 3:12; 21:2). The cumulative presence and prominence of these concepts has led Murray Harris to submit that the theology of the New Testament "could be written around this theocentric concept of 'newness,' which is summed up in the statement . . . 'See! I make everything

---

116. Galatians 5:6: "For in Christ Jesus neither circumcision nor uncircumcision counts for anything; the only thing that counts is faith working through love" (NRSVA); Gal 6:15: "For neither circumcision nor uncircumcision is anything; but a new creation is everything!" (NRSVA). See Keener, *Galatians*, 458 for a discussion of this equivalence.

117. Indeed, as Beale (*New Testament Biblical Theology*, 687) concludes, there are "hints of a fecund new creation in Gal. 5:22–25, especially when seen against an Isaianic background," and according to N. T. Wright (*Galatians*, 339), Paul's overall purpose in Gal 5 is "to clear the ground for the genuine new humanity to emerge."

118. Roy A. Harrisville, "The Concept of Newness in the New Testament," *Journal of Biblical Literature* 74, no. 2 (1955): 73.

new!' [Rev 21:5]"[119]—indeed, the very name "New" Testament is itself testimony to the importance of this emerging "newness."[120]

The pervasive renewal themes in the New Testament have sometimes been referred to under the umbrella term of "new creation." This usage is generally broader than Paul's use of the term in 2 Cor 5:17 and Gal 6:15—the only two places in the canon where the actual phrase occurs—since the phrase is typically understood to refer to the whole ongoing process of transformation leading to the final eschatological consummation; as Mark Stephens summarises, it reflects "common scholarly parlance in which the term functions as a conceptual label to collate a range of cosmic eschatological images, not only within early Christian texts, but also in the Hebrew Bible and Second Temple Judaism."[121]

On the basis of these considerations, we may see the fruit of the Spirit as a summary of the values that humans are to acquire in new creation in order to develop into citizens of the eschatological kingdom of God. This explains why Schreiner, for example, calls the fruit of the Spirit a "new quality of life," also adding that "the old age no longer reigns over believers."[122] This also explains the declaration in Rom 14:17 that "the

---

119. Murray J. Harris, *The Second Epistle to the Corinthians: A Commentary on the Greek Text*, NIGTC (Grand Rapids: Eerdmans, 2005), 433.

120. Steve Motyer, "New, Newness," in *Evangelical Dictionary of Theology*, ed. Walter A. Elwell (Grand Rapids: Baker Academic, 2001), 824.

121. Mark B. Stephens, *Annihilation or Renewal? The Meaning and Function of New Creation in the Book of Revelation* (Tübingen: Mohr Siebeck, 2011), 1. A good illustration of this broader usage is offered by Hubbard: "The motif of 'new creation,' however, is not confined to the opening and closing chapters of the Christian Scriptures. The prophets, the psalmists, the evangelists, and so on, all exhibit a robust faith in the creative activity of God, and this faith was not focused solely on the remote past or the distant future. The prayer of the penitent sinner that God would 'create a pure heart, and grant a new spirit' (Ps 51:10), as well as the bold declaration of the prophet that Yahweh was, even now, 'making something new' (Isa 43:18), reflect a deep-seated belief in the continuing new-creative work of God, and form part of the vibrant, if variegated, biblical witness to new creation." Moyer V. Hubbard, *New Creation in Paul's Letters and Thought* (Cambridge: Cambridge University Press, 2002), 1.

122. Schreiner, *Galatians*, 352.

kingdom of God is not a matter of eating and drinking, but of righteousness, peace and joy in the Holy Spirit."[123]

Summary: The Fruit of the Spirit and the Kingdom of God

We have seen in this chapter that the Bible depicts the spiritual transformation process of humans through a variety of concepts, metaphors, and images, without offering a single unified specification of the economy of moral/spiritual growth and salvation. This diversity has been reflected by the fluidity of the scholarly understanding of the various terms related to this domain and by the absence of a robust, overarching theoretical model of human transformation in the theological mainstream. This lacuna has formed a barrier to the full recognition of the significance of the fruit of the Spirit, because there has been no obvious theological framework that could have naturally accommodated the fruit as the ultimate end-state of a transformation process.

Despite the fragmented and rather kaleidoscopic picture of human formation, there is a common theme running through the Bible involving all the relevant construals, an emphasis on the *ongoing* moral/spiritual development of the believer that follows the initial first step of becoming a Christian disciple. The Scriptures witness to the fact again and again that full spiritual maturity is not reached by the initial act of turning to God, but continues after the believer's conversion/justification. This process of spiritual growth towards Christian maturity has been referred to under different labels—most notably sanctification, deification, and being conformed to the divine image—and the current chapter has examined the main biblical paradigms of spiritual formation with a view of their relationship to the fruit of the Spirit.

The principal argument of the chapter drew on a passage in Paul's

---

123. Cohick ("Fruit of the Spirit," 332) states in this respect: "Fruit of the Spirit (love, joy, peace, patience, kindness, goodness, faithfulness, gentleness, self-control) demonstrates moral transformation consistent with those who will inherit the kingdom of God."

first letter to the Corinthians (1 Cor 3:1–3), which construes spiritual formation in terms of a transformation from being "fleshly" to becoming "people who live by the Spirit." That is, this passage presents Paul's vision of developing Christian maturity as a journey from a primarily flesh-bound towards an increasingly Spirit-bound existence. This tenet was then related to the fruit of the Spirit, because the flesh–Spirit antithesis is also at the centre of Gal 5:19–23. This contrast has traditionally been interpreted as the believer's struggle between two opposite tendencies, and we have seen that 1 Cor 3:1–3 adds to this picture a *developmental dimension*: growing spiritual maturity involves increasingly choosing the Spirit over the flesh; that is, the process results in an increased proclivity to attune to the Spirit in one's daily conduct rather than to succumb to the temptations and influences of the flesh. Within this paradigm, the picture painted by Paul in Gal 5 can be seen as a graphic description of two poles of a fundamental human transformation process, spelling out in rich detail the starting point and the final destination of moral/spiritual growth, with the latter being represented by the fruit of the Spirit.

This reading received further confirmation when we examined how the fruit was related to the three principal theological references to Christian formation: sanctification, deification, and being conformed to the divine image. It was shown that the diversity of these metaphors only concerns the *process* of spiritual development, whereas the metaphors converge in presenting the *outcome* of this development as a unified target: the believer's empowerment to lead a religious/ethical life,[124] always implying, and often specifically mentioning, the fruit of the Spirit.

Finally, it was suggested that taking the fruit as the descriptor of the desired target of human transformation also makes sense when extrapolated to a broader creational level, as part of the process of new creation whereby God's stewards are turned into citizens of the eschatological kingdom of God. Indeed, the link between the fruit of the Spirit and the kingdom of God receives indirect confirmation in Gal 5:19–21, where the

---

124. See Rabens, "The Holy Spirit and Deification in Paul," 200.

apostle Paul declares that the kingdom of God will be denied to those whose conduct is defined by the works of flesh—that is, by the opposite of the fruit of the Spirit: "The acts of the flesh are obvious. . . . I warn you, as I did before, that those who live like this will not inherit the kingdom of God" (see also 1 Cor 6:9–10).

7

CULTIVATING THE
FRUIT OF THE SPIRIT

Can you tell me, Socrates, whether virtue is acquired by teaching
or by practice; or if neither by teaching nor practice, then
whether it comes to man by nature, or in what other way?
—Plato, *Meno*

The final chapter of this book explores the practical implications of
the fruit of the Spirit, and the initial question in Plato's philosophical fiction, *Meno*, written at the beginning of the fourth century BC,
sums up the relevant themes in masterful brevity. As the quote above
shows, Socrates is asked how virtue can be cultivated, and he is offered
three possible options: through teaching, through practice, or "by nature"
(i.e., genetically endowed). In the current chapter we shall ask the same
question about biblical virtues in general and then the fruit of the Spirit
in particular, and the options will not be dissimilar: Are the facets of
the fruit of the Spirit divine endowments (corresponding in a way to
Plato's "by nature") or attributes that need to be consciously developed in
humans (i.e., through teaching and practice)? The discussion will start
by exploring the potential tension between divine and human agency in

cultivating virtues, arguing that the two options are not exclusive. Next we shall survey how scholars of various backgrounds have traditionally understood the promotion of virtues in general and what contemporary psychology can contribute to the discussion. Following this, the second half of the chapter will focus specifically on the three dimensions of the fruit of the Spirit—loving compassion, spiritual contentment, and steadfast perseverance—and will summarise the most important biblical and psychological approaches to their cultivation.

Divine Gift or the Outcome of Human Effort?

A long-standing dilemma in biblical studies has concerned the fact that the facets of the fruit of the Spirit are described in the Scriptures both as endowments/benefits received from the sovereign Holy Spirit and as virtues that need to be consciously cultivated by humans. That is, while Fung rightly points out that "the phrase directly ascribes the power of fructification not to the believer himself but to the Spirit,"[1] elsewhere in the Bible all the facets of the fruit of the Spirit are commanded of the believer (as will be shown in table 3 in the next section); for example, as C. Wright illustrates, in John's Gospel Jesus is reported to command his disciples to love one another three times (13:34; 15:12, 17), and 1 John urges the readers to exercise love five times (3:11, 18, 23; 4:7, 11).[2] Accordingly, Christian Miller and his colleagues rightly conclude, "It is not clear how to understand the contribution that both human beings and God are supposed to make in fostering them [virtues in general]. Some Christian theologians have maintained that not only faith, hope, and love but also the moral virtues cannot be acquired by human effort but must be infused by God."[3]

---

1. Fung, *Galatians*, 262.
2. C. Wright, *Cultivating the Fruit of the Spirit*, 24–25.
3. Miller et al., "Introduction," 5.

The crucial question therefore is in this respect how proactive one needs to be to acquire or appropriate the fruit of the Spirit: Does it happen automatically as one leads an increasingly Spirit-filled life, or do people have to consciously strive for it in one way or another?[4] N. T. Wright calls this biblical tension between divine and human agency a "mystery,"[5] elaborating on this point as follows: "We are here, as so often in theology, at the borders of language, because we are trying to talk at the same time about 'something God does' and 'something humans do' as if God were simply another character like ourselves, as though (in other words) the interplay of God's work and our work could be imagined on the model of two people collaborating on a project."[6]

Before we examine any further the various biblical and scholarly positions regarding this paradox, we should note that the divine/ human duality has also emerged in theology with regard to the notion of sanctification (which is, in fact, not unexpected given that the previous chapter directly linked the process of sanctification to the fruit of the Spirit as its outcome): Blocher, amongst several other scholars, points out that while some biblical passages highlight the Holy Spirit as the divine author of sanctification (e.g., 2 Thess 2:13; 1 Pet 1:2), elsewhere believers are encouraged to actively seek sanctification (e.g., Heb 12:14).[7]

Understanding the relationship between the divine and human agencies is undoubtedly a crucial question regarding the cultivation of the fruit of the Spirit, because any consideration of consciously developing biblical virtues will only make sense if such human efforts can be realistically expected to bring about concrete benefits. So, let us look at the issue of

---

4. This question is sometimes referred to as the issue of the "indicative and imperative" in Pauline theology and ethics; see e.g., Volker Rabens, "'Indicative and Imperative' as the Substructure of Paul's Theology-and-Ethics in Galatians? A Discussion of Divine and Human Agency in Paul," in *Galatians and Christian Theology: Justification, the Gospel, and Ethics in Paul's Letter*, ed. Mark W. Elliott, Scott J. Hafemann, and John Frederick (Grand Rapids: Baker Academic, 2014).

5. N. T. Wright, *After You Believe*, 197.

6. N. T. Wright, 197.

7. Blocher, "Sanctification by Faith?," 61. For a similar argument, see Hoekema, "The Reformed Perspective," 77.

agency more closely, examining the various positions and possible ways of reconciling them with each other.

Various Emphases in the Divine versus Human Agency Debate

The most prominent marker of the fruit of the Spirit in Scripture is that it is "*of the Spirit*," and therefore it is fitting to begin by considering the Holy Spirit's involvement in producing the fruit. Dockery makes the valid point that in introducing the nine virtues in Gal 5:22, Paul does not speak about "the fruit of faith" but specifically of the fruit of the Spirit,[8] and by doing so he highlights the role of divine agency in a way that goes beyond merely living a righteous Christian life. The question that has divided interpreters is what this "divine role" might entail, and one group of commentators maintains that the facets of the fruit of the Spirit can be seen entirely as personality endowments bestowed on humans by the sovereign Holy Spirit. Such a position is not only consistent with the label "fruit of the Spirit," but it is also in harmony with Jesus's teaching in John 15:5: "If you remain in me and I in you, you will bear much fruit; apart from me you can do nothing." Accordingly, in an overview of Christian character formation, Ray Yeo for example states, "This chapter makes the claim that character and virtue formation in the Christian tradition is distinct from its non-religious counterparts in its foundational insistence that genuine Christian character formation can only be achieved through the gracious gift of God, and cannot be had simply through human endeavours."[9]

Variations on the same argument have been put forward by many scholars, all centred around the claim that the qualities of the fruit are not the product of human strength.[10] Most modern commentators, however,

---

8. Dockery, "Fruit of the Spirit," 316.

9. Yeo, "Christian Character Formation," 538.

10. E.g., Hays ("Galatians," 328) argues, "Fruit cannot be humanly manufactured; it can grow only organically, as God gives the growth—in this case, through the life-giving energy of the Spirit." Alston (*Divine Nature and Human Language*, 233) mentions in this respect the traditional Catholic view that "by grace we are 'infused' with the theological virtues of faith, hope, and love, and endowed with such 'gifts of the Spirit' as wisdom, fortitude, and piety," and calls this the "fiat model." See also J. V. Fesko, *Galatians*, Lectio Continua Expository Commentary on the New

would qualify this stance by also adding that accepting the Spirit's pivotal role does not mean that the growth of the fruit requires no human cooperation at all. After all, as table 3 demonstrates, all the nine facets of the Spirit mentioned in Gal 5:22–23 are specifically expected elsewhere in the New Testament to be promoted one way or another by the believer. The classic biblical example to show that divine and human agencies are interrelated is a passage in Philippians, which exhorts the readers to "continue to work out your salvation with fear and trembling, for it is God who works in you to will and to act in order to fulfil his good purpose" (2:12–13). Here the command to work out one's own salvation is juxtaposed with the declaration that it is God who will deliver the task, leading Cole to conclude that "progressive sanctification is a cooperative venture."[11] Indeed, in this passage Paul appears to underline the need to maintain a fine balance between divine and human agency,[12] and this balanced partnership is also evidenced in Col 1:29: "To this end I strenuously contend with all the energy Christ so powerfully works in me." We find indications of a combination of agencies also in the epistle to the Galatians itself: although the fruit is "of the Spirit" (5:22), believers are instructed to "live by the Spirit" (v. 16), to "keep in step with the Spirit" (v. 25), to "sow" to the Spirit rather than the flesh (6:8), and to "do good to all people" (v. 10).

In the light of the above considerations as well as the multiple biblical calls for conscious cultivation of the various facets of the fruit (table 3), contemporary theology has shifted towards giving more credit to human efforts in Christian character building.[13] After all, as N. T. Wright rightly asks, if the growing of the fruit were automatic, why would self-control be needed?[14] Tidball also highlights Eph 4:22–24 in this respect—"You were *taught* . . . to be made new in the attitude of your minds; and to put on the

---

Testament (Powder Springs, GA: Tolle Lege Press, 2012), 169; Fung, *Galatians*, 262; Schreiner, *Galatians*, 348.

11. G. A. Cole, "Sanctification," 722.

12. See e.g., Elwell and Comfort, *Tyndale Bible Dictionary*, 1164. As Alston (*Divine Nature and Human Language*, 232) points out, "The Pauline love of paradox is such that this passage can be used to illustrate everything from the ultra-Pelagian view that it is all our doing to the ultra-Augustinian view that God has simply taken over and displaced the human agent."

13. See e.g., Davids, "Adoption," 179; Fee, *God's Empowering Presence*, 370; Grudem, *Systematic Theology*, 989; Keener, "Fruit of the Spirit," 579; N. T. Wright, *Galatians*, 337–338.

14. N. T. Wright, *After You Believe*, 196.

Table 3: Biblical Calls for the Cultivation of the Nine Facets of the Fruit of the Spirit

Facet of the Fruit of the Spirit	Calls for Conscious Cultivation
Love	Matt 22:37–39; Mark 12:29–31; John 13:34; 15:12, 17; 1 Cor 16:14; Eph 5:2; Col 3:14; 1 Tim 6:11; 2 Tim 2:22; 2 Pet 1:7; 1 John 3:11, 18, 23; 4:7, 11
Joy	Rom 12:12, 15; 2 Cor 13:11; Phil 3:1; 4:4; Jas 1:2; 1 Pet 4:13
Peace	2 Cor 13:11; Eph 4:3; Col 3:15; 2 Tim 2:22
Patience	Eph 4:2; Col 3:12; 2 Tim 4:2
Kindness	Col 3:12; 2 Tim 2:24
Goodness	Rom 12:9, 21; Gal 6:9, 10; Eph 4:28
Faithfulness	Rom 12:12; 1 Cor 4:2; 1 Tim 6:11; Rev 2:10; 14:12
Gentleness	Eph 4:2; Col 3:12; 1 Tim 6:11
Self-control	2 Pet 1:6; Titus 1:8

new self, created to be like God in true righteousness and holiness" (emphasis added)—because this passage suggests that human transformation into the image of God can be "taught"—that is, consciously generated.[15]

Regarding the question of how this human involvement can be harmonised with the role of the Holy Spirit in the process, it appears that setting up an either/or contrast between divine and human agency may constitute a false choice. We saw in chapter 2, when we defined the notion of a "virtue," that similar to other personality characteristics, virtues also have several layers of "situatedness": a trait-like level, which is not unlike top-down endowment, a state-like level, which is more under human control, and a narrative level, which is fully dependent on the personal stories that people develop to organise their experiences and to make sense

---

15. Tidball, *The Message of Holiness*, 179–180.

of their lives. This implies that some aspects of a virtue can be divinely infused in someone and some others consciously shaped by the person (we shall return to the narrative aspect later in this chapter). It is indeed possible to think of several possible ways of reconciling the influence of the divine and the human agency in a manner that can accommodate the dual involvement naturally; let us have a look at four such options:

(1) Believers consciously create access to the Spirit's power. Even if one considers the Spirit's role paramount in developing the fruit of the Spirit, this role may be dependent on the believer's action to gain access to the Spirit's impact. It is not unreasonable to expect that believers need to successfully attune themselves to the power of the indwelling Spirit for him to be able to start working in them, not unlike having to tune into a radio station before one can receive its broadcast or putting a plug into a socket to receive electricity.[16] An analogy of this is the Eastern Orthodox view, reported by Olson, that "deification is not the result of human striving or merit or virtue; these only *open one up to the divinizing power of the Holy Spirit.*"[17] In practical terms, such an "opening up" may involve keeping the channels of one's mind and heart open through prayer, worship, praise, and thanksgiving (as suggested by Eph 5:18–20 as ways of being filled with the Spirit), and in general trying to spend time in Jesus's presence, for example by reading Scripture and forming a personal relationship with him. In Bruce Atkinson's words, "The closer we are to Jesus, the more the Spirit can flow through us in fruit and gifts. . . . The more we live in the Spirit the more we should also open up and allow his divine nature to be diffused through our lives."[18] Such an understanding appears to be consistent with Rom 8:6, which states that "the mind *governed* by the flesh is death, but the mind *governed* by the Spirit is life and peace" (emphasis added), because being "governed" by the Spirit may be understood as being

---

16. Dörnyei, *Progressive Creation*, 243. N. T. Wright (*After You Believe*, 259) offers the analogy of "the man in the old Jewish joke who constantly prayed that he would win the lottery. Eventually, he shook his fist heavenward and demanded that God explain why he wasn't answering the man's fervent prayer. 'My son,' God replied, 'you need to come halfway to meet me. You could at least buy a ticket!'"

17. Olson, "Deification," 190; emphasis added.

18. Bruce Atkinson, *No More Law! A Bold Study in Galatians* (Milton Keynes: Paternoster, 2012), 197.

attuned to or aligned with the Spirit (as it is unlikely to mean being "controlled"). Even more closely related to the fruit of the Spirit, Paul submits in Gal 5:25: "Since we live by the Spirit, let us keep in step with the Spirit," with the NRSVA translating the Greek verb for "keep in step with" (*stoicheō*) as "be guided by" and N. T. Wright rendering it into "line up with."[19]

(2) The Spirit creates a potential that humans need to realise. This option goes one step further than the previous one in that not only does one need to receive and discern the Spirit's guidance (i.e., create access to the Spirit), but one also needs to *follow* him obediently, in line with Keener's argument: "A believer should cooperate with what the Spirit births (as in Phil 2:12–13); . . . the fruit grows as believers *respond* to the Spirit's moral direction (Gal 5:16–18)."[20] Talking about the love component of the fruit of the Spirit, De Boer expresses the same view when he asks: "Is love something the Galatians must decide to do, or is it the natural outcome of the Spirit's presence?" His answer is that the Spirit creates the "condition" in which loving action can be exercised,[21] which is another example of realising the potential created by the Holy Spirit.

(3) Believers cooperate with God to nurture growth. We saw in chapter 2 that commentators have often used biological analogies related to fruits in general in interpreting various aspects of the fruit of the Spirit. The analogy of fruit-bearing lends itself to explaining the divine–human cooperation: for the divine seed to grow, the ground needs to be prepared and the plant needs to be nurtured by the farmer. This option thus adds to the previous two points a "nurturing" element: even after the seed has been received and successfully planted, the fully-formed fruit will only emerge if the tree is "watered, tended and pruned, protected against the elements and various kinds of disease, and defended against attack from predators."[22] In practical terms, such nurturing duties involve removing

---

19. N. T. Wright, *After You Believe*, 196–197. Speaking about self-control, Packer expresses a similar view: "The discipline and effort must be blessed by the Holy Spirit, or they would achieve nothing. So all our attempts to get our lives in shape need to be soaked in constant prayer that acknowledges out inability to change ourselves." James I. Packer, *Keep in Step with the Spirit: Finding Fullness in Our Walk with God*, 2nd ed. (Grand Rapids: Baker Books, 2005), 91.

20. Keener, *Galatians*, 517; emphasis added.

21. de Boer, *Galatians*, 364.

22. N. T. Wright, *Galatians*, 338.

obstacles by resisting temptations and avoiding sin as much as possible, as well as creating a spiritual context for the growth of the fruit in terms of ongoing prayer for blessing and protection.[23] For our current purpose, the main point is not so much the exact nature of how to tend the growth of the fruit as the fact that such a practice offers a natural cooperation of divine and human effort.

(4) God replenishes depleted inner resources. The final option for the reconciliation of divine and human agency originates in psychology. When we examined psychological research on self-control in chapter 3, the intriguing notion of "ego depletion" emerged as one of the most relevant aspects underpinning self-discipline. According to recent findings, the capacity for self-control is a limited resource, which, with repeated use, can become depleted. When this happens, performance on subsequent tasks that require self-control becomes impaired, which becomes highly relevant to our discussion if we recall that performing all the virtues—and especially loving compassion—are sustained by self-control. Indeed, Klodiana Lanaj and her colleagues report in an article aptly entitled "When Lending a Hand Depletes the Will" that helping behaviour does exhaust people's resources,[24] and according to Baumeister and colleagues' results, so do other impeding factors such as interpersonal conflict, illness, physical pain, and even insufficient sleep.[25] The consequence is that when one's inner resources are depleted, "people are less able to restrain their selfish impulses and therefore will express less willingness to help strangers."[26]

Thus, as Baumeister and Exline conclude, by reducing one's capacity of self-control, ego depletion can lead to *moral deterioration.*[27] However, the Bible is laced with verses of encouragement and exhortation related

---

23. E.g., following an Eastern Orthodox tradition, Olson ("Deification," 190) illustrates the process of removing obstacles by "faithfully participating in the sacraments and praying without ceasing."

24. Klodiana Lanaj, Russell E. Johnson, and Mo Wang, "Costs and Benefits of Helping," 1100.

25. Roy F. Baumeister, Bradley R. E. Wright, and David Carreon, "Self-Control 'in the Wild': Experience Sampling Study of Trait and State Self-Regulation," *Self and Identity* 18, no. 5 (2019): 520.

26. DeWall et al., "Depletion," 1660.

27. Baumeister and Exline, "Virtue," 1189.

to strength: people are repeatedly reassured that it is the Lord who gives strength to his people,[28] urging believers to turn to God in prayer at times of exhaustion, a message that is expressively articulated in Isa 40:29–31:

> He gives strength to the weary
>> and increases the power of the weak.
> Even youths grow tired and weary,
>> and young men stumble and fall;
> but those who hope in the LORD
>> will renew their strength.
> They will soar on wings like eagles;
>> they will run and not grow weary,
>> they will walk and not be faint.

This would suggest that the Holy Spirit might counteract ego depletion and replenish inner resources to renew compassion; indeed, 1 Pet 4:11 specifically affirms, "If anyone serves, they should do so with the strength God provides." This message is reiterated at the end of the same letter: "And the God of all grace . . . will himself restore you and make you strong, firm and steadfast" (1 Pet 5:10).

In summary, the fruit of the Spirit may be seen as the joint product of divine and human agency, without these necessarily excluding each other. Such divine–human cooperation is expressed in Prov 21:31—"The horse is made ready for the day of battle, but victory rests with the LORD"— where it is made clear that attributing the outcome of the battle to the Lord does not shift all responsibility to God, because the horse needs to be "made ready." Accordingly, Elwell and Comfort submit that "perhaps the real 'secret' of holiness consists precisely in learning to keep that balance: relying thoroughly on *God* as the true agent in sanctification while faithfully discharging one's *personal* responsibility."[29] Jennifer Herbst explains that this productive tension lay at the heart of the Christian

---

28. E.g., 1 Chr 29:12; Ps 18:32; 68:35; 89:21; Isa 58:11; Ezek 34:16; Hab 3:19; Phil 4:13; 2 Tim 4:17.

29. Elwell and Comfort, *Tyndale Bible Dictionary*, 1164.

tradition of character formation over the centuries, balancing between reliance on divine power and virtuous striving for excellence.[30] Since both themes have a strong scriptural basis, she concludes that it was rare for one to be elevated at the expense of the other.

Cultivating Virtues

Let us begin to explore the specific ways of cultivating virtues by surveying psychological research on the question as to whether personality traits can be changed. As we shall see, there has been a flurry of research on this topic recently, offering many practical implications. Drawing on these findings we shall then summarise the main mechanisms whereby virtues can undergo positive change through conscious cultivation, before narrowing down our focus to the three specific dimensions of the fruit of the Spirit.

Can Personality Traits Be Changed?

In a recent article on personality stability and change, Jenny Wagner and her colleagues conclude that the traditional differentiation between genetic and environmental influences on one's personality (i.e., nature vs. nurture) still holds sway, even though it is increasingly clear that genetic and contextual factors are interwoven in a dynamic manner: for example, life experiences can alter genetic activity, whilst genetic sensitivity can affect the way people engage with their environment.[31] From a practical perspective, all this boils down to the question of whether "personality is fate," or whether personality traits can be changed.[32] For example, can people become more sociable, more compassionate, more empathic, more conscientious, or more self-disciplined? In an attempt to address this matter comprehensively, Brent Roberts and his

---

30. Herdt, "Cultivation of Christian Virtue," 229.

31. Jenny Wagner et al., "Toward an Integrative Model of Sources of Personality Stability and Change," *Current Directions in Psychological Science* 29, no. 5 (2020): 439.

32. See e.g., Brent W. Roberts et al., "A Systematic Review of Personality Trait Change through Intervention," *Psychological Bulletin* 143, no. 2 (2017): 117.

colleagues have conducted a meta-analysis of the relevant research in both clinical and personality psychology and provided unambiguous evidence that personality traits are amenable to change across the life span. They found that made-to-measure training programmes appear to be effective in bringing about personality changes, and these changes in turn are retained for relatively long time intervals.[33] However, such focused interventions are not the only source of change, as studies have shown that ageing and new life experiences and events (most notable related to work, love, and health) can also have a robust impact on personality.[34]

The fact that personality features are malleable is consistent with lay beliefs; after all, as Hudson and Frawley point out, people spend tens of billions of dollars each year buying self-help books or participating in self-help programmes[35] (a point that is also supported by the popularity of Christian books on how to improve the various facets of the fruit of the Spirit). The changeability hypothesis has received further confirmation from biopharmaceutical investigations in which neurochemicals (e.g., oxytocin) have been successfully applied to heighten empathy, generosity, and the capacity for compassion,[36] indicating that the relevant neural structures are changeable through conscious manipulation. Thus, research has made considerable strides in understanding how human character can be modified for the better, and the investigations conducted in the various psychological domains have identified a number of prerequisites for successful personality change to take place:

(1) There needs to be a strong desire for change, amplified by challenges to one's basic assumptions. Recent research on volitional personality change has produced evidence that if people are sufficiently motivated, they may be able to successfully attain desired changes to their personality

---

33. Roberts et al., 126. For similar findings, see Nathan W. Hudson et al., "Change Goals Robustly Predict Trait Growth: A Mega-Analysis of a Dozen Intensive Longitudinal Studies Examining Volitional Change," *Social Psychological and Personality Science* 11, no. 6 (2020): 729.

34. Nathan W. Hudson and R. Chris Fraley, "Volitional Personality Trait Change: Can People Choose to Change Their Personality Traits?," *Journal of Personality and Social Psychology* 109, no. 3 (2015): 490–491; Wagner et al., "Personality Stability and Change," 439–440.

35. Hudson and Fraley, "Volitional Personality Trait Change," 501.

36. For an overview, see Hughes, "Moral Enhancement," 89–90.

traits—that is, develop their character in the direction of their desired trait levels.[37] For having a tangible impact, the underlying motivation needs to be *strong* and *sincere*, comprising major life goals that will motivate people by placing rewards, punishments, and contingencies on certain traits.[38] Moreover, it appears that for best effect, the desire to change needs also to be accompanied by fundamental *challenges* to the individual's established (often entrenched) views and dispositions. Cognitive theories of conceptual change suggest that for people to embark on the often risky course of transformation, they need a certain amount of *dissonance* to "dislodge" them from their comfort zone.[39] In other words, to facilitate change, not only does one need to make the "there" (i.e., the future vision) attractive but also the "here" (the present state of affairs) intolerable—this was indeed a common biblical practice exercised by the prophets to engender transformation by contrasting positive and negative imagery.[40] Thus, in psychology, Allemand and Flückiger argue that challenging basic assumptions, beliefs, expectations, and motives of the individual are likely to be critical prerequisites of change, and they point out that an instructive approach in this respect might involve learning from successful and failed past experiences.[41]

(2) The desire needs to be acted upon. Research has found that even a strong desire for change is insufficient to result in a tangible outcome unless one *actively pursues it* by implementing change-related behaviours.[42] The results of Hudson and his colleagues suggest that taking even small but consistent steps towards aligning one's behaviours with

---

37. Hudson and Fraley, "Volitional Personality Trait Change," 502; Hudson et al., "Change Goals," 729; Wagner et al., "Personality Stability and Change," 439.

38. Olivia E. Atherton, Emily Grijalva, Brent W. Roberts, and Richard W. Robins, "Stability and Change in Personality Traits and Major Life Goals from College to Midlife," *Personality and Social Psychology Bulletin* 47, no. 5 (2021): 855.

39. See Magdalena Kubanyiova, *Teacher Development in Action: Understanding Language Teachers' Conceptual Change* (Basingstoke, UK: Palgrave Macmillan, 2012).

40. Zoltán Dörnyei, *Vision, Mental Imagery and the Christian Life: Insights from Science and Scripture* (Abingdon: Routledge, 2020), 195.

41. Mathias Allemand and Christoph Flückiger, "Changing Personality Traits: Some Considerations from Psychotherapy Process-Outcome Research for Intervention Efforts on Intentional Personality Change," *Journal of Psychotherapy Integration* 27, no. 4 (2017): 489.

42. Marie Hennecke et al., "A Three-Part Framework for Self-Regulated Personality Development across Adulthood," *European Journal of Personality* 28 (2014): 289.

one's desired traits can produce trait growth.[43] These findings are reminiscent of the call in the letter of James to be "doers of the word" (1:22 NRSVA), because without becoming a "doer," a person's faithful mindset will be as transient as a forgettable image of oneself in the mirror: "Anyone who listens to the word but does not do what it says is like someone who looks at his face in a mirror and, after looking at himself, goes away and immediately forgets what he looks like" (1:23–24). In other words, James emphasizes that "doing" is necessary to make the faithful mindset a *lasting* part of one's identity; the mindset needs to be backed up by action so as not to fade away like a dim reflection in the mirror. The implication is that even if a person *can* tune into the Spirit-centred mindset, this state can only prevail in the person's life if it is internalised to such an extent that it is also manifested in his or her actions.[44] This point is also made in Gal 6:8–10: "Whoever sows to please their flesh, from the flesh will reap destruction; whoever sows to please the Spirit, from the Spirit will reap eternal life. Let us not become weary in doing good, for at the proper time we will reap a harvest if we do not give up. Therefore, as we have opportunity, let us do good to all people, especially to those who belong to the family of believers."

(3) Personality growth requires sustained, habitual engagement. Even when change-related action has been successfully initiated, it will only evoke enduring personality trait growth if it is sustained habitually for an extended period; in Hudson and Frawley's words, "when maintained for an extended period of time, changes in state-level patterns of thoughts, feelings, and behaviours can calcify into abiding personality trait change."[45] These scholars reported that individuals' desire to become more outgoing and extraverted predicted growth in their daily behaviour, which, when sustained long enough, led to changes in

---

43. Nathan W. Hudson et al., "You Have to Follow Through: Attaining Behavioral Change Goals Predicts Volitional Personality Change," *Journal of Personality and Social Psychology* 117, no. 4 (2019): 839.

44. The "practice what you preach" message is a recurring injunction in the Scriptures (e.g., Ezek 33:31–32; Matt 7:24–27; 25:31–46; Luke 6:47–49; 11:28; Rom 2:13; 1 John 3:18), suggesting that faith without action is of little value.

45. Hudson and Fraley, "Volitional Personality Trait Change," 503.

their trait-level extraversion.[46] This finding is consistent with Roberts and colleagues' conclusion about personality-change programmes, that interventions lasting less than approximately four weeks tend to have small effects. Interestingly, they also found that interventions longer than eight weeks do not induce greater personality change, which therefore points to the requirement of having a period of 4–8 weeks of behavioural change to have a salient impact.[47] We find several Bible passages that underline a similar importance of sustained effort to advance in the maturation process. James 1:4 for example states, "Let perseverance *finish* its work so that you may be mature and complete, not lacking anything" (emphasis added), and Isa 1:16–17 similarly teaches, "Wash and make yourselves clean. . . . Stop doing wrong. *Learn* to do right; seek justice" (emphasis added). Galatians 6:9–10 is particularly explicit about the importance of sustained, habitual engagement: "Let us *not become weary* in doing good, for at the proper time we will reap a harvest if we do not give up. Therefore, *as we have opportunity*, let us do good to all people" (emphasis added).

(4) Community-level intervention and the role of the church community. There is growing evidence that "character is conditioned by communities"[48]—that is, the broader social structures surrounding a person have the potential to alter personality.[49] Parenting and familial influences have long been known to have enduring effects on personality development, and in a similar way, the social networks a person is part of can have a positive impact. In a study of contemporary virtue education in Canada and South Korea, Michael Ferrari and his colleagues rightly remind us that it is informal education through socialisation into a community that develops one's sense of identity,[50] and given that in most

46. Hudson and Fraley, 499.

47. Roberts et al., "Personality Trait Change," 128.

48. Tomlin, *Spiritual Fitness*, 66.

49. See e.g., Benjamin P. Chapman, Sarah Hampson, and John Clarkin, "Personality-Informed Interventions for Healthy Aging: Conclusions from a National Institute on Aging Work Group," *Developmental Psychology* 50, no. 5 (2014): 1432.

50. Michel Ferrari et al., "Educating for Virtue: How Wisdom Coordinates Informal, Nonformal and Formal Education in Motivation to Virtue in Canada and South Korea," *Journal of Moral Education* 48, no. 1 (2019): 48.

countries in the modern world Christian virtues are just as countercultural as they were in NT times, the role of the *church community* as the informal venue of moral formation becomes paramount. Indeed, in the first century, Paul specifically wrote to the Thessalonian believers that they should "encourage one another and build each other up, just as in fact you are doing" (1 Thess 5:11), and Heb 10:24–25 conveys a similar call: "And let us consider how we may spur one another on towards love and good deeds, not giving up meeting together, . . . but encouraging one another." Paul also urged Timothy to "command and teach" his congregation about godliness (1 Tim 4:7, 11; 6:6), humility (6:17), doing good (v. 18), and being generous (v. 18). Even more pertinently, 2 Tim 2:22 also encourages Timothy to "pursue righteousness, faith, love and peace, along with those who call on the Lord out of a pure heart," thereby foregrounding the communal practice of virtues. In a similar vein, Titus is also instructed to teach virtues in his church: "Teach the older men to be temperate, worthy of respect, self-controlled, and sound in faith, in love and in endurance" (2:2). There is therefore no doubt that Paul saw the local Christian community as the arena in which spiritual formation was facilitated, and accordingly Samra concludes, "Paul expected believers to be conformed to Christ in community."[51]

These considerations have obvious implications for contemporary churches. Herdt concludes about the character-building role of church communities that "this is another way in which to view the characterological significance of Christian churches and their many liturgical and paraliturgical practices—as offering social sustenance for the practice of virtue."[52] In agreement with this position, Hauerwas also emphasises that "the most important social task of Christians is to be nothing less than a community capable of forming people with virtues sufficient to witness to God's truth in the world."[53]

---

51. Samra, *Being Conformed to Christ*, 133. J. Green makes a similar point: "Restoration to the likeness of God is the work of the Spirit within the community of God's people, the fellowship of Christ-followers set on maturation in Christ." Joel B. Green, *Body, Soul, and Human Life: The Nature of Humanity in the Bible* (Grand Rapids: Baker Academic, 2008), 70.

52. Herdt, "Cultivation of Christian Virtue," 241.

53. Hauerwas, *A Community of Character*, 3.

Mechanisms of Cultivating Virtues

As seen above, psychological research on personality change supports the possibility of consciously developing biblical virtues, because it shows that in optimal conditions even entrenched, trait-like personality features can be altered or enhanced. We have seen that such a trait change has four prerequisites: the individual's motivation to change, corresponding change-related action, a sustained period of engagement, and appropriate community support. Let us now explore further the question of character formation by examining the specific mechanisms whereby virtues can be promoted. We shall start with the traditional understanding of virtue development in antiquity (shared also by Aristotle), *habit formation*, to be followed by the approach most emphasised in the Scriptures, *role modelling*. We shall then inspect the role of *strategic knowledge* and *motivational strategies* in the spiritual formation process, before concluding with a description of a novel avenue for virtue development opened up by modern psychological research on *narratives* and *narrative identity*.

Virtues Seen as Habits and Skills

Aristotle in his seminal work on virtues, *Nicomachean Ethics*, regarded habit formation through training as the primary mechanism for becoming a virtuous person. Although we saw earlier (e.g., in chapter 2) that his views on what a virtue entails differed considerably from how the biblical authors construed virtues, this divergence did not concern the *process* whereby a virtue could be formed. Indeed, Aristotle's understanding of habit formation is still considered valid both in philosophy and moral psychology,[54] and the notion of a *habit*, which constituted a cornerstone of behaviourist psychology in the twentieth century, remains a central construct in explaining human action and learning.[55] So what is a "habit"? It is an established behaviour pattern that becomes auto-

---

54. See e.g., McAdams, "Psychological Science and the Nicomachean Ethics," 311–312; MacIntyre, *After Virtue*, 182–184; N. T. Wright, *After You Believe*, 33–36.

55. See e.g., Bas Verplanken, ed., *The Psychology of Habit: Theory, Mechanisms, Change, and Contexts* (Cham, Switzerland: Springer, 2018); Wendy Wood and Dennis Rünger, "Psychology of Habit," *Annual Review of Psychology* 67 (2016): 289–314.

matic through practice, so that habitual action is performed with little or no conscious awareness. Aristotle believed that young people needed to be provided with extensive opportunities to practice virtuous behaviours in order to master the arts of virtue—that is, to develop virtuous conduct.[56] According to this thesis, therefore, we become good by doing good things.[57] Curiously, such a learning process shares some features in common with the "fake it till you make it" aphorism (CONCEPT 7.1).

Concept 7.1: "Fake It Till You Make It?"

The English aphorism "fake it till you make it" suggests that people can realise certain qualities in their lives by first only imitating/pretending them, and in this sense the process shares some features in common with forming habits through practice. C. S. Lewis summarises the essence of this process with regard to love: "The rule for all of us is perfectly simple. Do not waste time bothering whether you 'love' your neighbour; act as if you did. As soon as we do this we find one of the great secrets. When you are behaving as if you loved someone, you will presently come to love him."[58]

One may rightly wonder, however, whether merely putting on virtuous acts without the right motive—that is, "faking" them—will indeed lead to genuine personality change or merely to hypocrisy.[59] N. T. Wright's response is that "if we wait to start practicing these things until we 'mean them' from the bottom of our hearts, we will wait a long time and probably mess up a lot of lives, includ-

---

56. McAdams, "Psychological Science and the Nicomachean Ethics," 311.

57. See e.g., Tomlin, *Spiritual Fitness*, 90. In psychology a recent finding supporting this view is that helping is beneficial for helpers because it also improves their own well-being rather than only that of the person helped; Klodiana Lanaj, Russell E. Johnson, and Mo Wang, "Costs and Benefits of Helping," 1097.

58. Lewis, *Christian Behaviour*, 131.

59. See e.g., James A. Van Slyke, "Moral Psychology, Neuroscience, and Virtue: From Moral Judgment to Moral Character," in *Virtues and Their Vices*, ed. Kevin Timpe and Craig A. Boyd (New York: Oxford University Press, 2014), 466–467.

ing our own, in the process."[60] While this does make sense, what about the further objection that this practice carries the danger of church life becoming all habit and no virtue? Wright agrees that this may indeed happen regrettably, but he also adds, "But those of us who live in a land where churchgoing used to be a habit of the many and is now a hobby of the few should not scorn such habits as still remain."[61] This is undoubtedly a contentious issue, and yet the theory of habit formation does suggest a pathway from the uninternalised (i.e., the "not-fully-meant") virtuous behaviour to the internalised (i.e., the "fully-assumed-and-adopted") virtue through the process of extended practice.

The "learning by doing" principle involved in habit formation is also at the heart of contemporary skill learning theory,[62] which holds that the essence of the progression of learning any skill—from playing a musical instrument to riding a bicycle or driving a car—is a gradual move from the laboured, conscious, and overtly controlled processes of the novice to the smooth, unconscious, and covertly controlled processes of the expert (see CONCEPT 7.2). The similarity has prompted scholars to conceptualise virtues as a type of skill.[63] As Matt Stichter points out, the correspondence between virtues and skills is made particularly meaningful by the fact that "virtue" as a notion is similar to "skill" in that it implies a desired end and acquired excellence.[64] This virtue–skill analogy is especially useful when examining how virtuous competencies are developed, because reaching expertise in both areas requires "deliberate practice"—that is, striving to engage with activities that one currently cannot do perfectly, in order to receive feedback and

---

60. N. T. Wright, *After You Believe*, 224.

61. N. T. Wright, 278.

62. E.g., John R. Anderson, *Learning and Memory: An Integrated Approach*, 2nd ed. (Hoboken, NJ: Wiley, 2000).

63. Matt Stichter, "Virtue as Skill," in *The Oxford Handbook of Virtue*, ed. Nancy E. Snow (New York: Oxford University Press, 2018), 58.

64. Stichter, 59.

thus make corrections and improve. To illustrate the increased stability of a virtue as it becomes habitual through practice, Jennifer Wright and her colleagues offer the following illustration: if someone who wants to overcome his or her inclination to stray from the truth keeps practicing responding honestly in all circumstances, this will result in the person's honesty becoming habituated and engrained to such an extent that eventually giving an honest response will not require much effort or thought.[65]

Concept 7.2: Skill Learning Theory and the Development of Virtues

Skill learning theory is based on the recognition that the learning of a wide variety of skills such as cooking or playing the guitar shows remarkable similarity in terms of its development. The central premise of the theory is that skill acquisition proceeds through three characteristic stages:

(1) Declarative stage: Learners need to be prepared for the task by being offered explicit guidelines and facts about the skill in question. This initial *declarative knowledge* ("knowing what") can be conveyed through various forms of instruction and explanation, as well as by modelling the skill through illustration or demonstration. Regarding virtues, we saw in chapter 2 that they are by definition related to achieving something "good," and therefore, the "good" element needs to be unpacked before the virtue can be fully internalised. Specific details of this "unpacking" will be provided when discussing the role of strategic knowledge and narrative identity in virtue development.

(2) Procedural stage: The first trials of the new skill are inevitably error prone, but subsequent guided practice gradually transforms the initial declarative knowledge to *procedural*

---

65. J. Wright, Warren, and Snow, *Understanding Virtue*, 49.

knowledge ("knowing how") so that the skill becomes established though not yet fully spontaneous, as it still requires considerable attention. This corresponds to the process of learning a virtue by doing—that is, solidifying virtuous conduct by repeatedly putting it into practice, reminiscent to some extent of the "fake it till you make it" principle discussed in CONCEPT 7.1.

(3) Automatic stage: The skill is further improved and fine-tuned through extended practice in diverse situations. The level of automaticity and fluency in performing the skill increases while the required cognitive involvement decreases. We saw in chapter 2 that virtues are situation-specific—implying that people are often inconsistent in applying the same virtue in different situations—and Herdt, for example, points out that "if practicing being nice to folks at coffee hour following worship cultivates nothing more than a reliable disposition to be nice to folks at coffee hour, it isn't much to brag about."[66] Therefore, this final stage can be seen in virtue terms as trying to extend positive Christlike personality traits to a wide range of social situations, thereby developing "robust" virtues that transfer across different contexts.[67]

The process of forming good habits also has biblical warrants. For example, Paul instructs the Philippians, "Whatever you have learned or received or heard from me, or seen in me—put it into practice. And the God of peace will be with you" (4:9), and he tells Timothy: "Train yourself to be godly. For physical training is of some value, but godliness has value for all things" (1 Tim 4:7–8).[68] Even more specific is the point made in Hebrews that ongoing practice is the key to moral development: "But solid food is for the mature, who *by constant use* have *trained themselves*

---

66. Herdt, "Cultivation of Christian Virtue," 241.

67. See e.g., N. T. Wright, *Galatians*, 54–55.

68. There are also several warnings in Scripture about developing bad habits; e.g., Jer 13:23: "Can an Ethiopian change his skin or a leopard its spots? Neither can you do good who are accustomed to doing evil"; see also 1 Tim 5:13; Heb 10:25.

to distinguish good from evil" (5:14; emphases added); it is then further explained that "no discipline seems pleasant at the time, but painful. Later on, however, it produces a harvest of righteousness and peace for those who have been trained by it" (12:11). William Lane rightly emphasises that this image in the Hebrews passage has been borrowed from athletics, where systematic training and discipline are the key to success,[69] and the next verse specifically urges believers to engage in such training: "Therefore, strengthen your feeble arms and weak knees" (v. 12), using an image that goes back to Isa 35:3 ("Strengthen the feeble hands, steady the knees that give way").

In addition, the main driving force of habit formation in behaviourist psychology is that good habits need to be reinforced and bad habits punished—which is technically referred to as "operant conditioning"—and Lasure and Mikulas rightly point out that not only are praises common in the Scriptures (e.g., 1 Cor 11:2; Phlm 7), but "one of the most prominent themes in the Bible relates to heaven (reinforcement) and hell (punishment). These are dependent on specific behaviours, such as those related to following the commandments and opening the heart."[70]

Finally, it follows from understanding the learning of a virtue as a skill (CONCEPT 7.2) that practicing the virtuous skill under strain—that is, under difficult circumstances—makes virtue stronger and more permanent (similar to how physical muscles are strengthened). This would partly explain the recurring biblical teaching that people can be morally perfected through suffering (e.g., Rom 5:3–4; Heb 2:10; 5:7–10; 12:1–11; Jas 1:2–4).[71] Taking all these considerations together, we can indeed see that habit formation is a viable avenue for developing virtues, thereby supporting Packer's conclusion: "The fruit of the Spirit itself is, from one standpoint, a series of habits of action and reaction: love, joy, peace, patience, kindness, goodness, faithfulness, gentleness,

---

69. William L. Lane, *Hebrews 9–13*, WBC 47b (Dallas: Word, 1991), 426.

70. Linda C. Lasure and William L. Mikulas, "Biblical Behavior Modification," *Behaviour Research and Therapy* 34, no. 7 (1996): 563.

71. Charles H. Cosgrove, "Moral Formation," in *Dictionary of Scripture and Ethics*, ed. Joel B. Green (Grand Rapids: Baker Academic, 2011), 529.

self-control are all of them habitual . . . ways of thinking, feeling, and behaving."[72]

Virtues and Role Modelling

Acts 20:18–35 presents the apostle Paul's farewell message delivered to the Ephesian elders on his way to Jerusalem. He knew he would not see them again (v. 25), and in many ways the speech constitutes his parting words to the churches in general.[73] As such, Luke Timothy Johnson characterises it as a "kind of paraenetic discourse, in which the main point is the instruction of the listener in certain moral values."[74] The special significance of this farewell address for the current discussion lies in the way Paul delivers this moral instruction: he does not offer a list of specific exhortations, recommendations, and advice—in fact, his only directive of this sort in the whole speech consists of the appeal, "So be on your guard!" (20:31)—but rather he devotes most of the message talking about *himself.* That is, the legacy he leaves is not a set of tried-and-tested strategies to follow but rather the *example of himself.* While the call to imitate someone's faithful service was not out of line with farewell addresses of the time,[75] the strategy Paul applies here—*role modelling*—is of a more general nature, highly esteemed both in antiquity and modern times as an effective instructional method.

In an overview of role models in the Roman world, Sinclair Bell summarises that the Roman practice of identifying mythical or historical figures as *exempla* in terms of their actions and attributes was a characteristic cultural pattern of the time: "Rome's literary and material culture was thick with precedent, its inscriptions and art signposting individuals

---

72. Packer, *Keep in Step with the Spirit,* 90–91.

73. I. Howard Marshall, *The Acts of the Apostles: An Introduction and Commentary* (Nottingham: Inter-Varsity, 1980), 347. Moreover, as Wall underlines, because it is Paul's only speech addressed to believers, it also carries a paradigmatic value. Robert W. Wall, "The Acts of the Apostles: Introduction, Commentary, and Reflections," in *The New Interpreter's Bible,* ed. Leander E. Keck (Nashville: Abingdon, 2002), 280.

74. Luke Timothy Johnson, *The Acts of the Apostles,* SP 5 (Collegeville, MN: Liturgical Press, 1992), 367.

75. See e.g., Ajith Fernando, *Acts,* The NIV Application Commentary (Grand Rapids: Zondervan, 1998), 532; Johnson, *Acts,* 367.

and acts that the populace was enjoined to imitate in their own lives."[76] Indeed, *exempla* constituted the basic means of moral instruction and character building in antiquity, with the role models drawn both from the distant past and contemporary life; and while elite adult males were most often selected, *exempla* represented all classes, ages, and genders.[77] These role models shared in common the fact that their characters had been invested with moral authority, thereby forming the ethical base of Greco-Roman life.[78]

Modern scholarship has also recognised that role models can exert considerable influence on shaping individuals' values, attitudes, and beliefs. The term "role model" was originally coined by sociologist Robert Merton in his 1957 book on social theory,[79] but the theoretical basis of the phenomenon was developed by Albert Bandura in his seminal work on social learning theory in 1977 (see CONCEPT 7.3). Significantly, in this book Bandura submits that "virtually *all learning phenomena* resulting from direct experience occur on a vicarious basis by observing other people's behaviour and its consequences for them."[80] James Van Slyke describes how vicarious learning applies to the attainment of virtues very clearly: "Imitation is the starting point for virtuous behaviour in that the moral learner copies or reproduces the types of behaviour that the moral *exemplar* performs. Secondly, the moral learner begins to simulate the reasons, motives, and feelings of the moral *exemplar* until those states become their own and the moral learner acts based on their own internalized characteristics."[81]

---

76. Bell, "Role Models," 2.

77. Bell, 2.

78. E.g., as Fiore and Blanton summarise, "The use of example as a device to persuade or dissuade has been shown above to be constant in Greek and Roman usage. Those engaged in deliberative oratory found it to be a particularly appropriate strategy to move their audiences to action by illustrations with examples." Benjamin Fiore and Thomas R. Blanton, "Paul, Exemplification, and Imitation," in *Paul in the Greco-Roman World: A Handbook*, ed. J. Paul Sampley (London: Bloomsbury T&T Clark, 2016), 180.

79. Robert K. Merton, *Social Theory and Social Structure*, rev. ed. (New York: Free Press, 1957), 302.

80. Albert Bandura, *Social Learning Theory* (Englewood Cliffs, NJ: Prentice-Hall, 1977), 12; emphasis added.

81. Van Slyke, "Moral Psychology, Neuroscience, and Virtue," 460.

Concept 7.3: Vicarious Learning in Role Modelling

At the heart of Bandura's theory of role modelling[82] is the notion of "vicarious learning," that is, learning from the experience of others. The theory posits that the vicarious experience of observing models involves four key processes:

- First, behaviour will only be learned from models to whom individuals *pay attention*, which underlines the importance of highlighting potential role models (as is often done in the Bible).
- The second and third processes—*retention* and *motor reproduction*—concern the importance of the way the observed stimulus is stored and processed, involving the strengthening of this information by repeated exposure (e.g., by further observation and analysis) and various forms of practice (e.g., by repetition, imitation, and even mental rehearsal in one's imagination) through which these "symbolic representations" can be converted into action.
- The final aspect relates to accompanying *motivational processes*, as people are more likely to enact a modelled action if they observe the action resulting in positive consequences for others. Indeed, Bandura emphasises that "seeing or visualising people similar to oneself perform successfully typically raises efficacy beliefs in observers that they themselves possess the capabilities to master comparable activities."[83]

Role modelling was the biblical authors' preferred choice for moral instruction. Indeed, Gerd Theissen submits that the unique significance

---

82. Bandura, *Social Learning Theory*.
83. Bandura, 87.

of the Bible in this respect—what enabled it to become one of the most important textbooks of human behaviour and experience—"rests in part on the fact that it contains a large selection of realistic models, from Adam to Paul."[84] Table 4 contains an extensive list of biblical passages where role modelling is consciously applied. The list demonstrates well the pervasive nature of purposeful role modelling, not only by containing over twenty passages from sixteen different NT books, but also by the variety of the selected role models: the self-evident models are God and his earthly image, Jesus, but the teaching role of modelling is applied more widely by also highlighting models that were closer to the audience's lives: first the prophets of the past, then the apostle Paul and other church leaders (e.g., Timothy and Titus), and finally whole church communities and their members. First Thessalonians 1:6–8 is a good illustration of the latter: "You became imitators of us. . . . And so you became a model to all the believers in Macedonia and Achaia. The Lord's message rang out from you not only in Macedonia and Achaia—your faith in God has become known everywhere."

Fiora and Blanton summarise the general pattern underlying this passage as follows: "God and/or Christ are portrayed as exemplifying some trait, which in turn is exemplified by Paul; in their imitation of Paul, God, or Christ, the members of local assemblies may be depicted as exemplary models themselves."[85] This indicates that Paul recommending himself as a model has nothing to do with self-promotion but rather with the desire to become a mediator of Christlike values.[86] Willis De Boer argues in this respect that Paul's calling the disciples to the imitation of himself was a means to "maturing them to the maturity of direct imitation of Christ."[87] Indeed, Paul specifically states in 1 Cor 11:1, "Follow my example, as I

---

84. Gerd Theissen, *Psychological Aspects of Pauline Theology*, trans. John P. Galvin (Edinburgh: T & T Clark, 1987), 9.

85. Fiore and Blanton, "Paul, Exemplification, and Imitation," 189.

86. E.g., Hoekema ("The Reformed Perspective," 68) states, "One is amazed at Paul's willingness to hold himself up as an example. But Paul, in turn, was trying to pattern his life after that of Christ, who is our ultimate example."

87. Willis P. De Boer, *The Imitation of Paul: An Exegetical Study* (Eugene, OR: Wipf and Stock, 1962/2016), v; he also suggests that by performing this nurturing role Paul acted as a spiritual father modelling Christlike behaviour to his spiritual children (pp. 214–15).

follow the example of Christ," and in 1 Cor 4:16–17 he sets up an imitation chain linking Timothy through himself to Jesus: "I appeal to you, then, be imitators of me. For this reason I sent you Timothy, who is my beloved and faithful child in the Lord, to remind you of my ways in Christ Jesus, as I teach them everywhere in every church" (NRSVA).

Table 4: Biblical Passages Representing Conscious Role Modelling

- "I have set you an example that you should do as I have done for you" (John 13:15).
- "A new command I give you: love one another. As I have loved you, so you must love one another" (John 13:34).
- "In everything I did, I showed you that by this kind of hard work we must help the weak" (Acts 20:35).
- "May the God who gives endurance and encouragement give you the same attitude of mind toward each other that Christ Jesus had. . . . Accept one another, then, just as Christ accepted you" (Rom 15:5, 7).
- "Therefore I urge you to imitate me" (1 Cor 4:16).
- "Follow my example, as I follow the example of Christ" (1 Cor 11:1).
- "Your enthusiasm has stirred most of them to action" (2 Cor 9:2).
- "I plead with you, brothers and sisters, become like me" (Gal 4:12).
- "Be kind and compassionate to one another, forgiving each other, just as in Christ God forgave you" (Eph 4:32).
- "Follow God's example, therefore, as dearly loved children and live a life of love, just as Christ loved us and gave himself up for us as a fragrant offering and sacrifice to God" (Eph 5:1–2).
- "In your relationships with one another, have the same mindset as Christ Jesus" (Phil 2:5).

- "Join together in following my example, brothers and sisters, and just as you have us as a model, keep your eyes on those who live as we do" (Phil 3:17).
- "Whatever you have learned or received or heard from me, or seen in me—put it into practice" (Phil 4:9).
- "You became imitators of us and of the Lord, for you welcomed the message in the midst of severe suffering with the joy given by the Holy Spirit. And so you became a model to all the believers in Macedonia and Achaia" (1 Thess 1:6–7).
- "For you, brothers and sisters, became imitators of God's churches in Judea" (1 Thess 2:14).
- "For you yourselves know how you ought to follow our example. . . . We did this, not because we do not have the right to such help, but in order to offer ourselves as a model for you to imitate" (2 Thess 3:7–9).
- "Set an example for the believers in speech, in conduct, in love, in faith and in purity" (1 Tim 4:12).
- "In everything set them an example by doing what is good" (Titus 2:7).
- "Imitate those who through faith and patience inherit what has been promised" (Heb 6:12).
- "Remember your leaders, who spoke the word of God to you. Consider the outcome of their way of life and imitate their faith" (Heb 13:7).
- "Brothers and sisters, as an example of patience in the face of suffering, take the prophets who spoke in the name of the Lord" (Jas 5:10).
- "Christ suffered for you, leaving you an example, that you should follow in his steps" (1 Pet 2:21).
- "Be shepherds of God's flock that is under your care, . . . not lording it over those entrusted to you, but being examples to the flock" (1 Pet 5:2–3).
- "Since God so loved us, we also ought to love one another" (1 John 4:11).

The fact that Paul was mindful of the instructional value of role modelling is revealed in 2 Thess 3:7–9, where he writes (regarding supporting oneself through work), "We did this . . . in order to offer ourselves *as a model for you to imitate*" (emphasis added). Thus, using oneself and others around him as *exempla* has been the application of the instructional technique employed by both ancient and contemporary leaders and educators to good effect along the "practice what you preach" principle.

While the list in table 4 is extensive, it represents only the tip of the iceberg, because role modelling is even more widespread in the New Testament at a less direct or more abstract level:

- In many cases Christ's example is implied *indirectly*, without using explicit "imitation" or "example" language; Willis De Boer highlights instances where Christ's example is held up before Christians implicitly, for example in Rom 15:1–3 ("We who are strong ought to bear with the failings of the weak and not to please ourselves. . . . For even Christ did not please himself") or in 2 Cor 10:1 ("By the humility and gentleness of Christ, I appeal to you").[88] De Boer then rightly concludes that the question is how broadly one is to apply the notion of imitation, because Jesus's life and ministry "established a certain pattern which has significance for his people."[89]

- Paul also offers *negative examples* representing behaviour to be avoided (e.g., Rom 16:17–18; 1 Cor 10:1–12; Phil 3:18–19), and Heb 12:16 further presents Esau as a deterrent case of irresponsible conduct. Third John 11 is also relevant in this respect: "Dear friend, do not imitate what is evil but what is good."

- An *overarching theme* in several of Paul's letters is his presentation of himself as "an apostolic ideal."[90] For example, Samra points out that in 1 Corinthians the list of Paul's self-referencing offers an almost complete outline of the whole letter,[91] and in 2 Cor 6:4

---

88. De Boer, *The Imitation of Paul*, 62–64.
89. De Boer, 68.
90. Harris, *Second Corinthians*, 470.
91. Samra, *Being Conformed to Christ*, 130, where he draws on Margaret Mitchell's work.

Paul specifically "commends" himself "in every way," with Guthrie pointing out that this act of commending himself is a "vitally important thread that has been woven through the book (3:1; 4:2; 5:12; 7:11; 10:12, 18; 12:11), one that lies at the heart of the apostle's intentions for 2 Corinthians."[92] Samra also submits that the whole of Phil 2–3 can be seen as a parallel pattern of imitation of both Christ and Paul, with explicit commands to imitate Paul found in 3:17 and 4:9, alongside references to his own life to form the background in 1:19–26 and 1:29–30.[93]

Finally, an even broader conception of role modelling involves cases when it is not the specific attributes of a person that are modelled, but rather the transformation that God performs in the person's life. Reflecting on such cases, N. T. Wright suggests, "We may suspect that there is something more than mere imitation going on here. One recent writer speaks of 'cascading grace': when God does something in one person's life and through his or her work, other people see it and think, 'Do you suppose that could happen here?' and a spark turns into a flame."[94]

The Bible is, unsurprisingly, packed with such broader models/witnesses, in accordance with Jesus's teaching to his disciples: "You are the salt of the earth. . . . You are the light of the world. . . . Let your light shine before others, that they may see your good deeds and glorify your Father in heaven" (Matt 5:13–16). Paul's awareness of the significance of this modelling/witnessing function is evidenced in his instruction to the Philippian believers: "Do all things without murmuring and arguing, so that you may be blameless and innocent, children of God without blemish in the midst of a crooked and perverse generation, in which you shine like stars in the world" (Phil 2:14–15 NRSVA).

First Peter 2:12 reiterates this message: "Live such good lives among the pagans that, though they accuse you of doing wrong, they may see your good deeds and glorify God on the day he visits us." All this

---

92. Guthrie, *2 Corinthians*, 325.
93. Samra, *Being Conformed to Christ*, 130, where he draws on William Kurz's work.
94. N. T. Wright, *After You Believe*, 269–270.

underlines the significance of the fruit of the Spirit as the essence of the Christlike character and the shining outcome of human transformation through the empowering presence of the Holy Spirit; as Russell succinctly summarises, "We imitate God through the practice of virtue; we also imitate him by clothing ourselves in Christ."[95]

Virtues and Strategic Knowledge

Chapter 5 presented a less-known side of virtues—namely, that an excessive use of a virtue might become counterproductive, and that exercising one virtue may sometimes cause conflict with regard to other virtues. Therefore, striking the right balance in a specific life situation requires a great deal of wisdom and discernment on the part of the actor, which explains why Phil 1:9–10 states that the virtue of love needs to be combined with "knowledge" and "depth of insight" to achieve righteous conduct. In fact, the point that some kind of "knowledge" needs to accompany virtues comes up in several places in the Bible (e.g., Rom 15:14; Col 3:10; 2 Pet 1:5–7), raising the question of what exactly this "knowledge" entails and how it can enhance the cultivation of virtues. The obvious place to start the discussion is the notion of "practical wisdom" (*phronesis*), a key component in Aristotle's virtue theory, as it can be seen to represent a central cognitive element.

Philosophers often interpret Aristotle's master virtue of practical wisdom as "the ability to properly apply the other virtues in a variety of contexts."[96] This is a useful reminder that being virtuous in a social situation will inevitably impact others one way or another. Accordingly, it stands to reason that the required "practical wisdom" presupposes some knowledge about the nature of the specific context, including the participants affected, in order to avoid causing unintended harm when the virtue is translated into concrete action.[97] In concrete terms, such knowledge

---

95. Russell, *The Doctrine of Deification*, 13.

96. Root Luna, Tongeren, and vanOyen Witvliet, "Virtue, Positive Psychology, and Religion," 300. We should note that there is no uniform interpretation of the Aristotelian construct; as Lapsley ("Phronesis," 133) summarises, "There is no question that phronesis does heavy lifting in virtue ethics. It is also true that there is no univocal understanding of what it is and how it works."

97. See Neal Krause and R. David Hayward, "Virtues, Practical Wisdom and Psychological Well-Being: A Christian Perspective," *Social Indicators Research* 122, no. 3 (2015): 735.

may concern issues such as cultural appropriateness, relevance, specificity, as well as awareness of potential problems and challenges that may arise when virtuous action is implemented. Krause and Hayward further argue that there may be even more to practical wisdom than merely guiding and coordinating virtues: it can also "initiate, activate, or motivate the exercise of virtues in general."[98] This is well illustrated by the popular Serenity Prayer, attributed to American theologian Reinhold Niebuhr: "God, grant me the serenity to accept the things I cannot change, courage to change the things I can, and wisdom to know the difference." Commenting on this prayer, Dale Floody underlines the fact that the challenge is knowing what things one can or cannot change, which is where the wisdom part comes into play.[99]

To summarise, exercising loving compassion requires careful consideration about when and how to initiate action that is both effective and sustainable. There is undoubtedly a need for some kind of practical wisdom to allow the actor to see clearly, to discern key ethical aspects of the social situation, and to regulate one's emotional response when making concrete decisions.[100] N. T. Wright relates this need for practical wisdom to the development of the fruit of the Spirit by underlining that "the different varieties of fruit are, like the virtues, characteristics that need to be thought through, chosen with an act of mind and will, and implemented with determination even when the emotions may be suggesting something quite different. That is how you acquire a taste. Or a skill."[101]

In addition to practical wisdom, relevant knowledge may also facilitate the development of the fruit of the Spirit in at least four other areas discussed earlier in this chapter:

---

98. Krause and Hayward, 739.

99. Floody, "Serenity and Inner Peace," 112.

100. Lapsley, "Phronesis," 133. Darnell, et al. ("Phronesis," 116–119) propose a four-component model of phronesis: (a) *constitutive function*, referring to the ability to discern the ethical relevance of applying virtue in a situation; (b) *integrative function*, involving weighing and adjusting the priority of virtues; (c) *blueprint*, which is related to "moral identity" (discussed in the current chapter under narrative identity); (d) emotional regulation, concerning the appropriate control of emotions by reason.

101. N. T. Wright, *After You Believe*, 206.

- First, a reasoned understanding of the cooperation of divine and human agencies in growing the fruit will ensure that one will not be deterred by uncertainties concerning whether the fruit can be consciously cultivated.
- Second, knowing that personality traits *can* be changed will encourage people to exert effort in this area.[102] Carol Dweck's influential "mindset theory"[103] in psychology posits that some people constrain their own personal development by the belief that their potentials are limited, for example by birth, early education, or manner of upbringing; the fundamental maxim of the theory is that it is people's personal beliefs about how much they can change and learn that will influence what they can actually achieve and become.
- Third, in skill learning theory the initial stage preceding guided practice requires "declarative" (i.e., explicit) input about the nature of the skill and its learning. As Stichter emphasises, learning a skill involves a process of acquiring the practical knowledge of how to do something, and he adds that "with virtue, the practical knowledge is the knowledge of how to act well, like acting honestly."[104]
- Fourth, Bandura's theory of role modelling includes the prerequisite that in order for people to benefit from someone else's experience, they need to pay specific attention to the person as a useful model. Therefore, some explicit information about a role model and the relevant attribute to imitate is needed for effective moral learning to take place (which is exactly the kind of conscious messaging that the Bible often provides about *exempla*).

---

102. As Hudson and Fraley ("Volitional Personality Trait Change," 505) emphasise, people's beliefs about whether their personality can be changed will moderate the efficacy of any one type of personality-trait change intervention.

103. E.g., Carol S. Dweck, *Mindset: Changing the Way You Think to Fulfil Your Potential*, rev. ed. (London: Robinson, 2017).

104. Stichter, "Virtue as Skill," 57.

Virtues and the Motivation to Change

We have seen earlier in this chapter that the primary condition for any personality change is the individual's sincere desire for change. The good news is that psychology has produced strong evidence that genuine life goals *can* result in desired trait change, provided these goals are accompanied by change-related behaviour that is consistently implemented over a sustained period.[105] How can we evoke the necessary motivation to promote such long-term engagement with regard to moral virtues? A useful way of understanding the biblical approach in this respect is to examine the biblical context of how virtues are presented and modelled in the Scriptures. After reexamining the biblical material presented in table 2 in chapter 4 (containing a list of virtues in the New Testament) and in table 4 in the current chapter (containing verses of Scripture representing conscious role modelling), three broad motivational strategies emerge: (1) *linking virtue to divine rewards*, (2) *contrasting moral darkness and light* (i.e., desired and undesired states), and (3) *amplifying the attraction value of role models*. Let us examine these strategies more closely.

(1) Linking virtues to divine rewards. Table 2 (in chapter 4) offered an extensive list of virtuous characteristics in the New Testament. An analysis of the immediate scriptural context of the listed passages (presented in table 5) reveals that every single one of them was accompanied by some motivational device, and that these motivational tools fell into one of two categories: the virtue was either related to some *divine reward* or it was *contrasted with some undesired state of affair* (to be discussed below). The archetype of a divine reward occurs at the beginning of the Beatitudes: "Blessed are the meek, for they will inherit the earth" (Matt 5:5) or "Blessed are the pure in heart, for they will see God" (v. 8), and in v. 12 Jesus specifically states, "Rejoice and be glad, because great is your reward in heaven." Elsewhere, virtues are linked to the kingdom of God (Rom 14:17; also in Matt 5:10). As can be seen in table 5, although some of the links to divine rewards are admittedly less obvious than some others, on balance they all share an

---

105. Hennecke et al., "Self-Regulated Personality Development," 289.

overarching tenor of grace, and taken together, they represent a general biblical motivational strategy, the raising of the hope of eternal life in the presence of God.

Table 5: Biblical Promises of Divine Rewards Accompanying the Virtue Passages Listed in Table 2[106]

Matt 5:5–12: "Blessed are the meek, for *they will inherit the earth.* / . . . Blessed are the merciful, for *they will be shown mercy.* / Blessed are the pure in heart, for *they will see God.* / Blessed are the peacemakers, for *they will be called children of God.* / Blessed are those who are persecuted because of righteousness, for *theirs is the kingdom of heaven.* / . . . Rejoice and be glad, because *great is your reward in heaven.*"

Rom 14:17–18: "For the *kingdom of God* is not a matter of eating and drinking, but of righteousness, peace and joy in the Holy Spirit, because anyone who serves Christ in this way is *pleasing to God* and receives *human approval.*"

Rom 15:13: "May the God of hope fill you with all joy and peace as you trust in him, so that *you may overflow with hope by the power of the Holy Spirit.*"

1 Cor 13:10–12: "When *completeness* comes, what is in part disappears. . . . For now we see only a reflection as in a mirror; then *we shall see face to face.* Now I know in part; then *I shall know fully.*"

Eph 4:7–8: "But to each one of us *grace has been given* as Christ apportioned it. This is why it says: 'When he ascended on high, he . . . *gave gifts to his people.*'"

Eph 5:14: "Wake up . . . and *Christ will shine on you.*"

1 Tim 3:13: "Those who have served well gain an *excellent standing* and *great assurance in their faith in Christ Jesus.*"

---

106. The virtue passages in Table 2 that are not mentioned here are featured in Table 6, which focuses on contrasting darkness and light.

1 Tim 4:14: "Do not neglect your *gift, which was given you* through prophecy."

1 Tim 6:12: "Take hold of the *eternal life to which you were called.*"

1 Tim 6:19: "In this way they will lay up treasure for themselves as a *firm foundation for the coming age*, so that they may *take hold of the life that is truly life.*"

Heb 6:11–12: "Show this same diligence to the very end, so that *what you hope for may be fully realized.* . . . Imitate those who through faith and patience *inherit what has been promised.*"

2 Pet 1:8: "For if you possess these qualities in increasing measure, *they will keep you from being ineffective and unproductive* in your knowledge of our Lord Jesus Christ."

Jude 2: "Mercy, peace and love be yours *in abundance.*"

(2) Contrasting moral darkness and light. It was mentioned earlier in this chapter that the motivational incentive of virtue attainment needs to be a combination of the "pulling power" of attractive goals (like the divine rewards discussed above) and the "pushing power" of trying to avoid the alternative immoral state. In general, people tend to find change difficult, regardless of its nature, and in order to embark on some radical personal transformation they may need to be "dislodged" from the entrenched comfort/complacency of their current state. Old Testament prophets regularly relied on this strategy,[107] and we also find a similar contrasting of good/evil or light/darkness in the presentation of virtue lists in the Bible. Table 6 presents verses of Scripture contrasting moral darkness and light that accompany the relevant virtue passages listed in table 2. The archetypical example is of course the list of vices in Gal 5:19–21 that precede the list of virtues making up the fruit of the Spirit, where it is explicitly spelled out that such sinful conduct will exclude someone from the kingdom of God. Similar categorical warnings are also included in some other passages (e.g., Eph 5:5; Col 3:6), but in most

---

107. See e.g. Dörnyei, *Vision*, 195.

other cases the mere description of moral darkness—or a reference to it—serves as a deterrent. Similar to the examples in table 5, some of the verses demonstrate this motivational strategy more clearly than some others, but the overall picture of deliberate contrasting is distinctive.

Table 6: Verses of Scripture Contrasting Aspects of Moral Darkness Accompanying the Virtue Passages Listed in Table 2[108]

> **2 Cor 6:9–10:** "Dying, and yet we live on; beaten, and yet not killed; sorrowful, yet always rejoicing; poor, yet making many rich; having nothing, and yet possessing everything."
>
> **Gal 5:19–21:** "The acts of the flesh are obvious: sexual immorality, impurity and debauchery; idolatry and witchcraft; hatred, discord, jealousy, fits of rage, selfish ambition, dissensions, factions and envy; drunkenness, orgies, and the like. I warn you, as I did before, that those who live like this will not inherit the kingdom of God."
>
> **Eph 5:3–5:** "But among you there must not be even a hint of sexual immorality, or of any kind of impurity, or of greed, because these are improper for God's holy people. Nor should there be obscenity, foolish talk or coarse joking, which are out of place, but rather thanksgiving. For of this you can be sure: no immoral, impure or greedy person—such a person is an idolater—has any inheritance in the kingdom of Christ and of God."
>
> **Eph 5:11:** "Have nothing to do with the fruitless deeds of darkness."
>
> **Col 3:5–10:** "Put to death, therefore, whatever belongs to your earthly nature: sexual immorality, impurity, lust, evil desires and greed, which is idolatry. Because of these, the wrath of God is coming. You used to walk in these ways, in the life you once lived. But now you must also rid yourselves of all such things as these: anger, rage, malice, slander, and filthy language from your

---

108. The virtue passages in Table 2 that are not mentioned here are featured in Table 5, which focuses on divine rewards.

lips. Do not lie to each other, since you have taken off your old self with its practices and have put on the new self."

1 Tim 3:2–3: "Now the overseer is to be above reproach, faithful to his wife, temperate, self-controlled, respectable, hospitable, able to teach, not given to drunkenness, not violent but gentle, not quarrelsome, not a lover of money."

1 Tim 6:4–5: "They are conceited and understand nothing. They have an unhealthy interest in controversies and quarrels about words that result in envy, strife, malicious talk, evil suspicions and constant friction between people of corrupt mind, who have been robbed of the truth and who think that godliness is a means to financial gain."

1 Tim 6:9–11: "Those who want to get rich fall into temptation and a trap and into many foolish and harmful desires that plunge people into ruin and destruction. For the love of money is a root of all kinds of evil. Some people, eager for money, have wandered from the faith and pierced themselves with many griefs. But you, man of God, flee from all this."

2 Tim 2:22: "Flee the evil desires of youth."

2 Tim 2:25–26: "Opponents must be gently instructed, in the hope that . . . they will come to their senses and escape from the trap of the devil, who has taken them captive to do his will."

2 Tim 3:13: "Evildoers and impostors will go from bad to worse, deceiving and being deceived."

Titus 1:7: "He must be blameless—not overbearing, not quick-tempered, not given to drunkenness, not violent, not pursuing dishonest gain."

Titus 1:15–2:1: "To those who are corrupted and do not believe, nothing is pure. In fact, both their minds and consciences are corrupted. . . . They are detestable, disobedient and unfit for doing anything good. You, however, must teach."

Titus 3:3: "At one time we too were foolish, disobedient, deceived and enslaved by all kinds of passions and pleasures. We lived in malice and envy, being hated and hating one another."

2 Pet 1:9: "But whoever does not have them is short-sighted and blind."

Jas 3:14–15: "But if you harbour bitter envy and selfish ambition in
your hearts, do not boast about it or deny the truth. Such 'wisdom' does not come down from heaven but is earthly, unspiritu-
al, demonic."

(3) Amplifying the attraction value of role models. Role models by definition have a normative character—that is, motivational value—and in the
contemporary usage of the term "role model," it is taken for granted that
people chose their models for themselves (e.g., celebrities). Therefore, role
models in the modern era carry, by definition, a positive connotation. The
exempla in the Greco-Roman world, however, were often socially nomi-
nated rather than personally chosen, and they embraced a fuller spectrum
by also including deterrent cases, which suggests that they required further motivational backing.[109] Bandura highlighted two aspects of making
role models genuinely inspiring for people: (1) the extent to which the
modelled action appears to result in positive consequences, particularly if
(2) it is performed by people similar to the observer (because this makes
the success seem more transferable).[110] Table 7 presents the role modelling
passages listed in table 4, this time also including follow-up motivational
amplifiers. As can be seen, every single instance is accompanied by some
addition that foregrounds or augments the inherent motivational capacity
of the modelling act. We may divide these motivational amplifiers into
six categories, the first three types being variations on Bandura's first
point, the fourth and the fifth on Bandura's second point, and the sixth
type simply multiplying the role models:

Highlighting Positive Consequences
- Offering some link to the divine (e.g., no. 6: "The head of every
  man is Christ. . . . And the head of Christ is God"; also: nos. 2,
  3, 4, 5, 9, 10, 11, 12, 14, 19, 23)

---

109. Bell, "Role Models," 4.
110. Bandura, *Social Learning Theory*, 87.

- Mentioning a reward (e.g., no. 22: "You will receive the crown of glory"; also: nos. 1, 11, 16, 17, 18, 20, 21)
- Offering some form of praise (e.g., no. 13: "Your faith in God has become known everywhere"; also: no. 7)

Relating the Role Model More Closely to the Observer

- Emphasising the personal relationship with the role model (e.g., no. 8: "For I became like you. You did me no wrong"; also: nos. 2, 7)
- Mentioning a mediating peer role model (e.g., no. 5: "I have sent to you Timothy. . . . He will remind you of my way of life in Christ Jesus")

Multiplying the Role Models

- Double or repeated role models (e.g., no. 9: "just as in Christ God forgave you. Follow God's example . . . just as Christ loved us"; also: no. 15)

Table 7: Role Modelling Passages with Follow-Up Motivational Amplifiers in Bold (Emphases Added)

1. "I have set you an example that you should do as I have done for you" (John 13:15). "**Now that you know these things, *you will be blessed* if you do them**" (v. 17).

2. "A new command I give you: love one another. As I have loved you, so you must love one another. **By this everyone will know that *you are my disciples*, if you love one another**" (John 13:34–35).

3. "In everything I did, I showed you that by this kind of hard work we must help the weak, **remembering the words the *Lord Jesus* himself said: 'It is more blessed to give than to receive'**" (Acts 20:35).

4. "May the God who gives endurance and encouragement give you the same attitude of mind toward each other that Christ Jesus had, **so that with one mind and one voice you may** *glorify the God and Father of our Lord Jesus Christ.* Accept one another, then, just as Christ accepted you, **in order to** *bring praise to God*" (Rom 15:5-7).

5. "Therefore I urge you to imitate me. **For this reason I have** *sent to you Timothy.... **He will** *remind you* **of my way of life** *in Christ Jesus*" (1 Cor 4:16-17).

6. "Follow my example, as I follow the example of Christ" (1 Cor 11:1). *"The head of every man is Christ ... **and** the head of Christ is God"* (v. 3).

7. "Your enthusiasm has stirred most of them to action . . . **in order that** *our boasting about you* **in this matter should not prove hollow, . . . we—not to say anything about you—would be ashamed of having been so confident**" (2 Cor 9:2–4).

8. "I plead with you, brothers and sisters, become like me, **for** *I became like you. You did me no wrong*" (Gal 4:12).

9. "Be kind and compassionate to one another, forgiving each other, just as in Christ *God* forgave you. Follow *God's example*, therefore, as dearly loved children and live a life of love, just *as Christ* loved us and gave himself up for us as a fragrant offering and sacrifice to God" (Eph 4:32–5:2; **repeated role model: God; double role models: God and Christ**).

10. "In your relationships with one another, have the same mindset as Christ Jesus: **who, being in** *very nature God*" (Phil 2:5-6).

11. "Join together in following my example, brothers and sisters, and just as you have us as a model, keep your eyes on those who live as we do. . . . *But our citizenship is in heaven.* **And we eagerly await a Saviour from there, the Lord Jesus Christ, who . . . will** *transform our lowly bodies* **so that they will be** *like his glorious body*" (Phil 3:17, 20–21).

12. "Whatever you have learned or received or heard from me, or seen

in me—put it into practice. **And the** *God of peace will be with you*" (Phil 4:9).

13. "You became imitators of us and of the Lord, for you welcomed the message in the midst of severe suffering with the joy given by the Holy Spirit. And so you became a model to all the believers in Macedonia and Achaia. . . . **Your faith in God** *has become known everywhere*" (1 Thess 1:6–8).

14. "For you, brothers and sisters, became imitators of God's churches in Judea, **which are** *in Christ Jesus*" (1 Thess 2:14).

15. "For you yourselves know how you ought to follow *our example*. . . . We did this, not because we do not have the right to such help, but in order to offer ourselves *as a model for you to imitate*" (2 Thess 3:7, 9; **repeated role model**).

16. "Set an example for the believers in speech, in conduct, in love, in faith and in purity" (1 Tim 4:12). **"If you do, you will** *save both yourself and your hearers*" (v. 16).

17. "In everything set them an example by doing what is good . . . **so that** *those who oppose you may be ashamed* **because they have nothing bad to say about us**" (Titus 2:7–8).

18. "Imitate those who through faith and patience *inherit what has been promised*" (Heb 6:12; **the descriptor of the model carries the reward**).

19. "Remember your leaders, who spoke the word of God to you. Consider the outcome of their way of life and imitate their faith. *Jesus Christ* **is the same yesterday and today and forever**" (Heb 13:7–8).

20. "Brothers and sisters, as an example of patience in the face of suffering, take the prophets who spoke in the name of the Lord. . . . **You have heard of Job's perseverance and have seen** *what the Lord finally brought about*" (Jas 5:10–11).

21. "Christ suffered for you, leaving you an example, that you should follow in his steps" (1 Pet 2:21). **"'He himself bore our sins'** . . . **so that we might die to sins and** *live for righteousness*; **'by his wounds** *you have been healed*'" (v. 24).

22. "Be shepherds of God's flock that is under your care, . . . not lording it over those entrusted to you, but being examples to the flock. **And when the Chief Shepherd appears,** *you will receive the crown of glory* **that will never fade away**" (1 Pet 5:2–4).

23. "Since God so loved us, we also ought to love one another. . . . **If we love one another,** *God lives in us* **and his love is made complete in us**" (1 John 4:11–12).

Virtues and Narratives

We saw in chapter 2 that one way of distinguishing a virtue from other personality traits is by emphasising its moral nature: a virtue serves by definition some morally good purpose. However, "morality" is an elusive and context-dependent term, and earlier it was shown, for example, that Christian virtues in the New Testament era differed considerably from the Greco-Roman virtues of antiquity. This implies that a prerequisite for the cultivation of virtues is to describe the moral framework within which the virtue in question operates. Research in psychology has shown that autobiographical life narratives offer an effective vehicle for conveying such a moral framework, thereby forming the person's narrative identity.[111]

How does this work in practice? An "integrative life narrative" is a coherent personal story that connects together disparate elements of someone's psychology such as memories, values, everyday experiences, and future visions through various forms of autobiographical reasoning (e.g., explanations, justifications, interpretations, prioritisations, rationalisations, excuses, and other forms of self-analysis). A simple example is that past failure can be narrated both in a constructive way (e.g., *I failed the exam because I didn't prepare enough—I'll do better next time*) and in a demotivating way (e.g., *I failed because I'm not clever enough*). If people succeed in crafting a constructive life story, it can become the foundation

---

111. E.g., Dan P. McAdams and Kate C. McLean, "Narrative Identity," *Current Directions in Psychological Science* 22, no. 3 (2013): 233.

of their self-concept in the sense that it provides their life with a sense of unity.[112] As Jerome Bruner, a pioneer of narrative psychology, has succinctly summarised, "In the end, we become the autobiographical narratives by which we 'tell about' our lives."[113]

Regarding *biblical virtues*, Schnitker and her colleagues emphasise the need to also add a spiritual element to the life narrative; as they argue, virtues are given meaning by a "transcendent narrative identity"[114]—that is, a spiritual life story that encompasses moral engagement.[115] This practice is in harmony with the nature of Scripture, which contains a large amount of narrative material, and narratives have been known to be effective in construing meaning in theology (for a brief overview of narrative theology, see CONCEPT 7.4). Significantly, Vanhoozer and Treier point out in this respect that stories not only help to make sense of one's experiences by configuring characters and events, but they also play a crucial role in articulating worldviews,[116] which can provide virtues with the critical cultural context. In agreement, Brueggemann further explains that "biblical morality is in a story rather than a set of rules. It is like that in our families as well. How we act is generally not determined by what our parents told us to do, but by the events that shaped our growing up in the family."[117]

As such, biblical narratives are effective in configuring the specific meaning of Christian virtues, and indeed, narrative illustrations of personal values are not only an integral part of Scripture but are also

---

112. McAdams, "Psychological Science and the Nicomachean Ethics," 324; as he elaborates, "As a selective reconstruction of the past and an imagined vision for the future, a person's narrative identity tells a story, for the self and for others, regarding how the person believes he or she came to be the person that he or she is becoming. It is my story about how the 'me' of my past became the 'me' of my present, and will become the anticipated 'me' of the future" (324–325).

113. Jerome Bruner, "Life as Narrative," *Social Research* 54, no. 1 (1987): 15.

114. Schnitker, King, and Houltberg, "Religion, Spirituality, and Thriving," 276.

115. McAdams ("Psychological Science and the Nicomachean Ethics," 325) concurs: "The construction of a life story is both a psychological and a moral project, for authors always position themselves within an assumptive world regarding what they (explicitly and implicitly) believe to be good and true."

116. Kevin J. Vanhoozer and Daniel J. Treier, *Theology and the Mirror of Scripture: A Mere Evangelical Account* (London: Apollos, 2016), 95–96.

117. Brueggemann, *Peace*, 67.

regularly utilised in sermons and other forms of Bible teaching.[118] We should note, however, that narratives do not replace rules and regulations (i.e., more doctrinal teaching); for example, regarding Brueggemann's picture above, how one acts is *also* determined by what one's parents explicitly instruct or forbid to do. The main strength of narratives is that they contextualise moral principles and bring them to life, whereas rules and regulations ensure that the narrative interpretation accurately reflects the biblical message.

Concept 7.4: Narrative Theology

The 1970s saw a new movement emerging in theology which highlighted the significance of biblical narratives for theological reflection.[119] This loose but influential theological orientation—often referred to as *narrative theology*—drew attention to the central role of narratives within the biblical canon, arguing that they are instrumental in creating coherence in the patchwork of different genres, discourse types, and voices in Scripture. Following developments in the social sciences,[120] it was also recognised that narratives constitute a fundamental human interpretive schema that allows people to process theological messages by relating to the biblical stories in an immediate and personal way. This recognition

---

118. See e.g., Ferrari et al., "Educating for Virtue," 48.

119. See, e.g., Richard J. Bauckham, "Reading Scripture as a Coherent Story," in *The Art of Reading Scripture*, ed. Ellen F. Davis and Richard B. Hays (Grand Rapids: Eerdmans, 2003); Hans W. Frei, *The Eclipse of Biblical Narrative: A Study in Eighteenth and Nineteenth Century Hermeneutics* (New Haven, CT: Yale University Press, 1974); John Goldingay, "Biblical Narrative and Systematic Theology," in *Between Two Horizons: Spanning New Testament Studies and Systematic Theology*, ed. Joel B. Green and Max Turner (Grand Rapids: Eerdmans, 2000); Stanley Hauerwas and L. Gregory Jones, "Introduction: Why Narrative?," in *Why Narrative? Readings in Narrative Theology*, ed. Stanley Hauerwas and L. Gregory Jones (Grand Rapids: Eerdmans, 1989); L. Gregory. Jones, "Narrative Theology," in *The Blackwell Encyclopedia of Modern Christian Thought*, ed. Alister E. McGrath (Malden, MA: Blackwell, 1993).

120. E.g., the seminal paper by Bruner, which is often seen as one of the main instigators of the narrative turn in the social sciences: Bruner, "Life as Narrative."

shifted the focus of hermeneutical exegesis towards considering how larger blocks of biblical narrative can offer more holistic theological meaning; in Hans Frei's words, "It is not going too far to say that the story is the meaning or, alternatively, that the meaning emerges from the story form, rather than being merely illustrated by it."[121] Thus, a basic assumption of narrative theology is that the impact of the Bible is achieved because readers can personally relate to the biblical stories: once they are caught up in the world that the narrative proposes, they can perceive God's timeless truths and moral principles that would be lost on them if they were conveyed in a propositional form.[122]

In concrete terms, if people succeed in crafting life narratives that feature certain biblical virtues—for example, they highlight generosity by cherishing key scenes or plot lines in their lives that exemplify it—such a life story will "eventually layer over goals and values, which layer over dispositional traits,"[123] thereby promoting ethical and moral ideals.[124] Schnitker and her colleagues summarise this process expressively by comparing it to people "sanctifying" their own stories so that those take on "deeper and transcendent meaning."[125]

Cultivating the Components of the Ideal Christlike Character

In chapter 5 we saw that the ideal Christlike character outlined by the fruit of the Spirit can be understood in terms of three broad dimensions:

---

121. Frei, *Eclipse of Biblical Narrative*, 280.
122. Brian Horne, "Theology in the Narrative Mode," in *Companion Encyclopedia of Theology*, ed. Leslie Houlden (London: Routledge, 1995), 967.
123. McAdams, "Psychological Science and the Nicomachean Ethics," 328.
124. As McAdams argues, such a life narrative may even enable some people "to affirm a vocation in virtue—a life in full dedicated . . . to the fulfilment of a personal destiny or calling toward virtue" (329).
125. Schnitker, King, and Houltberg, "Religion, Spirituality, and Thriving," 283.

loving compassion, spiritual contentment, and steadfast perseverance. It was argued that having such broad virtue dimensions possess positive pragmatic value, because they highlight straightforward priorities and offer a limited number of critical targets rather than foregrounding a relatively large number of personality features where people fall short of the mark. Let us therefore conclude this chapter by examining how we may specifically cultivate these three broad dimensions of the fruit of the Spirit.

Fostering Loving Compassion

We have seen earlier that compassionate love is the primary—or "supreme"—virtue within the ideal Christlike character. However, Paul adds eight further descriptors to the character sketch in Gal 5:22–23, which are helpful in unpacking what the command to love involves in practical terms, particularly when it is applied to the hard-to-love, such as one's enemies (Luke 6:27): one can make a start at becoming more loving by exercising kindness, gentleness, and patience, as well as being generous and doing good. Recall also C. S. Lewis's argument that "the rule for all of us is perfectly simple. Do not waste time bothering whether you 'love' your neighbour; act as if you did."[126] Jesus in fact taught the same strategy: "Love your enemies, do good to those who hate you, bless those who curse you, pray for those who ill-treat you. If someone slaps you on one cheek, turn to them the other also. If someone takes your coat, do not withhold your shirt from them. Give to everyone who asks you, and if anyone takes what belongs to you, do not demand it back. Do to others as you would have them do to you" (Luke 6:27–31).

An important point to recognise for the current discussion is that stepping out in such a compassionate manner towards someone is not merely selfless service, as it also paves the way to coming to love the person in question. That is, the "coming-to-love" approach involves a stepwise process to experiencing genuine love,[127] and a passage in 2 Peter charts such a step-

---

126. Lewis, *Christian Behaviour*, 131.

127. Winward (*Fruit of the Spirit*, 76) makes this point clearly: "We can love our enemies in what we do for them, say to them, and pray for them. If we begin with the third, it may lead on to the other two. There is nothing that makes us love a man so much as praying for him; and when you

by-step route: "For this very reason, make every effort to add to your faith goodness; and to goodness, knowledge; and to knowledge, self-control; and to self-control, perseverance; and to perseverance, godliness; and to godliness, mutual affection; and to mutual affection, love" (1:5–7).

This passage uses a literary device that was popular in NT times[128] called *sorite*, which includes a chain-like succession that progresses towards the culmination, which in this case is love.[129] Commentators point out that the verb rendered "add" in the English translation (*epichorēgeō*) has the sense of "supply," "furnish," "supplement," or even "sponsor."[130] Therefore, the passage represents a string of attributes that are interconnected in such a way that each develops from exercising the previous one.[131] Given that the starting point of this progression is faith, it unquestionably represents Christian moral development, but unlike Gal 5:22–23, which includes *specific* virtues to complement the broad initial notion of love, here the attributes following from faith tend to be rather *generic*, higher-order factors:

- "Virtue" (*aretē*; translated as "goodness") is a broad umbrella term for moral excellence, possibly subsuming the cardinal virtues in philosophy.[132]
- "Knowledge" again has a potentially wide-ranging meaning, from the knowledge of God to the wisdom required to implement virtues (as discussed earlier).[133]

---

do this sincerely for any man, you have fitted your soul for the performance of anything that is kind and civil towards him."

128. See also Rom 5:3–5; Jas 1:15.

129. See e.g., Gene L. Green, *Jude and 2 Peter*, BECNT (Grand Rapids: Baker Academic, 2008), 191; Robert Harvey and Philip H. Towner, *2 Peter and Jude*, IVP New Testament Commentary (Downers Grove, IL: InterVarsity, 2009), 42–43.

130. E.g., Daniel J. Harrington, *1 Peter, Jude and 2 Peter*, SP 15 (Collegeville, MN: Liturgical Press), 244; Norman Hillyer, *1 and 2 Peter, Jude*, Understanding the Bible (Grand Rapids: Baker Books, 2011), 164.

131. E.g., Bauckham, *Jude, 2 Peter*, 184; Warren W. Wiersbe, *The Bible Exposition Commentary* (Wheaton: Victor Books, 1996), 438.

132. Daryl J. Charles, "2 Peter," in *The Expositor's Bible Commentary: Hebrews–Revelation*, rev. ed., ed. Tremper Longman III and David E. Garland (Grand Rapids: Zondervan, 2006), 387; Jerome H. Neyrey, *2 Peter, Jude: A New Translation with Introduction and Commentary*, AB 37c (New Haven, CT: Yale University Press, 2008), 156; e.g., Wis 8:7 states, "And if anyone loves righteousness, her labours are virtues; for she teaches self-control and prudence, justice and courage" (NRSVA).

133. Bauckham, *Jude, 2 Peter*, 186; G. Green, *Jude and 2 Peter*, 193.

- "Self-control" and "perseverance" together represent the steadfast perseverance dimension of the fruit of the Spirit, and it was argued in chapter 5 that this dimension is necessary for covering the inevitable costs of compassionate other-centredness.
- "Godliness" involves "respect for God's will and the moral way of life,"[134] as well as "due reverence and loyalty to the gods, parents, relatives, ancestors, social institutions, and fellow citizens."[135] Moo reminds us that godliness was already mentioned a few verses earlier in the same letter (in 2 Pet 1:3), as the quality of life towards which believers should move,[136] and indeed, 1 Tim 4:8 states that "godliness has value for all things, holding promise for both the present life and the life to come."
- "Mutual affection" and "love" together represent the loving compassion dimension of the fruit of the Spirit.

Thus, looking at the broad content and connotations of the components of the chain in 2 Pet 1:5–7, it appears that the purpose of this passage is not so much to offer specific details about the anatomy of the process as to highlight the robust and gradual nature of one's *progression* towards appropriating the ultimate aspect of the Christian character, love. Indeed, several scholars have interpreted this passage as a programme for Christian moral formation or a précis of Christian discipleship.[137] The primary relevance of this passage to our current discussion is twofold: First, the listing of these broad, composite factors underpinning the development of a loving personality parallels closely the argument in chapter 5 that the first dimension of the fruit of the Spirit, loving compassion, is sustained and strengthened by the two other dimensions, spiritual contentment and steadfast perseverance. Second, the developmental element in 2 Pet 1 teaches us that loving compassion

---

134. Bauckham, *Jude, 2 Peter*, 178.

135. G. Green, *Jude and 2 Peter*, 194.

136. Douglas J. Moo, *2 Peter and Jude*, The NIV Application Commentary (Grand Rapids: Zondervan, 1996), 46.

137. E.g., Harrington, *1 Peter, Jude and 2 Peter*, 244–245; David R. Helm, *1 & 2 Peter and Jude: Sharing Christ's Sufferings*, Preaching the Word (Wheaton: Crossway, 2008), 199.

can be achieved gradually, by internalising and practicing other virtues first. In doing so, the human involvement is paramount, as believers are called to "make every effort" (v. 10) to "possess these qualities in *increasing measure*" (v. 8; emphasis added).

Fostering Spiritual Contentment and Communal Harmony

In Phil 4:11–13, Paul testifies that he has achieved lasting spiritual peace in the broad sense of joyous contentment discussed in chapter 5: "I have learned to be content whatever the circumstances. I know what it is to be in need, and I know what it is to have plenty. I have learned the secret of being content in any and every situation, whether well fed or hungry, whether living in plenty or in want. I can do all this through him who gives me strength." It is clear from the last sentence that this tranquil disposition is sustained spiritually, and yet its development also requires human agency, as indicated by Paul starting the passage with "I've learned . . ." He then reiterates this point by also adding that there is a "secret" to be learnt, and we may therefore conclude that discerning and internalising this secret of spiritual contentment forms an important part of growing the fruit of the Spirit in one's life. So, what does this "secret" involve?

The secret about Paul's contentment is rooted in spiritual serenity and eschatological hope, as expressed so clearly in his prayer in Rom 15:13: "May the God of hope fill you with all joy and peace as you trust in him, so that you may overflow with hope by the power of the Holy Spirit." However, this dimension of the fruit of the Spirit can be further strengthened through conscious effort in a number of areas, some related to *inner joy and peacefulness* and others to *peace in the community* (which are the two dynamically interrelated aspects of biblical "shalom" that presuppose each other). The following selection cannot be comprehensive but is intended to offer a taste of the varied approaches:

- **Thanksgiving.** Ephesians 5:18–20 states that in order to "be filled with the Spirit"—that is, to adopt a Spirit-filled mindset—one should be "giving thanks to God the Father for everything," and in Rom 1:21 Paul directly links the absence of thanksgiving to God to "futile" thinking and "darkened" hearts. Barth goes one step further and relates thanksgiving to the "readiness for joy," adding that "to be joyful means to look out for opportunities for gratitude."[138] In a similar vein, when Miroslav Volf was asked what he would suggest to someone who would "want to lead a joyful life," he responded: "I would say, open your eyes to the goodness, to what is good in your life and in the lives of others."[139] In psychology, Watkins and his colleagues confirm that gratitude is conducive to joy, and their findings also indicate that dispositional joy in turn predicts further gratitude, thereby initiating an upward spiral.[140] Examining joy as spiritual fruit, Johnson also highlights its correlation with "a deep, spiritual sense of satisfaction, confidence, or gratitude."[141]

- **Remembering and reminding ourselves of the good news.** C. Wright suggests that even though as Christians we have hope and the good news, sometimes we simply forget these; therefore, a way of enhancing spiritual contentment is "to make ourselves remember the great truths of the gospel from the Bible itself."[142] This has been echoed by Ryken, who defined spiritual contentment as the ability to "take good cheer from the gospel. It is not, therefore, a spontaneous response to some temporary pleasure. It does not depend on circumstance at all. It is based rather on rejoicing in one's eternal identity in Jesus Christ."[143] Active remembrance of Jesus and the gospel can take many forms, with some powerful traditional techniques involving "gospel meditation,"[144] "contemplative prayer,"[145]

---

138. Barth, *Church Dogmatics IV/3.4*, 378.
139. Adelle M. Banks, "Miroslav Volf Delves into the Theology of Joy: A Q&A," *Religion News Service*, 21 May 2018, https://religionnews.com/2018/05/21/miroslav-volf-delves-into-the-theology-of-joy-a-qa/.
140. Watkins et al. "Joy," 534.
141. Johnson, "Joy," 10.
142. C. Wright, *Cultivating the Fruit of the Spirit*, 53.
143. Ryken, *Galatians*, 233.
144. See e.g., Dörnyei, *Vision*, 132–135.
145. Thomas H. Green, *Opening to God: A Guide to Prayer*, rev. ed. (Notre Dame, IN: Ave Maria, 2006), 103–104.

and "imaginative prayer."[146] Guided imagery and visualisation have also been regularly applied in psychotherapy to generate inner tranquillity and serenity.[147]

- **Accepting others.** Communal harmony is enhanced by increasing the community members' acceptance for each other even if they do not agree on everything. Paul's teaching about this in Rom 14:1–4 is unambiguous: "Accept the one whose faith is weak, without quarrelling over disputable matters . . . for God has accepted them. Who are you to judge someone else's servant?" The concept of "acceptance" is a well-established notion in psychology, referring to a feeling towards another individual which is non-evaluative in nature, has nothing to do with likes and dislikes, but which can be characterised as an "unconditional positive regard" towards the individual, acknowledging that the person is, in Carl Rogers's words, "an imperfect human being with many feelings, many potentialities."[148] Significantly for the current chapter, the field of group dynamics has developed several techniques to enhance group members' acceptance of each other, ranging from helping people to learn about and interact with each other to facilitating cooperation and working towards common goals.[149]

- **Communal worship and celebration.** Communal harmony is strengthened by joyful collective worship and celebration—after all, as we have seen earlier, joyful festivals were a God-ordained feature of Israel's life and worship, and joy was also a critical aspect, the "dominant note,"[150] in the worldview of early Christians: believers were encouraged to experience joyful togetherness in collective action such as singing, shouting (with joy), and dancing.

- **Narrative techniques.** We have seen earlier the potential usefulness of crafting powerful personal narratives for providing the

146. Gregory A. Boyd, *Seeing Is Believing: Experience Jesus through Imaginative Prayer* (Grand Rapids: Baker Books, 2004), 15.

147. See e.g., Dörnyei, *Vision*, 38–40; Floody, "Serenity and Inner Peace," 125.

148. Carl Rogers, *Freedom to Learn for the 80's* (Columbus, OH: Merrill, 1983), 124.

149. See e.g., Zoltán Dörnyei and Tim Murphey, *Group Dynamics in the Language Classroom* (Cambridge: Cambridge University Press, 2003), 19–26.

150. N. T. Wright, "Joy," 46.

required moral/spiritual context of virtues, and Schnitker and her colleagues have suggested that one way of facilitating joyful spiritual contentment is through framing joy more consciously within a transcendent narrative identity.[151] The most obvious way for believers expanding the transcendent element of their narrative identities is through focused Bible study. Promoting spiritual and communal peace in different forms is a recurring instruction in Scripture, possibly because of the difficulty of implementing this aspect of the fruit of the Spirit in the turbulent social reality of the world. This being the case, the Bible offers several templates for "putting on the new self" in terms of spiritual contentment (see e.g., Eph 4:17–32, which contains several practical suggestions), and these can form the basis of formulating a Christian narrative that bridges the gap between the individual believer's life and God's vision of peace. As a result, believers can locate their individual narrative identities within the biblical narrative of spiritual contentment.

Fostering Steadfast Perseverance

Enduring persistence and sustained effort concern a broad psychological domain, involving a number of interrelated elements such as resisting temptation, generating and maintaining long-term motivation, possessing gritty character features, the capacity to bounce back after setbacks, displaying resilience under stress, and employing appropriate strategies to counter difficulties and to overcome obstacles.[152] Persistence also has uniquely theological aspects concerning how to overcome what the Litany

---

151. Schnitker, Ratchford, and Lorona, "How Can Joy Escape Jingle-Jangle," 45–46.

152. For psychological overviews, see e.g., Roy F. Baumeister, Dianne M. Tice, and Kathleen D. Vohs, "The Strength Model of Self-Regulation: Conclusions from the Second Decade of Willpower Research," *Perspectives on Psychological Science* 13, no. 2 (2018): 141–45; Zoltán Dörnyei and Alastair Henry, "Accounting for Long-Term Motivation and Sustained Motivated Learning: Motivational Currents, Self-Concordant Vision, and Persistence in Language Learning," in *Advances in Motivation Science*, vol. 9, ed. Andrew J. Elliot (Cambridge, MA: Academic Press, 2022); Duckworth et al., "Self-Control"; Howard and Crayne, "Persistence"; Mischel, *Marshmallow Test*; Hannah Moshontz and Rick H. Hoyle, "Resisting, Recognizing, and Returning: A Three-Component Model and Review of Persistence in Episodic Goals," *Social and Personality Psychology Compass* 15, no. e12576 (2021): 1–17; Peterson and Seligman, *Character Strengths and Virtues*, 229–247.

of the Anglican Book of Common Prayer calls the "deceits of the world, the flesh, and the devil" and how to "fight the good fight of the faith" (1 Tim 6:12), thereby touching upon the issues of spiritual warfare, the perseverance of faith, and the endurance-promoting nature of trials and suffering.[153] The following discussion will by necessity only focus on areas that are directly relevant to character formation and the fruit of the Spirit. The categories below have been drawn up on the basis of psychological research on the promotion of self-control and persistence, each having clear biblical representation.

Developing the "Self-Control Muscle"

The endurance required to fulfil one's calling has been expressively captured in several places in the Scriptures by the metaphor of an athlete running a race to the end.[154] For example, in his second letter to Timothy, Paul concludes about his life, "I have fought the good fight, I have finished the race, I have kept the faith" (4:7), and according to 1 Corinthians 9:25–27, the key factor in being able to finish the race is self-discipline: "Everyone who competes in the games goes into strict training. . . . Therefore I do not run like someone running aimlessly; I do not fight like a boxer beating the air. No, I strike a blow to my body and make it my slave so that . . . I myself will not be disqualified for the prize."

The important point to note is that although Paul's focus is on moral rather than physical strength, he draws a parallel between the training of the two. Contemporary psychological research fully echoes his approach by likening self-control to a muscle that can be developed with training. This association has emerged from research findings indicating that repeatedly exercising self-control led to an improvement in

153. See e.g., Clinton E. Arnold, *Three Crucial Questions about Spiritual Warfare* (Grand Rapids: Baker Academic, 1997); James K. Beilby and Paul Rhodes Eddy, eds., *Understanding Spiritual Warfare: Four Views* (Grand Rapids: Baker Academic, 2012); Dörnyei, *Progressive Creation*, 224–236; I. Howard Marshall, *Kept by the Power of God: A Study of Perseverance and Falling Away* (London: Epworth, 1969); Robert Ewusie Moses, *Practices of Power: Revisiting the Principalities and Powers in the Pauline Letters* (Minneapolis: Fortress, 2014); Sydney H. T. Page, *Powers of Evil: A Biblical Study of Satan and Demons* (Grand Rapids: Baker, 1995); Thomas R. Schreiner and Ardel B. Caneday, *The Race Set before Us: A Biblical Theology of Perseverance and Assurance* (Downers Grove, IL: InterVarsity, 2001).

154. E.g., Acts 20:24; 1 Cor 9:24–27; 2 Tim 4:7; see also Gal 5:7; Phil 3:14; Heb 12:1.

the participants' general self-regulatory strength;[155] in other words, as Baumeister and his colleagues conclude, "Just as muscles become stronger with exercise, self-control could be improved by frequent exertions."[156] The increased capacity of self-control thus gained could be used for a variety of tasks, which means that if one makes a conscious effort to be more disciplined in one domain, this will have a positive ripple effect in other aspects of the person's life.[157] Winward concurs when he submits that "self-control practised in any part of life helps one to achieve self-control in every other part," which implies that "a particular weakness is best overcome, not by direct assault, but by the practice of an all-round discipline."[158]

Replenishing Depleted Inner Resources

It was already mentioned in chapters 3 and 7 that self-control is fuelled by a limited inner resource of character strength that can be depleted with use. When such "ego depletion" occurs, performance on subsequent tasks that require self-control—including performing other virtues—becomes impaired until the pool of resource is replenished by rest. This being the case, one way of cultivating steadfast perseverance is by keeping up our mental energy reserves. How can we fill up the self's stock of this resource? One way is to counteract certain conditions that act as potent depleting factors:

- **Fatigue.** This may sound trivial, but research has revealed a significant negative correlation between ego depletion and how many hours participants slept the night before: the less one sleeps, the smaller one's reserves.[159] Moreover, depleted feelings were found to increase steadily from early morning until evening bedtime,

---

155. E.g., Heatherton and Wagner, "Cognitive Neuroscience of Self-Regulation Failure," 134; Mark Muraven, Roy F. Baumeister, and Dianne M. Tice, "Longitudinal Improvement of Self-Regulation through Practice: Building Self-Control Strength through Repeated Exercise," *Journal of Social Psychology* 139, no. 4 (1999): 453.

156. Baumeister, Tice, and Vohs, "The Strength Model of Self-Regulation," 141.

157. Baumeister, Tice, and Vohs, 141.

158. Winward, *Fruit of the Spirit*, 190.

159. Baumeister, B. Wright, and Carreon, "Self-Control 'in the Wild,'" 509–10.

indicating that inner resources are progressively drained as the day wears on.[160] Baumeister and his colleagues also add that they observed a significant reduction in depleted feelings after mealtimes. Taken together, all this suggests that sleep, rest, and food have some value for restoring self-regulatory resources.

- **Negative emotions, low morale, bad mood.** When people are upset, sad, or disheartened, they often let their guard down and are consequently more likely to engage in indulgences or to be overwhelmed with temptations, sometimes even relapsing into addictive behaviours or bad habits.[161] On the other hand, experiences of positive emotions have been found to increase resilience over time;[162] indeed, Barbara Fredrickson's "broaden-and-build" theory posits that regular experiences of positive emotions compound over time to build subsequent personal resources.[163] Given that research has shown that when people feel good, they do good,[164] a recursive cycle of increased well-being, self-control, and other-centredness can be triggered if one manages to perform some simple, brief positive activity despite being in a depleted state[165]—this may lead to increased momentum.

- **Physical pain, illness, and suffering** have been shown to contribute to feelings of depletion, thereby impairing prosocial behaviour.[166] We find an extreme example of this process in Deut 28:53–54, which reports on Moses describing how suffering (as a consequence of not obeying the Lord) can turn even the most gentle and sensitive person selfish: "Because of the suffering your enemy will inflict on you . . . even the most gentle and sensitive man among you will

---

160. Baumeister, B. Wright, and Carreon, 520.

161. Heatherton and Wagner, "Cognitive Neuroscience of Self-Regulation Failure," 132.

162. Fredrickson, "Positive Emotions," 25.

163. E.g., Barbara L. Fredrickson et al., "Open Hearts Build Lives: Positive Emotions, Induced through Loving-Kindness Meditation, Build Consequential Personal Resources," *Journal of Personality and Social Psychology* 95, no. 5 (2008): 1045.

164. Layous et al., "Prosocial Effort," 385.

165. Layous et al., 396; see also Patty Van Cappellen, Megan E. Edwards, and Barbara L. Fredrickson, "Upward Spirals of Positive Emotions and Religious Behaviors," *Current Opinion in Psychology* 40 (2021): 93.

166. Baumeister, B. Wright, and Carreon, "Self-Control 'in the Wild,'" 498.

have no compassion on his own brother or the wife he loves or his surviving children." Indeed, Kapic emphasises that the loss of health can commonly cause a loss of a sense of peace, and that even a spiritual warrior such as Luther struggled when he was severely limited by physical pain and weakness.[167] In 1527, after a period of serious illness, Luther explained in a letter how he "almost lost Christ in the waves and blasts of despair and blasphemy against God."[168] He could only rely on the prayers of other believers, and "God was moved by the prayers of saints and began to take pity on me and rescued my soul from the lowest hell."[169]

Although no general strategy can be offered on how to counteract the above conditions and thus replenish one's depleted inner resources, simply being aware of the negative impact of diminished inner reserves may be of benefit. Such knowledge might help to explain shameful experiences such as seemingly unexpected lapses in one's self-discipline or increased selfishness, thereby making it potentially easier to be self-forgiving and to bounce back when the energy stocks have been restored (rather than let minor lapses snowball into full-blown binges or breakdowns).

Forming Implementation Intentions

Earlier we saw that one long-standing aim of moral instruction—going back as far as Aristotle—has been to turn the performance of virtues into habitual behaviour (following the "one becomes good by doing good things" principle). This objective is highly relevant to promoting steadfast perseverance, because research has shown that a crucial aspect of self-control is the establishment of good habits and personal rules that help to reduce the demands on one's willpower.[170] In other words, effective self-regulation partly depends on minimising the testing of one's willpower through creating automatic virtuous habits: for example, "I go to church on Sunday morning even if I'm tired or busy."

---

167. Kapic, "Faith, Hope and Love," 217–218.
168. Cited by Kapic, 218.
169. Cited by Kapic, 218.
170. See e.g., Baumeister, B. Wright, and Carreon, "Self-Control 'in the Wild,'" 505.

In some way, even the oft-cited biblical instruction "Do not let the sun go down while you are still angry" (Eph 4:26) can be seen as a personal rule of this kind. Duckworth and her colleagues point out that the benefit of such categorical rules is that they help to avoid the "just this once" rationalising.[171] There is admittedly a fine line, however, between the kind of rigid legalism that the new covenant tried to avoid by having the law written on believers' hearts (Jer 31:33; Heb 8:10) and solidifying personal perseverance through adopting systematic resolutions not unlike an athlete's methodical training mentioned earlier. However, the evidence is strong: if people fortify their autonomous decisions and principles by forming specific "if-then" rules—usually referred to as "implementation intentions" in psychology (CONCEPT 7.5)—this will reinforce their ultimate goal pursuit and help them to attain desired changes to their personality traits.[172] Summarising decades of relevant research, Mischel concludes, "In life, employing If–Then implementation plans has helped adults and children control their own behaviour more successfully than they had imagined possible."[173]

Concept 7.5: Implementation Intentions

Implementation intentions, first introduced in psychology by Peter Gollwitzer, are rehearsed if-then plans to bridge the gap between a desired goal and relevant action along the lines of "whenever situation X arises, I will initiate the goal-directed response Y!"[174] They are also useful for developing a strategic response to overcome potential obstacles and combat distractions and temptations (e.g., "If I feel upset about something I've experienced, I'll first pray about it"). The benefit of having such ready-made plans in place is that after some practice the self-control response will

---

171. Duckworth et al., "Self-Control," 389.
172. Hudson and Fraley, "Volitional Personality Trait Change," 500–501.
173. Mischel, *Marshmallow Test*, 258.
174. Peter M. Gollwitzer, "Implementation Intentions: Strong Effects of Simple Plans," *American Psychologist* 54, no. 7 (1999): 493.

become automatically triggered, thereby "taking the effort out of effortful control."[175] In this way, employing implementation intentions can be seen as being strategic about utilising habits, and Moshontz and Hoyle conclude in a recent review that "implementation intentions are one of the most effective strategies for promoting persistence."[176]

Strengthening Perseverance through Trials

Several Bible passages state that personal trials, afflictions, and suffering may strengthen perseverance. For example, Jas 1:2–3 explicitly states, "Consider it pure joy, my brothers and sisters, whenever you face trials of many kinds, because you know that the testing of your faith produces perseverance." Likewise, Paul declares in Romans that "we also boast in our sufferings, knowing that suffering produces endurance, and endurance produces character, and character produces hope" (5:3–4 NRSVA), and several other biblical passages compare this maturation process to a "refining fire" in analogy with the smelting of mineral ore.[177] Indeed, we read in Heb 5:7–10 that even Jesus was perfected through suffering. So, how does this process fit in with the cultivation of virtues described in this chapter?

We saw earlier the relevance of the skill-learning theory to the internalisation of virtues, and the third stage of the process of acquiring skills—the *automatic stage*—concerns extended practice in diverse situations (see CONCEPT 7.2). It was mentioned there that this stage is particularly relevant to virtue learning because habitual virtues tend to be rather situation-specific (i.e., virtuous acts tend to be automatised in recurring situations in the believer's life), whereas moral maturity involves

---

175. Mischel, *Marshmallow Test*, 258.

176. Moshontz and Hoyle, "Persistence," 10.

177. One of the most striking examples of how the "refining fire" is applied for the sake of purifying and maturing God's people is Zech 13:8–9, and it is of note that Zechariah's prophecy points to the same conclusion as James's declaration: "Blessed is anyone who endures temptation. Such a one has stood the test and will receive the crown of life that the Lord has promised to those who love him" (1:12 NRSVA). See also Prov 17:3; 1 Pet 1:6–7.

a more all-round capacity to apply the virtue in question. Successfully exercising perseverance in adverse conditions may serve multiple purposes in the process of attaining the fruit of the Spirit:

1. It extends the situational relevance of the virtue, beyond the person's original comfort zone.
2. Practicing self-control under strain develops moral muscle (in the sense it was discussed in a previous section).
3. Extended practice that takes a person to one's limits offers valuable specific "know-how" and confidence about using the virtue, which is consistent with the significance of strategic knowledge and practical wisdom discussed earlier.
4. Arguably most importantly, success in resisting temptations and persisting in the face of adversity may play a central role not only in developing a powerful autobiographical life narrative that will guide someone in similar future situations, but potentially also in forming a "transcendent narrative identity" by linking one's experience to that of Jesus in the sense expressed by Phil 3:10–11: "I want to know Christ—yes, to know the power of his resurrection and participation in his sufferings, becoming like him in his death, and so, somehow, attaining to the resurrection from the dead."[178]

Exercising Cognitive Strategies to Promote Resilience

In their seminal paper on "self-control as the moral muscle," Baumeister and Exline point out that "*attention* is the first and often most effective line of defence in nearly every sphere of self-control."[179] This was also demonstrated in the famous marshmallow test (CONCEPT 3.5), and the principal investigator behind this project, Walter Mischel, highlights three strategies whose effective use helped the participants to persist: (1) actively reminding themselves of their chosen goal on a continual basis; (2) inhibiting thinking about the appealing nature of temptation;

---

178. This verse, as Cosgrove ("Moral Formation," 529) argues, expresses Paul's conviction that character is formed through "sharing Christ's sufferings and thus becoming conformed to the crucified Christ."

179. Baumeister and Exline, "Virtue," 1172; emphasis added.

and (3) monitoring goal progress and making necessary amendments. Each of these strategies are also commended in the Bible:

The strategy of *applying reminders* was first taught by God himself, when he said to Moses, "Speak to the Israelites, and tell them to make fringes on the corners of their garments throughout their generations and to put a blue cord on the fringe at each corner. You have the fringe so that, when you see it, you will remember all the commandments of the LORD and do them, and not follow the lust of your own heart and your own eyes" (Num 15:38–39 NRSVA). In many ways, with its numerous commands, exhortations, and imperatives, we can view the whole Bible itself as an ongoing reminder. As the above quote illustrates, reminders can come in all sorts of creative forms, from stickers and special objects to reminder letters and messages, and Moshontz and Hoyle emphasise that they can be surprisingly effective for helping people to stay the course in daily life.[180]

Exercising thought control is highlighted in 2 Cor 10:5, where Paul states that "we take captive every thought to make it obedient to Christ" and, more pertinently to the current discussion, in Phil 4:8: "Finally, brothers and sisters, whatever is true, whatever is noble, whatever is right, whatever is pure, whatever is lovely, whatever is admirable—if anything is excellent or praiseworthy—think about such things." We should note that the Greek term rendered "excellent" in this verse is *aretē*, which literally means "virtue" and which is used here (as in 2 Pet 1:5, discussed above) as a broad umbrella term for moral excellence; the passage is therefore a call to believers to consciously fill their minds with virtuous thoughts. In a detailed analysis, Paul Holloway shows that this passage is an example of an established consolatory method of the Greek philosopher Epicurus (341–270 BC) called *avocatio*, referring to the strategy of distracting the mind from hardship by the contemplation of pleasure. As Holloway explains, Cicero (106–43 BC) further developed this principle by stipulating that the distractor should not be "the false goods of pleasure but the real goods of virtue,"[181] which is directly applied here. Thus, Winward

---

180. Moshontz and Hoyle, "Persistence," 10.

181. Paul A. Holloway, "Bona Cogitare: An Epicurean Consolation in Phil 4:8–9," *Harvard Theological Review* 91, no. 1 (1998): 92; see also Paul A. Holloway, *Philippians: A Commentary*, Hermeneia (Minneapolis: Fortress, 2017), 184.

rightly points out in this respect that the antidote for negative thought is positive thought,[182] and likewise, Baumeister and Exline confirm that distracting oneself can be an effective vehicle of "escaping from angry impulses, lustful feelings, or envious cravings."[183]

Second Corinthians 10:5 and Phil 4:8 are therefore examples of virtuous cognitive thought regulation, which is well summarised in Col 3:2: "Set your minds on things above." The Colossian passage then goes on to exhort believers to "put to death . . . whatever belongs to your earthly nature" (v. 5), including "anger, rage" (v. 8). One may wonder why anger is seen as so conducive to losing control that it warrants a special warning in Eph 4:26: "In your anger do not sin." Baumeister and Heatherton explain that the power of anger lies in the fact that it keeps one's attention confined to the immediate, anger-provoking situation, which does not leave any mental space to activate cognitive strategies to restrain one's violent impulses.[184]

Finally, arguably the most dramatic form of *monitoring progress and making amendments* in the Bible can be found in the Sermon on the Mount, where Jesus teaches that "if your right eye causes you to stumble, gouge it out and throw it away" and "if your right hand causes you to stumble, cut it off and throw it away" (Matt 5:29–30). These can be seen as extreme examples of what Duckworth and colleagues describe as "removing temptations from sight rather than trying to resist them directly."[185]

Summary: Cultivating the Fruit
Works but Not in a Rush

This chapter began with a question by Plato concerning the origins of virtue: Does virtue come to people by nature or is it consciously acquired

---

182. Winward, *Fruit of the Spirit*, 109.

183. Baumeister and Exline, "Virtue," 1172.

184. Roy F. Baumeister and Todd F. Heatherton, "Self-Regulation Failure: An Overview," *Psychological Inquiry* 7, no. 1 (1996): 5.

185. Angela L. Duckworth et al., "A Stitch in Time: Strategic Self-Control in High School and College Students," *Journal of Educational Psychology* 108, no. 3 (2016): 335.

either by teaching or by practice? Rather than offering a choice between the options, the material presented in the chapter suggests an affirmative answer to each of these questions (and also to some further, unasked ones). The fruit of the Spirit was shown to grow as a combined function of divine agency and conscious, motivated human involvement, and human agency further subsumes a variety of potentially effective approaches, often working in tandem. If moral/spiritual development is energised by a genuine desire to change—which is a prerequisite—personality *can* be transformed for the better through the conscious cultivation of virtues via multiple channels: as learning from taught input, role models, and biblical narratives; forming habits through practice; and constructing a growth-oriented personal life narrative that includes a transcendent (i.e., God-focused) element.

Success in growing the fruit of the Spirit is therefore dependent on the coordinated operation of several parallel processes, and it will not happen in a rush: We saw that *loving compassion* develops gradually, through adding layer after layer onto the foundation of faith. *Spiritual contentment* emerges through the dynamic cooperation of finding inner joy and peace as well as developing communal harmony through processes such as thanksgiving, remembrance, acceptance, worship, celebration, and generating appropriate personal narratives. Finally, *steadfast perseverance* requires the ongoing replenishment of one's inner resources and the development of one's spiritual muscle in multiple ways, both inside and outside one's comfort zone, including applying cognitive strategies and forming made-to-measure personal rules, habits, and implementation intentions. Although this chapter could not undertake a comprehensive summary of the rich variety of pragmatic suggestions that practical work on the fruit of the Spirit has accumulated in the past,[186] the frameworks and templates presented above provide evidence of the possibility and also of the reality of growing the fruit of the Spirit in believers' lives. In conclusion, however, it needs to be reiterated that this growth is gradual, a point clearly articulated by N. T. Wright:

---

186. For two particularly useful, practically oriented summaries, see Winward, *Fruit of the Spirit*, and C. Wright, *Cultivating the Fruit of the Spirit*.

But these character strengths don't happen all in a rush. You have to work at them. Character is a slowly forming thing. You can no more force character on someone than you can force a tree to produce fruit when it isn't ready to do so. The person has to choose, again and again, to develop the moral muscles and skills which will shape and form the fully flourishing character. And so, . . . the long, steady program of working on the character strengths, the virtues, will enable you to live in a way you would never have thought possible, avoiding moral traps and pitfalls and exhibiting a genuine, flourishing human life.[187Pudandel]

---

187. N. T. Wright, *After You Believe*, 35.

CONCLUSION

The Fruit of the Spirit and a "Body Full of Light"

In the Sermon on the Mount, Jesus used the metaphors of "eye" and "light" in his teaching (Matt 6:22–23), and Luke 11:34–36 offers the most elaborate account of the Lord's message: "Your eye is the lamp of your body. When your eyes are healthy, your whole body also is full of light. But when they are unhealthy, your body also is full of darkness. See to it, then, that the light within you is not darkness. Therefore, if your whole body is full of light, and no part of it dark, it will be just as full of light as when a lamp shines its light on you." Commentators agree that Jesus is talking in this highly symbolic message about moral development.[1] The eyes represent someone's moral compass and they are equated with a lamp, because if they are sound—that is, if the person keeps his eyes on Jesus as the ultimate model of virtuous human conduct—the whole person will be "full of light." If, however, the eyes are "unhealthy," then one's body will be "full of darkness," and to leave no doubt about what this alternative denotes, the Greek word rendered "unhealthy" in the Luke

---

1. E.g., Darrell L. Bock, *Luke: 9:51–24:53*, BECNT (Grand Rapids: Baker Academic, 1996), 1101; R. Alan. Culpepper, "The Gospel of Luke: Introduction, Commentary, and Reflections," in *The New Interpreter's Bible*, ed. Leander E. Keck (Nashville: Abingdon, 1995), 244; David E. Garland, *Luke* (Grand Rapids: Zondervan, 2011), 486; Susan R. Garrett, "'Lest the Light in You Be Darkness': Luke 11:33–36 and the Question of Commitment," *Journal of Biblical Literature* 110, no. 1 (1991): 94; John Nolland, *Luke 9:21–18:34*, WBC 35b (Dallas: Word, 1993), 658.

passage, *ponēros*, means "wicked" or "evil," and is in fact the same word that is used, for example, in Luke 11:29 for "wicked generation" or in the Lord's Prayer for the "evil one" (Matt 6:13).[2] There is thus little doubt that Jesus is contrasting two diametrically opposed moral alternatives.

We gain further insight into the full significance of Jesus's message in Acts 26:16–18,[3] which narrates Jesus's commission of Paul on the road to Damascus and which uses the same "eye" and "light" metaphors: "I have appeared to you to appoint you as a servant and as a witness of what you have seen and will see of me. I will rescue you from your own people and from the Gentiles. I am sending you to them to open their eyes and turn them from darkness to light, and from the power of Satan to God, so that they may receive forgiveness of sins and a place among those who are sanctified by faith in me." This passage confirms in no uncertain terms that "darkness" represents the authority of Satan, and Jesus elaborates on the meaning of light by directly relating it to the "forgiveness of sins" and being "sanctified." Reading together the two passages allows us to draw certain general conclusions that capture some of the main points made in the current book:

- The essence of Paul's commission by Jesus was to *open people's eyes and turn them from darkness to light*—that is, to facilitate their moral/spiritual transformation, which has been a central theme in this book.
- The moral/spiritual maturity that concludes the transformation process is described by Jesus as being *sanctified*, which has been explicitly linked to the fruit of the Spirit in chapter 6.
- The prerequisite for the moral/spiritual transformation to take place is for the *eyes to be healthy*—that is, for the believers to receive, and be guided by, God's teaching.[4] After all, God is light (1 John 1:5)

---

2. However, *ponēros* could also be used in a medical sense; see e.g., Nolland, *Luke 9:21–18:34*, 658.

3. According to J. Green, the metaphorical use of the imagery of light and darkness throughout the Lukan narrative is most explicit in Acts 26:18. Joel B. Green, *The Gospel of Luke*, NICNT (Grand Rapids: Eerdmans, 1997), 466. Likewise, Garrett ("Lest the Light in You Be Darkness," 100–101) argues that Luke 11:34 needs to be viewed against Acts 26:18.

4. Bock, *Luke*, 1101.

and Jesus is the light of the world (John 8:12), and Ps 18:28 further underlines the divine involvement in the transformation process: "You, LORD, keep my lamp burning; my God turns my darkness into light." The role of divine agency in bringing about moral/spiritual formation is foregrounded by the phrase "fruit *of the Spirit*" and it has been duly emphasised in the current book.

• Finally, the call in Jesus's teaching to *see to it, then, that the light within you is not darkness* makes it clear that the process of moral/spiritual transformation requires active human involvement by placing responsibility on the moral choices and decisions that believers make.[5] This underlines the discussion of the final chapter of this book on cultivating the fruit of the Spirit.

Taken together, Jesus's teaching points to the conclusion that "a body full of light" involves a mature, Christlike character that has been formed to approximate the fruit of the Spirit. The fact that Jesus specifically calls for human engagement in this moral/spiritual formation process offers an important insight into the overall biblical story: humans are not born with a fully developed Christlike character but, just as a fruit needs to grow from a seed, they need to be actively nurtured and socialised into becoming citizens of the kingdom of God. Indeed, even the Son of God was born as a baby and had to reach maturity embedded in a human community before starting his earthly ministry. These considerations have significant social implications for the transformation of Christian believers, described by Joel Green as follows: "Persons are not saved in isolation from the world around them. Restoration to the likeness of God is the work of the Spirit within the community of God's people, the fellowship of Christ-followers set on maturation in Christ. From this vantage point, "image of God" points ultimately to the transformation of believers in resurrection, a transformation already at work in the creation of a new humanity."[6]

---

5. Luke Timothy Johnson, *The Gospel of Luke*, SP 3 (Collegeville, MN: Liturgical Press, 1991), 186.

6. J. Green, *Body, Soul, and Human Life*, 70.

The main message of the current book is that the fruit of the Spirit takes centre stage in this moral/spiritual transformation process of "new humanity." It presents an elaborate portrayal of the Christlike character that leads to "a body full of light." The Gospels declare that the "spirit is willing, but the flesh is weak" (Mark 14:38 and parallels), but Jesus demonstrated on the cross that the flesh can have the capability of withstanding the enemy's attempts to corrupt. In order to achieve this, Christian disciples need to develop a body full of light—that is, strengthen their flesh by forming a Christlike character as described by the fruit of the Spirit. This explains why the culmination of Paul's epistle to the Galatians is an exposition of Spirit-led living according to the fruit of the Spirit. By providing a detailed list of the key facets of the fruit, the apostle offers specific guidelines on how the "weak flesh" can be fortified. As such, the fruit of the Spirit is more than merely a useful vehicle for Christian character building; it is also a cornerstone of the general biblical portrayal of moral/spiritual formation and a central component of the human transformation process whereby believers are being "conformed to the image of his Son" (Rom 8:29; see also 2 Cor 3:18). We can therefore conclude that the fruit of the Spirit is inextricably linked to the theological understanding of new creation and the advancement of the kingdom of God.

REFERENCES

Akin, Daniel L. "Conversion." In *Holman Illustrated Bible Dictionary*, edited by Chad Brand, Charles Draper, Archie England, Steve Bond, E. Ray Clendenen, and Trent C. Butler, 335–36. Nashville: Holman Bible Publishers, 2003.

Allemand, Mathias, and Christoph Flückiger. "Changing Personality Traits: Some Considerations from Psychotherapy Process-Outcome Research for Intervention Efforts on Intentional Personality Change." *Journal of Psychotherapy Integration* 27, no. 4 (2017): 476–94.

Allen, Michael. *Sanctification*. New Studies in Dogmatics. Grand Rapids: Zondervan, 2017.

Allport, Gordon W. "Personality and Character." *Psychological Bulletin* 18, no. 9 (1921): 441–55.

Alston, William P. *Divine Nature and Human Language: Essays in Philosophical Theology*. Ithaca, NY: Cornell University Press, 1989.

Anderson, John R. *Learning and Memory: An Integrated Approach*. 2nd ed. Hoboken, NJ: John Wiley & Sons, 2000.

Aristotle, *Nicomachean Ethics,* trans. W. D. Ross, 350 BC. Available online: http://classics.mit.edu/Aristotle/nicomachaen.html.

Arnold, Clinton E. "Joy." In *ABD*, edited by David Noel Freedman, 1022–23. New York: Doubleday, 1992.

Arnold, Clinton E. *Three Crucial Questions about Spiritual Warfare*. Grand Rapids: Baker Academic, 1997.

Ashton, Michael C., and Kibeom Lee. "The HEXACO Model of Personality Structure." In *Personality Measurement and Testing*, edited by Gregory J. Boyle, Gerald Matthews, and Donald H. Saklofske, 239–60. Vol. 2 of *The SAGE Handbook of Personality Theory and Assessment*. London: Sage, 2008.

Ashton, Michael C., Kibeom Lee, and Reinout E. de Vries. "The HEXACO Honesty-Humility, Agreeableness, and Emotionality Factors: A Review of Research and Theory." *Personality and Social Psychology Review* 18, no. 2 (2014): 139–52.

Atherton, Olivia E., Emily Grijalva, Brent W. Roberts, and Richard W. Robins. "Stability and Change in Personality Traits and Major Life Goals from College to Midlife." *Personality and Social Psychology Bulletin* 47, no. 5 (2021): 841-58.

Atkinson, Bruce. *No More Law! A Bold Study in Galatians.* Milton Keynes: Paternoster, 2012.

Aycock, Don M. *Living by the Fruit of the Spirit.* Expanded ed. Grand Rapids: Kregel, 2016.

Bandura, Albert. *Social Learning Theory.* Englewood Cliffs, NJ: Prentice Hall, 1977.

Banks, Adelle M. "Miroslav Volf Delves into the Theology of Joy: A Q&A." *Religion News Service.* 21 May 2018. https://religionnews.com/2018/05/21/miroslav-volf-delves-into-the-theology-of-joy-a-qa/.

Barclay, John M. G. *Obeying the Truth: A Study of Paul's Ethics in Galatians.* Edinburgh: T&T Clark, 1988.

Barclay, William. *Flesh and Spirit: An Examination of Galatians 5.19–23.* London: SCM, 1962.

Barenbaum, Nicole B., and David G. Winter. "History of Modern Personality Theory and Research." In *Handbook of Personality: Theory and Research,* edited by O. P. John, R. W. Robins, and L. A. Pervin, 3–26. New York: Guilford, 2008.

Barth, Karl. *Church Dogmatics IV/3.4: The Doctrine of Creation.* Edinburgh: T&T Clark, 1961.

———. *The Christian Life: Church Dogmatics IV/4; Lecture Fragments.* Grand Rapids: Eerdmans, 1981.

Bartos, Emil, "Deification." In *New Dictionary of Theology: Historical and Systematic,* edited by Martin Davie, Tim Grass, Stephen R. Holmes, John McDowell, and T. A. Noble, 246–47. Downers Grove, IL: IVP Academic, 2016.

Bauckham, Richard J. *Jude, 2 Peter.* WBC 50. Waco: Word, 1983.

———. "Reading Scripture as a Coherent Story." In *The Art of Reading Scripture,* edited by Ellen F. Davis and Richard B. Hays, 38–53. Grand Rapids: Eerdmans, 2003.

Baumeister, Roy F., and Julie Juola Exline. "Virtue, Personality, and Social Relations: Self-Control as the Moral Muscle." *Journal of Personality* 67, no. 6 (1999): 1165–94.

Baumeister, Roy F., and Kathleen D. Vohs. "Self-Regulation, Ego Depletion, and Motivation." *Social and Personality Psychology Compass* 1, no. 1 (2007): 115–28.

Baumeister, Roy F., and Todd F. Heatherton. "Self-Regulation Failure: An Overview." *Psychological Inquiry* 7, no. 1 (1996): 1–15.

Baumeister, Roy F., Bradley R. E. Wright, and David Carreon. "Self-Control 'in the Wild': Experience Sampling Study of Trait and State Self-Regulation." *Self and Identity* 18, no. 5 (2019): 494–528.

Baumeister, Roy F., Dianne M. Tice, and Kathleen D. Vohs. "The Strength Model of Self-Regulation: Conclusions from the Second Decade of Willpower Research." *Perspectives on Psychological Science* 13, no. 2 (2018): 141–45.

Beale, G. K. *A New Testament Biblical Theology: The Unfolding of the Old Testament in the New.* Grand Rapids: Baker Academic, 2011.

Beasley-Murray, George R. *John.* Rev. ed. Dallas: Word, 1999.

Beilby, James K., and Paul Rhodes Eddy, eds. *Understanding Spiritual Warfare: Four Views.* Grand Rapids: Baker Academic, 2012.

Bell, Sinclair. "Role Models in the Roman World." In *Role Models in the Roman World: Identity and Assimilations,* edited by Sinclair Bell and Inge Lyse Hansen, 1–39. Ann Arbor, MI: University of Michigan Press, 2008.

Berenbaum, Howard, Alice B. Huang, and Luis E. Flores. "Contentment and Tranquillity: Exploring Their Similarities and Differences." *Journal of Positive Psychology* 14, no. 2 (2019): 252–59.

Berscheid, Ellen. "Love in the Fourth Dimension." *Annual Review of Psychology* 51 (2010): 1–25.

Betz, Hans Dieter. *Galatians: A Commentary on Paul's Letter to the Churches in Galatia.* Philadelphia: Fortress, 1979.

Bleidorn, Wiebke. "Moving Character beyond the Person-Situation Debate." In *Character: New Directions from Philosophy, Psychology, and Theology,* edited by Christian B. Miller, R. Michael Furr, Angela Knobel, and William Fleeson, 129–49. New York: Oxford University Press, 2015.

Blocher, Henri. "Sanctification by Faith?" In *Sanctification: Explorations in Theology and Practice,* edited by Kelly M. Kapic, 57–78. Downers Grove, IL: IVP Academic, 2014.

Boa, Kenneth. *Conformed to His Image: Biblical, Practical Approaches to Spiritual Formation.* Rev. ed. Grand Rapids: Zondervan Academic, 2020.

Bock, Darrell L. *Luke 1:1–9:50.* BECNT. Grand Rapids: Baker Academic, 1994.

———. *Luke: 9:51–24:53.* BECNT. Grand Rapids: Baker Academic, 1996.

Bowlby, John. *Attachment*. Vol. 1 of *Attachment and Loss*. New York: Basic Books, 1969.

Boyd, Gregory A. *Seeing Is Believing: Experience Jesus through Imaginative Prayer*. Grand Rapids: Baker Books, 2004.

Bray, Gerald L., ed. *Galatians, Ephesians*. Reformation Commentary on Scripture, New Testament 10. Downers Grove, IL: IVP Academic, 2011.

Bruce, F. F. *The Epistle to the Galatians: A Commentary on the Greek Text*. NIGTC. Grand Rapids: Eerdmans, 1982.

Brueggemann, Walter. *Peace*. St. Louis: Chalice, 2001.

Bruner, Jerome. "Life as Narrative." *Social Research* 54, no. 1 (1987): 11–32.

Byrne, Brendan. *Romans*. SP 6. Collegeville, MN: Liturgical Press, 1996.

Cacioppo, John T., Harry T. Reis, and Alex J. Zautra. "Social Resilience: The Value of Social Fitness with an Application to the Military." *American Psychologist* 66, no. 1 (2011): 43–51.

Campbell, Constantine R. "Metaphor, Reality, and Union with Christ." In *"In Christ" in Paul: Explorations in Paul's Theology of Union and Participation*, edited by Michael J. Thate, Kevin J. Vanhoozer, and Constantine R. Campbell, 61–86. Tübingen: Mohr Siebeck, 2014.

Canter, David, Donna Youngs, and Miroslava Yaneva. "Towards a Measure of Kindness: An Exploration of a Neglected Interpersonal Trait." *Personality and Individual Differences* 106 (2017): 15–20.

Chapman, Benjamin P., Sarah Hampson, and John Clarkin. "Personality-Informed Interventions for Healthy Aging: Conclusions from a National Institute on Aging Work Group." *Developmental Psychology* 50, no. 5 (2014): 1426–41.

Charles, Daryl J. "2 Peter." In *The Expositor's Bible Commentary: Hebrews–Revelation*, rev. ed., edited by Tremper Longman III and David E. Garland, 357–412. Grand Rapids: Zondervan, 2006.

Chiraparamban, Varghese P. "The Translation of Πίστις and Its Cognates in the Pauline Epistles." *Bible Translator* 66, no. 2 (2015): 176–89.

Christensen, Michael J., and Jeffery A. Wittung, eds. *Partakers of the Divine Nature: The History and Development of Deification in the Christian Traditions*. Grand Rapids: Baker Academic, 2007.

Christie, Daniel J., ed. *The Encyclopedia of Peace Psychology*. 3 vols. Malden, MA: Wiley-Blackwell, 2012.

Christie, Daniel J., Richard V. Wagner, and Deborah D. Winter. "Introduction to Peace Psychology." In *Peace, Conflict, and Violence: Peace Psychology for the 21st Century*, edited by Daniel J. Christie, Richard V.

Wagner, and Deborah D. Winter, 1–25. Upper Saddle River, NJ: Prentice Hall, 2001.

Chung, Miyon. "Conversion and Sanctification." In *The Cambridge Companion to Evangelical Theology*, edited by Timothy Larsen and Daniel J. Treier, 109–24. Cambridge: Cambridge University Press, 2007.

Cohen, Taya R., A. T. Panter, and Nazli Turan. "Guilt Proneness and Moral Character." *Current Directions in Psychological Science* 21, no. 5 (2012): 355–59.

Cohick, Lynn H. "Fruit of the Spirit." In *Evangelical Dictionary of Theology*, edited by Daniel J. Treier and Walter A. Elwell, 332–33. Grand Rapids: Baker Academic, 2017.

Cohrs, J. Christopher, Daniel J. Christie, Matthew P. White, and Chaitali Das. "Contributions of Positive Psychology to Peace: Toward Global Well-Being and Resilience." *American Psychologist* 68, no. 7 (2013): 590–600.

Cole, Brian P. "Good Life." In *The Encyclopedia of Positive Psychology*, edited by S. J. Lopez, 438–41. Chichester, UK: Wiley-Blackwell, 2009.

Cole, Graham A. "Sanctification." In *Dictionary for Theological Interpretation of the Bible*, edited by Kevin J. Vanhoozer, 720–22. London: SPCK, 2005.

Cole, R. Alan. *Galatians: An Introduction and Commentary*. TNTC 9. Downers Grove, IL: InterVarsity, 1989.

Collins, Paul M. *Partaking in Divine Nature: Deification and Communion*. London: Bloomsbury T&T Clark, 2010.

Cordaro, Daniel T., Marc Brackett, Lauren Glass, and Craig L. Anderson. "Contentment: Perceived Completeness across Cultures and Traditions." *Review of General Psychology* 20, no. 2 (2016): 221–35.

Cosgrove, Charles H. "Moral Formation." In *Dictionary of Scripture and Ethics*, edited by Joel B. Green, 528–31. Grand Rapids: Baker Academic, 2011.

Costa, Paul T., Jr., and Robert R. McCrae. "The Revised Neo Personality Inventory (Neo-Pi-R)." In *Personality Measurement and Testing*, edited by Gregory J. Boyle, Gerald Matthews, and Donald H. Saklofske, 179–99. Vol. 2 of *The SAGE Handbook of Personality Theory and Assessment*. London: Sage, 2008.

Costa, Paul T., Jr., Robert R. McCrae, and David A. Dye. "Facet Scales for Agreeableness and Conscientiousness: A Revision of the Neo Personality Inventory." *Personality and Individual Differences* 12, no. 9 (1991): 887–98.

Cousar, Charles B. *Galatians*. Interpretation. Louisville: John Knox, 1982.

Crowe, Michael L., Donald R. Lynam, and Joshua D. Miller. "Uncovering the Structure of Agreeableness from Self-Report Measures." *Journal of Personality* 86 (2018): 771–87.

Culpepper, R. Alan. *The Gospel of Luke: Introduction, Commentary, and Reflections.* In *The New Interpreter's Bible*, edited by Leander E. Keck, 1–490. Nashville: Abingdon, 1995.

Darley, John M., and C. Daniel Batson. ""From Jerusalem to Jericho": A Study of Situational and Dispositional Variables in Helping Behavior." *Journal of Personality and Social Psychology* 27, no. 1 (1973): 100–108.

Darnell, Catharine, Liz Gulliford, Kristján Kristjánsson, and Panos Paris. "Phronesis and the Knowledge–Action Gap in Moral Psychology and Moral Education: A New Synthesis?" *Human Development* 62, no. 3 (2019): 101–29.

Davids, Peter H. "Adoption." In *Evangelical Dictionary of Theology*, edited by Daniel J. Treier and Walter A. Elwell, 30–31. Grand Rapids: Baker Academic, 2017.

Davis, Creath. "Joy." In *Evangelical Dictionary of Theology*, edited by Daniel J. Treier and Walter A. Elwell, 450–51. Grand Rapids: Baker Academic, 2017.

de Boer, Martinus C. *Galatians: A Commentary.* NTL. Louisville: Westminster John Knox, 2011.

De Boer, Willis P. *The Imitation of Paul: An Exegetical Study.* Eugene, OR: Wipf and Stock, 2016. First published 1962 by J. H. Kok.

Deal, Paul J., and Gina Magyar-Russell. "Sanctification Theory: Is Nontheistic Sanctification Nontheistic Enough?" *Psychology of Religion and Spirituality* 10, no. 3 (2018): 244–53.

deSilva, David A. *The Letter to the Galatians.* NICNT. Grand Rapids: Eerdmans, 2018.

Despotis, Athanasios. "From Conversion according to Paul and 'John' to Theosis in the Greek Patristic Tradition." *Horizons in Biblical Theology* 38 (2016): 88–109.

DeWall, C. Nathan, Roy F. Baumeister, Matthew T. Gailliot, and Jon K. Maner. "Depletion Makes the Heart Grow Less Helpful: Helping as a Function of Self-Regulatory Energy and Genetic Relatedness." *Personality and Social Psychology Bulletin* 34, no. 12 (2008): 1653–62.

Dieter, Melvin E. "The Wesleyan Perspective." In *Five Views on Sanctification*, edited by Stanley N. Gundry, 11–52. Grand Rapids: Zondervan, 1987.

Dinkler, Erich. "Eirene: The Early Christian Concept of Peace." Translated by Walter Sawatsky. In *The Meaning of Peace: Biblical Studies*, edited by Perry B. Yoder and Willard M. Swartley, 164–207. Louisville: Westminster John Knox, 1992.

Dockery, D. S. "Fruit of the Spirit." In *Dictionary of Paul and His Letters*, edited by Gerald F. Hawthorne and Ralph P. Martin, 316–19. Downers Grove, IL: InterVarsity, 1993.

Dörnyei, Zoltán. *Progressive Creation and the Struggles of Humanity in the Bible: A Canonical Narrative Interpretation.* Eugene, OR: Pickwick, 2018.

———. *Research Methods in Applied Linguistics: Quantitative, Qualitative and Mixed Methodologies.* Oxford: Oxford University Press, 2007.

———. *Vision, Mental Imagery and the Christian Life: Insights from Science and Scripture.* Abingdon: Routledge, 2020.

Dörnyei, Zoltán, and Alastair Henry. "Accounting for Long-Term Motivation and Sustained Motivated Learning: Motivational Currents, Self-Concordant Vision, and Persistence in Language Learning." In *Advances in Motivation Science*, edited by Andrew J. Elliot. Vol. 9. Cambridge, MA: Academic Press, 2022.

Dörnyei, Zoltán, and Ema Ushioda. *Teaching and Researching Motivation.* 3rd ed. London: Routledge, 2021.

Dörnyei, Zoltán, and Tim Murphey. *Group Dynamics in the Language Classroom.* Cambridge: Cambridge University Press, 2003.

Duckworth, Angela L., and James J. Gross. "Self-Control and Grit: Related but Separable Determinants of Success." *Current Directions in Psychological Science* 23, no. 5 (2014): 319–25.

Duckworth, Angela L., Jamie L. Taxer, Lauren Eskreis-Winkler, Brian M. Galla, and James J. Gross. "Self-Control and Academic Achievement." *Annual Review of Psychology* 70 (2019): 373–99.

Duckworth, Angela L., Rachel E. White, Alyssa J. Matteucci, Annie Shearer, and James J. Gross. "A Stitch in Time: Strategic Self-Control in High School and College Students." *Journal of Educational Psychology* 108, no. 3 (2016): 329–41.

Dunn, James D. G. *The Epistle to the Galatians.* BNTC. Peabody, MA: Hendrickson, 1993.

———. "If Paul Could Believe Both in Justification by Faith and Judgment according to Works, Why Should That Be a Problem for Us?" In *Four Views on the Role of Works at the Final Judgment*, edited by Robert N. Wilkin, Thomas R. Schreiner, James D. G. Dunn, and Michael P. Barber, 119–41. Grand Rapids: Zondervan, 2013.

———. *New Testament Theology: An Introduction.* Nashville: Abingdon, 2009.

———. *The Theology of Paul the Apostle.* Grand Rapids: Eerdmans, 1998.

Dweck, C. S. *Mindset: Changing the Way You Think to Fulfil Your Potential.* Rev. ed. London: Robinson, 2017.

Edwards, Mark J., ed. *Galatians, Ephesians, Philippians.* ACCNT 8. Downers Grove, IL: InterVarsity, 1999.

Elwell, Walter A., and Philip Wesley Comfort. *Tyndale Bible Dictionary.* Wheaton: Tyndale, 2001.

Emmons, Robert A. "Joy: An Introduction to This Special Issue." *Journal of Positive Psychology* 15, no. 1 (2020): 1–4.

Emmons, Robert A., and Raymond F. Paloutzian. "The Psychology of Religion." *Annual Review of Psychology* 54 (2003): 377–402.

Esler, Philip F. *New Testament Theology: Communion and Community.* London: SPCK, 2005.

Evans, Craig A. *Mark 8:27–16:20.* WBC 34b. Nashville: Thomas Nelson, 2001.

Fee, Gordon D. *God's Empowering Presence: The Holy Spirit in the Letters of Paul.* Peabody, MA: Hendrickson, 1994.

Fehr, Beverley. "Everyday Conceptions of Love." In *The New Psychology of Love*, edited by Robert J. Sternberg and Karin Sternberg, 155–82. Cambridge: Cambridge University Press, 2019.

———. "The Social Psychology of Love." In *The Oxford Handbook of Close Relationships*, edited by Jeffry A. Simpson and Lorne Campbell, 201–33. Oxford: Oxford University Press, 2013.

Fehr, Beverley, and Susan Sprecher. "Compassionate Love: What We Know So Far." In *Positive Psychology of Love*, edited by Mahzad Hojjat and Duncan Cramer, 107–20. New York: Oxford University Press, 2013.

Fehr, Beverley, Susan Sprecher, and Lynn G. Underwood, eds. *The Science of Compassionate Love: Theory, Research, and Applications.* Malden, MA: Wiley-Blackwell, 2009.

Fernando, Ajith. *Acts.* The NIV Application Commentary. Grand Rapids: Zondervan, 1998.

Ferrari, Michel, Hyeyoung Bang, Monika Ardelt, and Zhe Feng. "Educating for Virtue: How Wisdom Coordinates Informal, Nonformal and Formal Education in Motivation to Virtue in Canada and South Korea." *Journal of Moral Education* 48, no. 1 (2019): 47–64.

Fesko, J. V. *Galatians.* Lectio Continua Expository Commentary on the New Testament. Powder Springs, GA: Tolle Lege, 2012.

Finlan, Stephen, and Vladimir Kharlamov. "Introduction." In *Theosis: Deification in Christian Theology*, edited by Stephen Finlan and Vladimir Kharlamov, 1–15. Eugene, OR: Pickwick, 2006.

Fiore, Benjamin, and Thomas R. Blanton. "Paul, Exemplification, and Imitation." In *Paul in the Greco-Roman World: A Handbook*, edited by J. Paul Sampley, 169–95. London: Bloomsbury T&T Clark, 2016.

Fleeson, William, R. Michael Furr, Eranda Jayawickreme, Erik G. Helzer, Anselma G. Hartley, and Peter Meindl. "Personality Science and the Foundations of Character." In *Character: New Directions from Philosophy, Psychology, and Theology*, edited by Christian B. Miller, R. Michael Furr, Angela Knobel, and William Fleeson, 41–72. New York: Oxford University Press, 2015.

Floody, Dale R. "Serenity and Inner Peace: Positive Perspectives." In *Personal Peacefulness: Psychological Perspectives*, edited by Gregory K. Sims, Linden L. Nelson, and Mindy R. Puopolo, 107–33. New York: Springer, 2014.

Forde, Garhard O. "The Lutheran View." In *Christian Spirituality: Five Views of Sanctification*, edited by L. Donald Alexander, 13–32. Downers Grove, IL: IVP Academic, 1988.

Fowers, Blaine J. "From Continence to Virtue: Recovering Goodness, Character Unity, and Character Types for Positive Psychology." *Theory and Psychology* 18, no. 5 (2008): 629–53.

Frame, John M. *Salvation Belongs to the Lord: An Introduction to Systematic Theology*. Phillipsburg, NJ: P&R, 2006.

Frederick, John. "Mercy and Compassion." In *Lexham Theological Wordbook*, edited by D. Mangum, D. R. Brown, R. Klippenstein, and R. Hurst. Bellingham, WA: Lexham, 2014.

Fredrickson, Barbara L. "Positive Emotions Broaden and Build." *Advances in Experimental Social Psychology* 47 (2013): 1–53.

Fredrickson, Barbara L., Michael A. Cohn, Kimberly A. Coffey, Jolynn Pek, and Sandra M. Finkel. "Open Hearts Build Lives: Positive Emotions, Induced through Loving-Kindness Meditation, Build Consequential Personal Resources." *Journal of Personality and Social Psychology* 95, no. 5 (2008): 1045–62.

Frei, Hans W. *The Eclipse of Biblical Narrative: A Study in Eighteenth and Nineteenth Century Hermeneutics*. New Haven, CT: Yale University Press, 1974.

Fung, Ronald Y. K. *The Epistle to the Galatians*. NICNT. Grand Rapids: Eerdmans, 1988.

Furnish, Victor Paul. *Theology and Ethics in Paul*. Nashville: Abingdon, 1968.

Garland, David E. *Luke*. Zondervan Exegetical Commentary on the New Testament. Grand Rapids: Zondervan, 2011.

Garrett, Susan R. "'Lest the Light in You Be Darkness': Luke 11:33–36 and the Question of Commitment." *Journal of Biblical Literature* 110, no. 1 (1991): 93–105.

Gartner, Corinne A. "Aristotle on Love and Friendship." In *The Cambridge Companion to Ancient Ethics*, edited by Christopher Bobonich, 143–62. Cambridge: Cambridge University Press, 2017.

Gaventa, Beverly Roberts. "Conversion." In *ABD*, edited by David Noel Freedman, 1131–33. New York: Doubleday, 1992.

Gavrilyuk, Paul L. "The Retrieval of Deification: How a Once-Despised Archaism Became an Ecumenical Desideratum." *Modern Theology* 25, no. 4 (2009): 647–59.

George, Timothy. *Galatians*. NAC 30. Nashville: Broadman & Holman, 1994.

Gerig, Wesley L. "Fruit of the Spirit." In *Baker Encyclopedia of the Bible*, edited by Walter A. Elwell and Barry J. Beitzel, 818–19. Grand Rapids: Baker, 1988.

———. "Fruit of the Spirit." In *Evangelical Dictionary of Biblical Theology*, edited by Walter A. Elwell. Grand Rapids: Baker, 1996.

Goldingay, John. "Biblical Narrative and Systematic Theology." In *Between Two Horizons: Spanning New Testament Studies and Systematic Theology*, edited by Joel B. Green and Max Turner, 123–42. Grand Rapids: Eerdmans, 2000.

Goldingay, John, and David Payne. *A Critical and Exegetical Commentary on Isaiah 40–55*. Vol. 2. ICC. London: T&T Clark, 2006.

Gollwitzer, Peter M. "Implementation Intentions: Strong Effects of Simple Plans." *American Psychologist* 54, no. 7 (1999): 493–503.

Grant, Adam M., and Barry Schwartz. "Too Much of a Good Thing: The Challenge and Opportunity of the Inverted U." *Perspectives on Psychological Science* 6, no. 2 (2011): 61–76.

Green, Gene L. *Jude and 2 Peter*. BECNT. Grand Rapids: Baker Academic, 2008.

Green, Joel B. *Body, Soul, and Human Life: The Nature of Humanity in the Bible*. Grand Rapids: Baker Academic, 2008.

———. *The Gospel of Luke*. NICNT. Grand Rapids: Eerdmans, 1997.

———. "Joy." In *Dictionary of Jesus and the Gospels*, edited by Joel B. Green, Jeannine K. Brown, and Nicholas Perrin, 448–50. 2nd ed. Downers Grove, IL: InterVarsity, 2013.

Green, Thomas H. *Opening to God: A Guide to Prayer*. Rev. ed. Notre Dame, IN: Ave Maria, 2006.

Gregory the Great. "The Book of Pastoral Rule." Translated by James Barmby. In Vol. 12b of *A Select Library of the Nicene and Post-Nicene*

Fathers of the Christian Church, edited by Philip Schaff and Henry Wace, 1–72. New York: Christian Literature Company, 1895.

Grever, Joshua M. "Peace." In *The Lexham Bible Dictionary*, edited by John D. Barry, David Bomar, Derek R. Brown, Rachel Klippenstein, Douglas Mangum, Carrie Sinclair Wolcott, Lazarus Wentz, Elliot Ritzema, and Wendy Widder. Bellingham, WA: Lexham, 2016.

Grudem, Wayne. *Systematic Theology: An Introduction to Biblical Doctrine*. 2nd ed. Grand Rapids: Zondervan Academic, 2020.

Gulliford, Liz, and C. Robert Roberts. "Exploring the 'Unity' of the Virtues: The Case of an Allocentric Quintet." *Theory and Psychology* 28, no. 2 (2018): 208–26.

Hamalis, Perry T., and Aristotle Papanikolaou. "Toward a Godly Mode of Being: Virtue as Embodied Deification." *Studies in Christian Ethics* 26, no. 3 (2013): 271–80.

Hansen, G. Walter. *Galatians*. IVP New Testament Commentary Series. Downers Grove, IL: InterVarsity, 1994.

Harrington, Daniel J. *1 Peter, Jude and 2 Peter*. SP 15. Collegeville, MN: Liturgical Press.

Harris, Murray J. *The Second Epistle to the Corinthians: A Commentary on the Greek Text*. NIGTC. Grand Rapids: Eerdmans, 2005.

Harrisville, Roy A. "The Concept of Newness in the New Testament." *Journal of Biblical Literature* 74, no. 2 (1955): 69–79.

Harvey, Robert, and Philip H. Towner. *2 Peter and Jude*. IVP New Testament Commentary. Downers Grove, IL: InterVarsity, 2009.

Hauerwas, Stanley. *A Community of Character: Toward a Constructive Christian Social Ethic*. Notre Dame, IN: University of Notre Dame Press, 1981.

Hauerwas, Stanley, and L. Gregory Jones. "Introduction: Why Narrative?" In *Why Narrative? Readings in Narrative Theology*, edited by Stanley Hauerwas and L. Gregory Jones, 1–18. Grand Rapids: Eerdmans, 1989.

Hawthorne, Gerald F. "Joy." In *Dictionary of the Later New Testament and Its Developments*, edited by Ralph P. Martin and Peter H. Davids, 600–605. Downers Grove, IL: InterVarsity, 1997.

Hays, Richard B. "Justification." In *ABD*, edited by David Noel Freedman, 1129–33. New York: Doubleday, 1992.

———. "The Letter to the Galatians." In *New Interpreter's Bible*, edited by L. E. Keck, vol. 11, 181–348. Nashville: Abingdon, 2000.

———. *The Moral Vision of the New Testament: A Contemporary Introduction to New Testament Ethics*. London: T&T Clark, 1996.

Heatherton, Todd F., and Dylan D. Wagner. "Cognitive Neuroscience of Self-Regulation Failure." *Trends in Cognitive Sciences* 15, no. 3 (2011): 132–39.

Helm, David R. *1 & 2 Peter and Jude: Sharing Christ's Sufferings*. Preaching the Word. Wheaton: Crossway, 2008.

Hennecke, Marie, Wiebke Bleidorn, Jaap J. A. Denissen, and Dustin Wood. "A Three-Part Framework for Self-Regulated Personality Development across Adulthood." *European Journal of Personality* 28 (2014): 289–99.

Herdt, Jennifer A. "Frailty, Fragmentation, and Social Dependency in the Cultivation of Christian Virtue." In *Cultivating Virtue: Perspectives from Theology, Philosophy, and Psychology*, edited by Nancy E. Snow, 227–49. New York: Oxford University Press, 2014.

Hillyer, Norman. *1 and 2 Peter, Jude*. Understanding the Bible. Grand Rapids: Baker Books, 2011.

Hilton, C. Thomas. *Ripe Life: Sermons on the Fruit of the Spirit*. Protestant Pulpit Exchange. Nashville: Abingdon, 1993.

Hoekema, Anthony A. "The Reformed Perspective." In *Five Views on Sanctification*, edited by Stanley N. Gundry, 61–97. Grand Rapids: Zondervan, 1987.

Holloway, Paul A. "Bona Cogitare: An Epicurean Consolation in Phil 4:8–9." *Harvard Theological Review* 91, no. 1 (1998): 89–96.

———. *Philippians: A Commentary*. Hermeneia. Minneapolis: Fortress, 2017.

Home, Brian. "Theology in the Narrative Mode." In *Companion Encyclopedia of Theology*, edited by Leslie Houlden, 958–75. London: Routledge, 1995.

Horton, Stanley M. "The Pentecostal Perspective." In *Five Views on Sanctification*, edited by Stanley N. Gundry, 105–38. Grand Rapids: Zondervan, 1987.

Howard, Matt C., and Matthew P. Crayne. "Persistence: Defining the Multidimensional Construct and Creating a Measure." *Personality and Individual Differences* 139 (2019): 77–89.

Hubbard, Moyer V. *New Creation in Paul's Letters and Thought*. Cambridge: Cambridge University Press, 2002.

Hudson, Nathan W., and R. Chris Fraley. "Volitional Personality Trait Change: Can People Choose to Change Their Personality Traits?" *Journal of Personality and Social Psychology* 109, no. 3 (2015): 490–507.

Hudson, Nathan W., Daniel A. Briley, William J. Chopik, and Jaime Derringer. "You Have to Follow Through: Attaining Behavioral Change Goals Predicts Volitional Personality Change." *Journal of Personality and Social Psychology* 117, no. 4 (2019): 839–57.

Hudson, Nathan W., R. Chris Fraley, William J. Chopik, and Daniel A.

Briley. "Change Goals Robustly Predict Trait Growth: A Mega-Analysis of a Dozen Intensive Longitudinal Studies Examining Volitional Change." *Social Psychological and Personality Science* 11, no. 6 (2020): 723–32.

Hughes, James J. "Moral Enhancement Requires Multiple Virtues: Toward a Posthuman Model of Character Development." *Cambridge Quarterly of Healthcare Ethics* 24 (2015): 86–95.

Hunt, Lester H. "Generosity." In *International Encyclopedia of Ethics* (online), edited by Hugh LaFollette, 1–3. Hoboken, NJ: John Wiley & Sons, 2019.

Inzlicht, Michael, and Malte Friese. "The Past, Present, and Future of Ego Depletion." *Social Psychology* 50, no. 5–6 (2019): 370–78.

Jacob, Haley Goranson. *Conformed to the Image of His Son: Reconsidering Paul's Theology of Glory in Romans.* Downers Grove, IL: IVP Academic, 2018.

Jeanrond, Werner G. *A Theology of Love.* London: T&T Clark, 2010.

Jervis, L. Ann. "Paul the Theologian." In *The Oxford Handbook of Pauline Studies* (online), edited by Matthew V. Novenson and R. Barry Matlock, 1–25. Oxford: Oxford University Press, 2017.

Johnson, Eric L. "Sanctification." In *Baker Encyclopedia of Psychology and Counseling,* edited by David G. Benner and Peter C. Hill, 1050–51. Grand Rapids: Baker Academic, 1999.

Johnson, Luke Timothy. *The Acts of the Apostles.* SP 5. Collegeville, MN: Liturgical Press, 1992.

———. *The Gospel of Luke.* SP 3. Collegeville, MN: Liturgical Press, 1991.

Johnson, Matthew Kuan. "Chasing Joy: A Retrospective Analysis of the Theology of Joy and the Good Life Project." *Journal of Psychology and Christianity* 39, no. 3 (2019): 166–71.

———. "Joy: A Review of the Literature and Suggestions for Future Directions." *Journal of Positive Psychology* 15, no. 1 (2020): 5–24.

Jones, L. Gregory. "Narrative Theology." In *The Blackwell Encyclopedia of Modern Christian Thought,* edited by Alister E. McGrath, 395–98. Malden, MA: Blackwell, 1993.

Joosten, Anne, Marius van Dijke, Alain Van Hiel, and David De Cremer. "Out of Control!? How Loss of Self-Control Influences Prosocial Behavior: The Role of Power and Moral Values." *PLoS One* 10, no. 5 (2015): 1–20.

Kapic, Kelly M. "Faith, Hope and Love: A Theological Meditation on Suffering and Sanctification." In *Sanctification: Explorations in Theology and Practice,* edited by Kelly M. Kapic, 212–31. Downers Grove, IL: IVP Academic, 2014.

Keating, Daniel A. "Typologies of Deification." *International Journal of Systematic Theology* 17, no. 3 (2015): 267–83.

Keener, Craig S. "A Comparison of the Fruit of the Spirit in Galatians 5:22–23 with Ancient Thought on Ethics and Emotion." In *The Language and Literature of the New Testament: Essays in Honor of Stanley E. Porter's 60th Birthday*, edited by Lois Fuller Dow, Craig A. Evans, and Andrew W. Pitts, 574–98. Leiden: Brill, 2017.

———. *Galatians: A Commentary*. Grand Rapids: Baker Academic, 2019.

———. *The Mind of the Spirit: Paul's Approach to Transformed Thinking*. Grand Rapids: Baker Academic, 2016.

Kenneson, Philip D. *Life on the Vine: Cultivating the Fruit of the Spirit in Christian Community*. Downers Grove, IL: InterVarsity, 1999.

King, Pamela Ebstyne. "Joy Distinguished: Teleological Perspectives on Joy as a Virtue." *Journal of Positive Psychology* 15, no. 1 (2020): 33–39.

———. "The Reciprocating Self: Trinitarian and Christological Anthropologies of Being and Becoming." *Journal of Psychology and Christianity* 35, no. 3 (2016): 215–32.

Klassen, William. "Peace: New Testament." In *ABD*, edited by David Noel Freedman, 207–12. New York: Doubleday, 1992.

Krause, Neal, and R. David Hayward. "Virtues, Practical Wisdom and Psychological Well-Being: A Christian Perspective." *Social Indicators Research* 122, no. 3 (2015): 735–55.

Kubanyiova, M. *Teacher Development in Action: Understanding Language Teachers' Conceptual Change*. Basingstoke, UK: Palgrave Macmillan, 2012.

Lanaj, Klodiana, Russell E. Johnson, and Mo Wang. "When Lending a Hand Depletes the Will: The Daily Costs and Benefits of Helping." *Journal of Applied Psychology* 101, no. 8 (2016): 1097–110.

Lane, William L. *The Gospel of Mark*. NICNT. Grand Rapids: Eerdmans, 1974.

———. *Hebrews 9–13*. WBC 47b. Dallas: Word, 1991.

LaPine, Matthew A. *The Logic of the Body: Retrieving Theological Psychology*. Bellingham, WA: Lexham, 2020.

Lapsley, Daniel. "Phronesis, Virtues and the Developmental Science of Character: Commentary on Darnell, Gulliford, Kristjánsson, and Paris." *Human Development* 62 (2019): 130–41.

Lasure, Linda C., and William L. Mikulas. "Biblical Behavior Modification." *Behaviour Research and Therapy* 34, no. 7 (1996): 563–66.

Layous, Kristin, Katherine Nelson, Jamie L. Kurtz, and Sonja Lyubomirsky.

"What Triggers Prosocial Effort? A Positive Feedback Loop between Positive Activities, Kindness, and Well-Being." *Journal of Positive Psychology* 12, no. 4 (2017): 385–98.

Levine, Emma E., T. Bradford Bitterly, Taya R. Cohen, and Maurice E. Schweitzer. "Who Is Trustworthy? Predicting Trustworthy Intentions and Behavior." *Journal of Personality and Social Psychology* 115, no. 3 (2018): 468–94.

Lewis, C. S. *Christian Behaviour.* London: William Collins, 2016. First published 1943.

Leys, Christophe, Camila Arnal, Robin Wollast, Heidi Rolin, Ilios Kotsoua, and Pierre Fossion. "Perspectives on Resilience: Personality Trait or Skill?" *European Journal of Trauma & Dissociation* 4, no. 2 (2020): 1–6.

Lightfoot, J. B. *Saint Paul's Epistle to the Galatians: A Revised Text with Introduction, Notes, and Dissertations.* 10th ed. London: Macmillan, 1890.

Litwa, M. David. *We Are Being Transformed: Deification in Paul's Soteriology.* Berlin: De Gruyter, 2012.

Longenecker, Bruce W. *The Triumph of Abraham's God: The Transformation of Identity in Galatians.* Edinburgh: T&T Clark, 1998.

Longenecker, Richard N. *Galatians.* WBC 41. Dallas: Word, 1990.

Lossky, Vladimir. *In the Image and Likeness of God.* New York: St Vladimir's Seminary Press, 1974.

Luz, Ulrich. "The Significance of the Biblical Witnesses for Church Peace Action." Translated by Walter Sawatsky. In *The Meaning of Peace: Biblical Studies*, edited by Perry B. Yoder and Willard M. Swartley, 234–52. Louisville: Westminster John Knox, 1992.

Macaskill, Grant. *Union with Christ in the New Testament.* New York: Oxford University Press, 2013.

MacIntyre, Alasdair. *After Virtue: A Study in Moral Theory.* 3rd ed. Notre Dame, IN: University of Notre Dame Press, 2007.

Majerus, Brian D., and Steven J. Sandage. "Differentiation of Self and Christian Spiritual Maturity: Social Science and Theological Integration." *Journal of Psychology and Theology* 38, no. 1 (2010): 41–51.

Malti, Tina. "Kindness: A Perspective from Developmental Psychology." *European Journal of Developmental Psychology* 18, no. 5 (2021): 629–57.

Marshall, I. Howard. *The Acts of the Apostles: An Introduction and Commentary.* Nottingham: Inter-Varsity, 1980.

———. *Kept by the Power of God: A Study of Perseverance and Falling Away.* London: Epworth, 1969.

Martyn, J. Louis. *Galatians: A New Translation with Introduction and Commentary.* AB 33a. New Haven, CT: Yale University Press, 1997.

Maslow, Abraham H. *Motivation and Personality.* New York: Harper and Row, 1954.

Matera, Frank J. *Galatians.* SP 9. Collegeville, MN: Liturgical Press, 2007.

Mayer, Roger C., James H. Davis, and F. David Schoorman. "An Integrative Model of Organisational Trust." *Academy of Management Review* 20, no. 3 (1995): 709–34.

McAdams, Dan P. "Psychological Science and the Nicomachean Ethics." In *Cultivating Virtue: Perspectives from Philosophy, Theology, and Psychology,* edited by Nancy E. Snow, 307–36. New York: Oxford University Press, 2014.

McAdams, Dan P., and Jennifer L. Pals. "A New Big Five: Fundamental Principles for an Integrative Science of Personality." *American Psychologist* 61, no. 3 (2006): 204–17.

McAdams, Dan P., and Kate C. McLean. "Narrative Identity." *Current Directions in Psychological Science* 22, no. 3 (2013): 233–38.

McFall, Lynne. "Integrity." *Ethics* 98, no. 1 (1987): 5–20.

McGrath, Alister E. *Christian Theology: An Introduction.* 6th ed. Oxford: Wiley-Blackwell, 2017.

McGrath, Robert E., Michael J. Greenberg, and Ashley Hall-Simmonds. "Scarecrow, Tin Woodsman, and Cowardly Lion: The Three-Factor Model of Virtue." *Journal of Positive Psychology* 13, no. 4 (2018): 372–92.

McKnight, Scot. *Galatians.* The NIV Application Commentary. Grand Rapids: Zondervan, 1995.

Meconi, David Vincent, and Carl E. Olson, eds. *Called to Be the Children of God: The Catholic Theology of Human Deification.* San Francisco: Ignatius, 2016.

———. "The Scriptural Roots of Christian Deification." In *Called to Be the Children of God: The Catholic Theology of Human Deification,* edited by David Vincent Meconi and Carl E. Olson, 17–39. San Francisco: Ignatius, 2016.

Merton, Robert K. *Social Theory and Social Structure.* Rev. ed. New York: Free Press, 1957.

Miller, Christian B. *Moral Character: An Empirical Theory.* Oxford: Oxford University Press, 2013.

Miller, Christian B., and Walter Sinnott-Armstrong, eds. *Virtue and Character.* Vol. 5 of *Mortal Psychology.* Cambridge, MA: MIT Press, 2017.

Miller, Christian B., R. Michael Furr, Angela Knobel, and William Fleeson.

"Introduction." In *Character: New Directions from Philosophy, Psychology, and Theology*, edited by Christian B. Miller, R. Michael Furr, Angela Knobel, and William Fleeson, 1–16. New York: Oxford University Press, 2015.

Miller, Christian B., R. Michael Furr, Angela Knobel, and William Fleeson, eds. *Character: New Directions from Philosophy, Psychology, and Theology.* New York: Oxford University Press, 2015.

Mischel, Walter. *The Marshmallow Test: Understanding Self-Control and How to Master It.* London: Corgi, 2014.

Moltmann, Jürgen. "Christianity: A Religion of Joy." In *Joy and Human Flourishing: Essays on Theology, Culture, and the Good Life*, edited by Miroslav Volf and Justin E. Crisp, 1–15. Minneapolis: Fortress, 2015.

Moo, Douglas J. *2 Peter and Jude.* The NIV Application Commentary. Grand Rapids: Zondervan, 1996.

———. "Creation and New Creation." *Bulletin for Biblical Research* 20, no. 1 (2010): 39–60.

———. *The Epistle to the Romans.* NICNT. Grand Rapids: Eerdmans, 1996.

———. *Galatians.* BECNT. Grand Rapids: Baker Academic, 2013.

Morrice, William G. "Joy." In *Dictionary of Paul and His Letters*, edited by Gerald F. Hawthorne and Ralph P. Martin, 511–12. Downers Grove, IL: InterVarsity, 1993.

———. *Joy in the New Testament.* Exeter: Paternoster, 1984.

Moses, Robert Ewusie. *Practices of Power: Revisiting the Principalities and Powers in the Pauline Letters.* Minneapolis: Fortress, 2014.

Moshontz, Hannah, and Rick H. Hoyle. "Resisting, Recognizing, and Returning: A Three-Component Model and Review of Persistence in Episodic Goals." *Social and Personality Psychology Compass* 15, no. e12576 (2021): 1–17.

Motyer, J. Alec. *Isaiah: An Introduction and Commentary.* TOTC. Nottingham: Inter-Varsity, 1999.

Motyer, Steve. "New, Newness." In *Evangelical Dictionary of Theology*, edited by Walter A. Elwell, 824. Grand Rapids: Baker Academic, 2001.

Muraven, Mark, Dianne M. Tice, and Roy F. Baumeister. "Self-Control as Limited Resource: Regulatory Depletion Patterns." *Journal of Personality and Social Psychology* 74, no. 3 (1998): 774–89.

Muraven, Mark, Roy F. Baumeister, and Dianne M. Tice. "Longitudinal Improvement of Self-Regulation through Practice: Building Self-Control Strength through Repeated Exercise." *Journal of Social Psychology* 139, no. 4 (1999): 446–57.

Murray, John. *Systematic Theology.* Vol. 2 of *The Collected Writings of John Murray.* Edinburgh: Banner of Truth, 1997.

Nadelhoffer, Thomas, and Jennifer Cole Wright. "The Twin Dimensions of the Virtue of Humility: Low Self-Focus and High Other-Focus." In *Virtue and Character,* edited by Walter Sinnott-Armstrong and Christian B. Miller, 309–42. Vol. 5 of *Moral Psychology.* Cambridge, MA: MIT Press, 2017.

Nelissen, Rob M. A. "The Motivational Properties of Hope in Goal Striving." *Cognition and Emotion* 31, no. 2 (2017): 225–37.

Nelson, Linden L. "Peaceful Personality: Psychological Dynamics and Core Factors." In *Personal Peacefulness: Psychological Perspectives,* edited by Gregory K. Sims, Linden L. Nelson, and Mindy R. Puopolo, 71–106. New York: Springer, 2014.

———. "Peacefulness as a Personality Trait." In *Personal Peacefulness: Psychological Perspectives,* edited by Gregory K. Sims, Linden L. Nelson, and Mindy R. Puopolo, 7–43. New York: Springer, 2014.

Neyrey, Jerome H. *2 Peter, Jude: A New Translation with Introduction and Commentary.* AB 37c. New Haven, CT: Yale University Press, 2008.

Ng, Vincent, and Louis Tay. "Lost in Translation: The Construct Representation of Character Virtues." *Perspectives on Psychological Science* 15, no. 2 (2020): 309–26.

Nolland, John. *Luke 9:21–18:34.* WBC 35b. Dallas: Word, 1993.

Oakes, Peter. "*Pistis* as Relational Way of Life in Galatians." *Journal for the Study of the New Testament* 40, no. 3 (2018): 255–75.

Olson, Roger E. "Deification in Contemporary Theology." *Theology Today* 64 (2007): 186–200.

Osgood, Jeffrey M., and Mark Muraven. "Self-Control Depletion Does Not Diminish Attitudes about Being Prosocial but Does Diminish Prosocial Behaviors." *Basic and Applied Social Psychology* 37 (2015): 68–80.

Packer, James I. "Conversion." In *New Bible Dictionary,* edited by I. Howard Marshall, A. R. Millard, J. I. Packer, and D. J. Wiseman, 222–23. Downers Grove, IL: InterVarsity, 1996.

———. *Keep in Step with the Spirit: Finding Fullness in Our Walk with God.* 2nd ed. Grand Rapids: Baker Books, 2005.

Page, Sydney H. T. *Powers of Evil: A Biblical Study of Satan and Demons.* Grand Rapids: Baker, 1995.

Pannenberg, Wolfhart. *Systematic Theology.* Translated by Geoffrey W. Bromiley. Vols. 1–3. Edinburgh: T&T Clark, 1991–1998.

Pargament, Kenneth I., and Annette Mahoney. "Sacred Matters:

Sanctification as a Vital Topic for the Psychology of Religion."
International Journal for the Psychology of Religion 15, no. 3 (2005): 179–98.

Peck, M. Scott. *The Road Less Travelled: A New Psychology of Love, Traditional Values and Spiritual Growth*. 25th anniversary ed. London: Rider Books, 2003.

Peterson, Christopher, and Martin E. P. Seligman. *Character Strengths and Virtues: A Handbook and Classification*. Washington, DC: American Psychological Association, 2004.

Pinches, Charles R. "Patience." In *Dictionary of Scripture and Ethics*, edited by Joel B. Green, 582–83. Grand Rapids: Baker Academic, 2011.

Porter, Stanley E. "Paul, Virtues, Vices, and Household Codes." In *Paul in the Greco-Roman World: A Handbook*, edited by J. Paul Sampley, 369–90. London: Bloomsbury T&T Clark, 2016.

Porter, Steven L. "The Gradual Nature of Sanctification: Σάρξ as Habituated, Relational Resistance to the Spirit." *Themelios* 39, no. 3 (2014): 470–83.

Rabens, Volker. "The Holy Spirit and Deification in Paul: A 'Western' Perspective." In *The Holy Spirit and the Church According to the New Testament*, edited by Predrag Dragutinovic, Karl-Wilhelm Niebuhr, James Buchanan Wallace, and Christos Karakolis, 187–220. Tübingen: Mohr Siebeck, 2016.

———. "'Indicative and Imperative' as the Substructure of Paul's Theology-and-Ethics in Galatians? A Discussion of Divine and Human Agency in Paul." In *Galatians and Christian Theology: Justification, the Gospel, and Ethics in Paul's Letter*, edited by Mark W. Elliott, Scott J. Hafemann, and John Frederick, 285–305. Grand Rapids: Baker Academic, 2014.

Rapa, Robert K. "Galatians." In *The Expositor's Bible Commentary: Romans–Galatians*, edited by Tremper Longman III and David E. Garland, 547–640. Rev. ed. Grand Rapids: Zondervan, 2008.

Robbins, Brent Dean. "What Is the Good Life? Positive Psychology and the Renaissance of Humanistic Psychology." *Humanistic Psychologist* 36 (2008): 96–112.

Roberts, Brent W., Jing Luo, Daniel A. Briley, Philip I. Chow, Rong Su, and Patrick L. Hill. "A Systematic Review of Personality Trait Change through Intervention." *Psychological Bulletin* 143, no. 2 (2017): 117–41.

Roberts, Robert C. *Spiritual Emotions: A Psychology of Christian Virtues*. Grand Rapids: Eerdmans, 2007.

Rogers, Carl. *Freedom to Learn for the 80's*. Columbus, OH: Merrill, 1983.

Root Luna, Lindsey M., Daryl R. Van Tongeren, and Charlotte vanOyen Witvliet. "Virtue, Positive Psychology, and Religion: Consideration of an Overarching Virtue and an Underpinning Mechanism." *Psychology of Religion and Spirituality* 9, no. 3 (2017): 299–302.

Runge, Steven E. *Galatians: A Textual Guide*. High Definition Commentary. Bellingham, WA: Logos Bible Software, 2019.

Russell, Norman. *The Doctrine of Deification in the Greek Patristic Tradition*. Oxford: Oxford University Press, 2006.

Ryken, Leland, James C. Wilhoit, and Tremper Longman III. *Dictionary of Biblical Imagery*. Downers Grove, IL: InterVarsity, 1998.

Ryken, Philip Graham. *Galatians*. Reformed Expository Commentary. Phillipsburg, NJ: P&R, 2005.

Samra, James George. *Being Conformed to Christ in Community: A Study of Maturity, Maturation and the Local Church in the Undisputed Pauline Epistles*. London: T&T Clark, 2006.

Schellenberg, Ryan S. "Peace." In *Dictionary of Jesus and the Gospels*, edited by Joel B. Green, Jeannine K. Brown, and Nicholas Perrin, 666–69. 2nd ed. Downers Grove, IL: IVP Academic, 2013.

Schnitker, Sarah A. "An Examination of Patience and Well-Being." *Journal of Positive Psychology* 7, no. 4 (2012): 263–80.

Schnitker, Sarah A., and Robert A. Emmons. "The Psychology of Virtue: Integrating Positive Psychology and the Psychology of Religion." *Psychology of Religion and Spirituality* 9, no. 3 (2017): 239–41.

Schnitker, Sarah A., Benjamin Houltberg, William Dyrness, and Nanyamka Redmond. "The Virtue of Patience, Spirituality, and Suffering: Integrating Lessons from Positive Psychology, Psychology of Religion, and Christian Theology." *Psychology of Religion and Spirituality* 9, no. 3 (2017): 264–75.

Schnitker, Sarah A., Juliette L. Ratchford, and Rosemond T. Lorona. "How Can Joy Escape Jingle-Jangle? Virtue and Telos Conceptualizations as Alternative Approaches to the Scientific Study of Joy." *Journal of Positive Psychology* 15, no. 1 (2020): 44–48.

Schnitker, Sarah A., Pamela E. King, and Benjamin Houltberg. "Religion, Spirituality, and Thriving: Transcendent Narrative, Virtue, and Telos." *Journal of Research on Adolescence* 29, no. 2 (2019): 276–90.

Schreiner, Thomas R. *Galatians*. Zondervan Exegetical Commentary on the New Testament. Grand Rapids: Baker Academic, 2010.

———. *Romans*. BECNT. Grand Rapids: Baker Academic, 1998.

Schreiner, Thomas R., and Ardel B. Caneday. *The Race Set before Us: A Biblical Theology of Perseverance and Assurance*. Downers Grove, IL: InterVarsity, 2001.

Schwartz, Barry, and Kenneth E. Sharpe. "Practical Wisdom: Aristotle Meets Positive Psychology." *Journal of Happiness Studies* 7 (2006): 377–395.

Sheir-Jones, A. "Sanctification." In *New Dictionary of Theology: Historical and Systematic*, edited by Martin Davie, Tim Grass, Stephen R. Holmes, John McDowell, and T. A. Noble, 804–8. Downers Grove, IL: IVP Academic, 2016.

Sheldon, Kennon M., Paul E. Jose, Todd B. Kashdan, and Aaron Jarden. "Personality, Effective Goal-Striving, and Enhanced Well-Being: Comparing 10 Candidate Personality Strengths." *Personality and Social Psychology Bulletin* 41, no. 4 (2015): 575–85.

Shryack, Jessica, Michael F. Steger, Robert F. Krueger, and Christopher S. Kallie. "The Structure of Virtue: An Empirical Investigation of the Dimensionality of the Virtues in Action Inventory of Strengths." *Personality and Individual Differences* 48 (2010): 714–19.

Silva, Moisés, ed. *New International Dictionary of New Testament Theology and Exegesis*. Vols. 1–5. 2nd ed. Grand Rapids: Zondervan, 2014.

Sims, Gregory K., Linden L. Nelson, and Mindy R. Puopolo, eds. *Personal Peacefulness: Psychological Perspectives*. New York: Springer, 2014.

Smalley, Stephen S. "Joy." In *New Dictionary of Biblical Theology*, edited by T. Desmond Alexander and Brian S. Rosner, 608–11. Leicester: Inter-Varsity, 2000.

Snapp, James. "Galatians 5:22–23: Have We Lost Some Fruit?" *The Text of the Gospels* (blog). 4 July 2019. https://www.thetextofthegospels.com/2019/07/galatians-522-23-have-we-lost-some-fruit.html.

Sreenivasan, Gopal. "Character Education and the Rearguard of Situationism." In *Virtue and Character*, edited by Walter Sinnott-Armstrong and Christian B. Miller, 131–62. Vol. 5 of *Mortal Psychology*. Cambridge, MA: MIT Press, 2017.

Stamoolis, James J. "Theosis." In *Evangelical Dictionary of Theology*, edited by Daniel J. Treier and Walter A. Elwell, 875–76. Grand Rapids: Baker Academic, 2017.

Starr, James M. *Sharers in Divine Nature: 2 Peter 1:4 in Its Hellenistic Context*. Stockholm: Almqvist & Wiksell International, 2000.

Stein, Robert H. *Mark*. BECNT. Grand Rapids: Baker Academic, 2008.

Stephens, Mark B. *Annihilation or Renewal? The Meaning and Function of New Creation in the Book of Revelation*. Tübingen: Mohr Siebeck, 2011.

Sternberg, Karin. *Psychology of Love 101*. New York: Springer, 2014.

Stich, Stephen, John M. Doris, and Erica Roedder. "Altruism." In *The Moral*

Psychology Handbook, edited by John M. Doris, 147–205. New York: Oxford University Press, 2010.

Stichter, Matt. "Virtue as Skill." In *The Oxford Handbook of Virtue*, edited by Nancy E. Snow, 57–81. New York: Oxford University Press, 2018.

Stobart, A. J. "Regeneration." In *New Dictionary of Theology: Historical and Systematic*, edited by Martin Davie, Tim Grass, Stephen R. Holmes, John McDowell, and T. A. Noble, 752–54. Downers Grove, IL: IVP Academic, 2016.

Stott, John R. W. *The Message of Galatians: Only One Way*. Downers Grove, IL: InterVarsity, 1968.

Strauss, Mark L. *Mark*. Zondervan Exegetical Commentary on the New Testament. Grand Rapids: Zondervan, 2014.

Swartley, Willard M. "Peace." In *Dictionary of Scripture and Ethics*, edited by Joel B. Green, 583–86. Grand Rapids: Baker Academic, 2011.

Tappin, Ben M., and Valerio Capraro. "Doing Good vs. Avoiding Bad in Prosocial Choice: A Refined Test and Extension of the Morality Preference Hypothesis." *Journal of Experimental Social Psychology* 79 (2018): 64–70.

Telzer, Eva H., Carrie L. Masten, Elliot T. Berkman, Matthew D. Lieberman, and Andrew J. Fuligni. "Neural Regions Associated with Self Control and Mentalizing Are Recruited During Prosocial Behaviors Towards the Family." *NeuroImage* 58 (2011): 242–49.

Theissen, Gerd. *Psychological Aspects of Pauline Theology*. Translated by John P. Galvin. Edinburgh: T&T Clark, 1987.

Thielmann, Isabel, and Benjamin E. Hilbig. "The Traits One Can Trust: Dissecting Reciprocity and Kindness as Determinants of Trustworthy Behavior." *Personality and Social Psychology Bulletin* 41, no. 11 (2015): 1523–36.

Thiselton, Anthony C. *The Thiselton Companion to Christian Theology*. Grand Rapids: Eerdmans, 2015.

Tidball, Derek. "Holiness: Restoring God's Image—Colossians 3:5–17." In *Sanctification: Explorations in Theology and Practice*, edited by Kelly M. Kapic, 25–32. Downers Grove, IL: IVP Academic, 2014.

———. *The Message of Holiness: Restoring God's Masterpiece*. Nottingham: Inter-Varsity, 2010.

Tomlin, Graham. *Spiritual Fitness: Christian Character in a Consumer Society*. London: Continuum, 2006.

Trask, Thomas E., and Wayde I. Goodall. *The Fruit of the Spirit: Becoming the Person God Wants You to Be*. Nashville: Emanate, 2000.

Treier, Daniel J. *Proverbs and Ecclesiastes*. Brazos Theological Commentary on the Bible. Grand Rapids: Brazos, 2011.

Underwood, Lynn G. "Compassionate Love: A Framework for Research." In *The Science of Compassionate Love: Theory, Research, and Applications*, edited by Beverley Fehr, Susan Sprecher, and Lynn G. Underwood, 3–25. Malden, MA: Wiley-Blackwell, 2009.

———. "Interviews with Trappist Monks as a Contribution to Research Methodology in the Investigation of Compassionate Love." *Journal for the Theory of Social Behaviour* 35, no. 3 (2005): 285–302.

Vainio, Olli-Pekka. *Virtue: An Introduction to Theory and Practice*. Eugene, OR: Cascade Books, 2016.

Van Cappellen, Patty. "The Emotion of Joy: Commentary on Johnson." *Journal of Positive Psychology* 15, no. 1 (2020): 40–43.

Van Cappellen, Patty, Megan E. Edwards, and Barbara L. Fredrickson. "Upward Spirals of Positive Emotions and Religious Behaviors." *Current Opinion in Psychology* 40 (2021): 92–98.

Van Slyke, James A. "Moral Psychology, Neuroscience, and Virtue: From Moral Judgment to Moral Character." In *Virtues and Their Vices*, edited by Kevin Timpe and Craig A. Boyd, 459–81. New York: Oxford University Press, 2014.

Vanhoozer, Kevin J. "In Bright Shadow: C. S. Lewis on the Imagination for Theology and Discipleship." In *The Romantic Rationalist: God, Life, and Imagination in the Work of C. S. Lewis*, edited by John Piper and David Mathis, 81–104. Wheaton: Crossway, 2014.

———. *Pictures at a Theological Exhibition: Scenes of the Church's Worship, Witness and Wisdom*. Downers Grove, IL: IVP Academic, 2016.

Vanhoozer, Kevin J., and Daniel J. Treier. *Theology and the Mirror of Scripture: A Mere Evangelical Account*. London: Apollos, 2016.

Verplanken, Bas, ed. *The Psychology of Habit: Theory, Mechanisms, Change, and Contexts*. Cham, Switzerland: Springer, 2018.

Vess, Matthew, Rebecca J. Brooker, Matt Stichter, and Jenae M. Neiderhiser. "Genes and Virtue: Exploring How Heritability Beliefs Shape Conceptions of Virtue and Its Development." *Behavior Genetics* 49 (2019): 168–74.

Vohs, Kathleen D., and Roy F. Baumeister, eds. *Handbook of Self-Regulation: Research, Theory, and Applications*. 3rd ed. New York: Guilford, 2016.

Volf, Miroslav. "The Crown of the Good Life: A Hypothesis." In *Joy and Human Flourishing: Essays on Theology, Culture, and the Good Life*, edited by Miroslav Volf and Justin E. Crisp, 127–36. Minneapolis: Fortress, 2015.

Volf, Miroslav, and Justin E. Crisp, eds. *Joy and Human Flourishing: Essays on Theology, Culture, and the Good Life.* Minneapolis: Fortress, 2015.

Wagner, Jenny, Ulrich Orth, Wiebke Bleidorn, Christopher J. Hopwood, and Christian Kandler. "Toward an Integrative Model of Sources of Personality Stability and Change." *Current Directions in Psychological Science* 29, no. 5 (2020): 438–44.

Walker, A. D. M. "The Incompatibility of the Virtues." *Ratio* 6, no. 1 (1993): 44–62.

Wall, Robert W. "The Acts of the Apostles: Introduction, Commentary, and Reflections." In *The New Interpreter's Bible*, edited by Leander E. Keck, 1–368. Nashville: Abingdon, 2002.

Walvoord, John F. "The Augustinian Dispensational Perspective." In *Five Views on Sanctification*, edited by Stanley N. Gundry, 199–229. Grand Rapids: Zondervan, 1987.

Watkins, Philip C., Robert A. Emmons, Madeline R. Greaves, and Joshua Bell. "Joy Is a Distinct Positive Emotion: Assessment of Joy and Relationship to Gratitude and Well-Being." *Journal of Positive Psychology* 13, no. 5 (2018): 522–39.

Watson, Gary. "Virtues in Excess." *Philosophical Studies* 46, no. 1 (1984): 57–74.

Wenham, David. "The Christian Life: A Life of Tension? A Consideration of the Nature of Christian Experience in Paul." In *Pauline Studies: Essays Presented to Professor F. F. Bruce on His 70th Birthday*, edited by Donald A. Hagner and Murray J. Harris, 80–94. Exeter: Paternoster, 1980.

Wessel, Walter W., and Mark L. Strauss. "Mark." In *The Expositor's Bible Commentary: Matthew–Mark*, edited by Tremper Longman III and David E. Garland, 671–989. Rev. ed. Grand Rapids: Zondervan, 2010.

Westermann, Claus. "Peace (Shalom) in the Old Testament." Translated by Walter Sawatsky. In *The Meaning of Peace: Biblical Studies*, edited by Perry B. Yoder and Willard M. Swartley, 16–48. Louisville: Westminster John Knox, 1992.

White, Reginald E. O. "Sanctification." In *Evangelical Dictionary of Theology*, edited by Daniel J. Treier and Walter A. Elwell, 770–72. Grand Rapids: Baker Academic, 2017.

Wiersbe, Warren W. *The Bible Exposition Commentary.* Wheaton: Victor, 1996.

———, ed. *Classic Sermons on the Fruit of the Spirit.* Grand Rapids: Kregel, 2002.

Wiese, Christopher W., Louis Tay, Angela L. Duckworth, Sidney D'Mello, Lauren Kuykendall, Wilhelm Hofmann, Roy F. Baumeister, and Kathleen D. Vohs. "Too Much of a Good Thing? Exploring the Inverted-U Relationship between Self-Control and Happiness." *Journal of Personality* 86 (2018): 380–96.

Williams, Anna N. *The Ground of Union: Deification in Aquinas and Palamas.* New York: Oxford University Press, 1999.

Winward, Stephen F. *Fruit of the Spirit.* Leicester: Inter-Varsity, 1981.

Witherington, Ben, III. *Grace in Galatia: A Commentary on St. Paul's Letter to the Galatians.* Grand Rapids: Eerdmans, 1998.

Wood, W. Jay. "Christian Theories of Virtue." In *The Oxford Handbook of Virtue*, edited by Nancy E. Snow, 281–300. New York: Oxford University Press, 2018.

Wood, Wendy, and Dennis Rünger. "Psychology of Habit." *Annual Review of Psychology* 67 (2016): 289–314.

Wright, Christopher J. H. *Cultivating the Fruit of the Spirit: Growing in Christlikeness.* Downers Grove, IL: IVP Books, 2017.

Wright, Jennifer Cole, Michael T. Warren, and Nancy E. Snow. *Understanding Virtue: Theory and Measurement.* New York: Oxford University Press, 2021.

Wright, N. T. *After You Believe: Why Christian Character Matters.* New York: HarperOne, 2010.

———. *Galatians.* Commentaries for Christian Formation. Grand Rapids: Eerdmans, 2021.

———. "Joy: Some New Testament Perspectives and Questions." In *Joy and Human Flourishing: Essays on Theology, Culture, and the Good Life*, edited by Miroslav Volf and Justin E. Crisp, 39–60. Minneapolis: Fortress, 2015.

———. "The Letter to the Romans: Introduction, Commentary, and Reflections." In *The New Interpreter's Bible: A Commentary in Twelve Volumes*, edited by Leander E. Keck, vol. 10. 395–770. Nashville: Abingdon, 2002.

Yeo, Ray S. "Christian Character Formation and the Infusion of Grace." In *Character: New Directions from Philosophy, Psychology, and Theology*, edited by Christian B. Miller, R. Michael Furr, Angela Knobel, and William Fleeson, 538–55. New York: Oxford University Press, 2015.

Youngblood, Ronald F. "Peace." In *The International Standard Bible Encyclopedia*, edited by Geoffrey W. Bromiley, 731–33. Rev. ed. Grand Rapids: Eerdmans, 1988.

Acknowledgments

From its inception, the writing of this book was backed by my home church, Grace Church Nottingham, and I would like to thank Ben Topliss and the other leaders for their ongoing support. I am grateful for the invaluable feedback that Derek Tidball and Jon Potter gave me at several stages of the manuscript; their insights have played a major role in shaping the final form of the discussion. Three other friends who deserve sincere thanks are Andrew Clegg, Carolyn Kristjansson, and Paul Tognarelli, who offered many useful comments to improve various aspects of the text. Without Daniel Treier's gracious encouragement and endorsement, this book simply would not have been written—thank you so much for your generosity! I am grateful to Katya Covrett from Zondervan Academic for her support throughout the whole publication process, from the initial proposal to the final printed version. Katya and a very helpful anonymous reviewer have also provided many specific suggestions and pointers on how to strengthen some of the arguments and how to clarify potentially ambiguous issues in the text. Finally, I owe a debt of gratitude to my wife, Sarah, who has stood by me throughout the years and has offered many valuable comments and insights (including remembering Bible verses when my memory failed me!).

SUBJECT INDEX

acceptance (of others), 70, 229, 240
Adam and Eve, 161
adoption, 145, 158n60, 162–63
agapē, the meaning of, 36–38
agreeableness, 81–82, 126n37
American Psychological Association (APA), 11, 62
American Psychologist, 11
ancient Greeks, the ultimate goal to achieve, 24
Annual Review of Psychology, 10–11, 48
Aristotle, 25, 39, 80, 83, 113, 119–20, 124, 194–95, 208, 234
Athanasius (church father), 158, 161
Augustine of Hippo, 158
bad mood, 233
Beatitudes, 211
benevolence, 70, 76, 130
    defined, 76
benign tolerance, 70
Bible
    "newness" and "new creation" in the, 173–74
    spiritual transformation in the. *See chapter 6, "The Fruit of the Spirit and Spiritual Transformation in the Bible"* (137–77)
Big Five (personality model), 20, 21–23, 81, 82, 126
Book of Common Prayer, 230–31
Book of Pastoral Rule, The (Gregory the Great), 120–22
"broaden-and-build" theory (Fredrickson), 233
Cappadocian Fathers, 169
cardinal sin, the paramount, 25
caring, 45, 66, 69, 111, 115, 127, 128, 131
catalogue of cardinal virtues, 14, 23
Catechism of the Catholic Church, 17, 31
Character (Miller et al.), 9
characteristic adaptations, 21, 22, 23

Character Strengths and Virtues (Peterson and Seligman), 11, 130n50
chastity, 73, 83
Christian living, the point of, 5
Christlike character, cultivating the components of the ideal, 223–39
church community, the role of the (in personality development), 192–93
Clement of Alexandria, 158, 169
communal harmony, fostering spiritual contentment and, 227–30
    narrative techniques for, 229–30
communal worship and celebration, 229
compassion, x, xi, 8, 36, 44–45, 46, 69, 75, 80n185, 90, 101, 102n19, 106, 110, 111, 128, 129, 130–31, 134–36, 170, 179, 186, 187, 189, 209, 218, 224–26, 234, 240. *See also specifically* compassionate love
compassionate love
    correlation with self-control, 133
    emergence of the label, 49
    and inner peace, the link between, 131
    the prime motivators of, 49
    the supreme virtue within the Christlike character, 224
    on the working definition of, 39
consequences (positive), 202, 216
"contemplative prayer," 128
conversion, derivation and meaning of the term, 154
Cornelius (Gentile convert), 75, 154
creation in the image and likeness of God, 160–61
Cultivating the Fruit of the Spirit (C. Wright), 12, 26n36, 80n180
darkness
    and light, xi, 211, 213

SCRIPTURE INDEX

Author Index